Making a Middle Class

Making a Middle Class

Student Life in English Canada during the Thirties

PAUL AXELROD

McGill-Queen's University Press
Montreal & Kingston • London • Buffalo

© McGill-Queen's University Press 1990
ISBN 0-7735-0753-1

Legal deposit 3rd quarter 1990
Bibliothèque nationale du Québec

Printed in Canada on acid-free paper

Canadian Cataloguing in Publication Data

Axelrod, Paul Douglas
Making a middle class: student life in English Canada
during the thirties
Includes bibliographical references.
ISBN 0-7735-0753-1
1. College students – Canada – History – 20th century.
2. Universities and colleges – Social aspects – Canada –
History – 20th century. I. Title.
LA417.7.A95 1990   378.1'98'097109043   C90-090259-0

This book was phototypeset in Sabon 10/12
by Caractéra inc.

*This book is dedicated to Lynne Raskin:
for a friendship rooted in childhood,
strengthened by the years,
and cherished always.*

Contents

Tables

Acknowledgments

A number of individuals helped to make parts of this study possible and other parts better than they otherwise would have been. University archivists across the country were unfailingly helpful. Assistance in computer programming was provided by Anne Oram of York University's Institute for Social Research. I received excellent research assistance from Hetty Armour, David Sobel, Neil Matheson, Myra Rutherdale, and Debbie Stewart. Portions of the manuscript were read and evaluated by Gina Feldberg, Bob Gidney, Patricia Jasen, Wyn Millar, Allen Pomfret, and Alison Prentice. For their perceptive comments on the entire manuscript, I am grateful to John Reid and Keith Walden. Tom Traves aided my search for an appropriate title. Susan Kent Davidson provided firm and expert editorial advice.

This book has been published with the help of a grant from the Canadian Federation for the Humanities, using funds provided by the Social Sciences and Humanities Research Council of Canada. Additional financial assistance was provided through research grants from the Social Sciences and Humanities Research Council and from York University.

Chapter 6 first appeared in Paul Axelrod and John G. Reid, eds., *Youth, University, and Canadian Society: Essays in the Social History of Higher Education* (Montreal: McGill-Queen's University Press 1989).

Making a Middle Class

Introduction

Historians traditionally have devoted little scholarly attention to the institutions within which they live their professional lives. There is no shortage of university histories, but so often they take the form of encyclopedic testimonials, are written by retiring administrators with scores to settle or records to defend, and attract more library dust than intellectual excitement. But in different hands employing creative scholarly tools, the study of higher learning is a promising, interesting, and significant field of inquiry. As historian Konrad Jarausch observes, "The history of higher education is too important to be left to the vagaries of anniversary tributes to yet another illustrious alma mater. Instead it needs to be firmly integrated into the general discussion of social change in order to determine the university's contribution to 'modernization' as well as to the perpetuation of traditional elites, values, and styles."[1]

In this book I attempt to take up that challenge, though I am not the only Canadian academic to have done so. In recent years a handful of historians, in novel and refreshing ways, have broken the antiquarian mould in their exploration of the social and intellectual life of Canadian universities. Some even share my belief that one can write about higher education for only so long without discussing students.[2] Hence the theme and preoccupation of *Making a Middle Class* – the first Canadian monograph to examine the history of student life on a multi-institutional basis.[3]

As the title suggests, the following portrait of the student experience is painted on a broad canvas. Students were not merely the passive depositories of their professors' intellectual output. Their lives on campus were shaped by their histories, their psychological and social needs, and their expected destinies. They came from particular social classes and communities; they cultivated a thriving associational life, sometimes over the objections of university authorities; and they entered an adult world where they were expected to fill social and occupational roles befitting their background and academic experience. Following this life-course in the midst of the Depression posed special challenges that heightened the insecurity, without destroying the prospects, of those bent on achieving professional standing, and middle-class lives.

To submit that university students were mostly middle-class in their origins and uniformly middle-class in their aspirations is neither a surprising nor exceptional statement. Complexity and controversy are quickly encountered, however, when one attempts to identify the membership and values of this social category. While the term is used frequently and loosely in both academic and popular literature, twentieth century Canadian historians have avoided rigorous investigation of the "middle class." Canadian sociologists and historians elsewhere have been somewhat more systematic and empirical, and as I explain in an extended discussion in Appendix A, I have drawn certain insights from such work.

By concentrating on students as opposed to administrators and faculty – who are by no means ignored – this study, like other recent work in social history, explores the collective life of a group considered relatively powerless. Youth certainly lacked status and authority, but to portray them as mere victims of adult demands and expectations is to ignore a critical dimension of their experience. It is important to understand how students, without achieving legitimated power within the university, asserted a degree of control over their environment and achieved a margin of autonomy. Unlike traditional histories of higher education, this book also investigates the unique culture of female students and seeks to contribute to the growing literature on the history of women.

Regional differences in university life are not overlooked in the pages that follow, but I hope that readers will become convinced, as I have, that English Canadian universities spawned a common student culture that transcended provincial borders. National boundaries were in some ways also eclipsed, but they scarcely disappeared from the consciousness of students, particularly with respect to the 49th parallel. By focusing on typical, as opposed to exceptional student attitudes and behaviour, it becomes possible to capture the essence and define the ingredients of English Canadian student life.

Pursuing these questions through the 1930s brings a perspective to the Depression that has been all but ignored by Canadian historians. Higher education has been treated only superficially in standard accounts of the thirties; indeed, most scholars have *completely* bypassed the culture and politics of youth, though Canadians of that era were by no means so uninterested, nor were the activities of youth so insignificant. In addition, while the Depression disrupted Canadian society, often in tragic ways, this book suggests that at least with respect to educational institutions, the theme of continuity deserves as much attention as the theme of disjunction. The impact of the Depression was more subtle than popular conceptions would suggest.

Chapter 1 surveys the historical background against which higher education and student life emerged between the two world wars. Chapter 2 identifies both the social origins of students with respect to class, gender, region, and religion and their occupational and career expectations. Chapters 3 and 4 examine the intellectual and academic culture of the university, with the former focusing on the liberal arts and the latter on professional programs and more broadly on professional culture. Chapter 5 shifts attention to the social and extra-curricular dimension of campus life, while chapter 6 traces the activities of those students participating in campaigns for political change, peace, and social justice. Chapter 7 both follows the destinies of students and serves as a conclusion by drawing together the book's major themes.

Thus, while the topic is narrowly defined, this study's conceptual and historiographical scope is wide, and the analysis aims to contribute to several fields of English Canadian scholarship: to the social history of higher education, to the history of youth, to the history of the middle class, and to the history of the Depression.

CHAPTER ONE

Youth, University, and the Canadian Middle Class

Throughout history universities have unfailingly expressed their devotion to the "pursuit of truth," yet they have engaged this task neither unconditionally nor in splendid isolation. The varieties of knowledge they have sought, the social conditions under which they have laboured, and the responsibilities assigned to them by outside forces have shaped their character and changed over time.[1] The first two English Canadian colleges – both called "King's" – were spawned in the Maritimes at the end of the eighteenth century by Christian loyalists seeking to demonstrate both their commitment to "British tradition" and their aversion to American republicanism. As cultural outposts in two emerging, though vulnerable colonies, they trained Anglican ministers, stressing to them and other students the importance of assimilating conservative, Christian values.[2] The growth and religious diversity of the English Canadian population in the mid-nineteenth century led to the founding of additional universities by Methodists, Catholics, Presbyterians, and Baptists in the Maritimes and the Canadas, though these institutions, like their Anglican counterparts, continued to promote loyalism, religious training, and "respectable" culture.[3]

By virtue of their small numbers and advanced education, university graduates enjoyed an envied social position. Still, with the exception of prospective ministers and professors, aspiring "professionals" were not normally required to hold university degrees.[4] College training would by no means damage one's chances for success, but in pioneering, predominantly rural communities, there were other roads to power, prestige, and prosperity, and the social and economic role of university education remained limited. In this environment the provision of basic elementary schooling was a far greater public preoccupation.[5] The social changes flowing from industrial and urban growth at the end of the nineteenth century gradually reshaped both the functions and the perceived value of Canadian universities. They remained accessible to only a small minority of Canadian youth, but for this select constituency and for the consumers of the services that graduates provided, university training assumed growing significance.

I

Middle-class British North Americans in the mid-nineteenth century secured their status in a variety of ways: by owning abundant land, by engaging in trade and commerce, by working as artisans, or by belonging to one of the "learned" professions – the clergy, medicine, or the law.[6] By the turn of the century, commercial and industrial change was transforming the Canadian occupational structure by destroying older forms of employment and creating new ones. The burgeoning factory system encouraged migration from abroad and from country to city, displaced artisan labour and apprenticeship training in many industries, expanded the working class, and gave birth to white-collar, supervisory, and administrative occupations. The need for trained management accompanied the growth of industry, the emergence of new consumer markets, and the consolidation of capital. Between 1900 and 1929 manufacturing production, now concentrated in central Canada, increased tenfold; corporate mergers continued apace, enlarging the size of individual firms and contributing to the "bureaucratization" of the workplace, in part through the employment of personnel instructed to institute scientific and systematic management.[7] In addition, a variety of newer professions augmented the traditional ones, reflecting active interest in applied science, growing concern about public health, and widespread efforts to regulate both civic affairs and the behaviour of the working class, immigrants, and the poor.[8]

A "new" middle class thus replaced the old. Those intent on avoiding manual or farm labour faced considerable pressure, particularly if their family wealth had come from patronage, land ownership, or artisan trade. Threatened with the prospect of a decline in their social status unless they adapted to new economic and vocational realities, they and a minority of upwardly mobile working-class Canadians sought employment in areas where standing and security seemed more assured.[9] Their options now included business, managerial, engineering, teaching, sales, and clerical work. Medicine, law, the clergy, the civil service, dentistry, and pharmacy also provided prestigious employment for the fortunate few in the early twentieth century. While women became increasingly involved in white-collar occupations – predominantly teaching, sales, clerical, and social work – and while they had finally been permitted to enrol in Canadian universities in the last third of the nineteenth

Table 1
Distribution of Canadian Men and Women in Selected Occupations, 1901–41

Occupation	1901				1911			
	Total	Men	Women		Total	Men	Women	
			No.	%			No.	%
Trade and finance: owners, managers (retail & wholesale)	48,467	46,410	2,057	4.3	83,127	79,037	4,090	4.9
Insurance agents	2,737	2,723	14	0.5	5,924	5,243	51	0.9
Salesmen and saleswomen	26,446	21,045	5,401	20.4	N.A.			
Architects	594	593	1	0.2	N.A.			
Clergymen & priests	8,653	8,653	0	0	9,905	9,905	0	0
Dentists	1,332	1,298	24	1.8	2,183	2,016	167	7.7
Engineers, professional	2,608	2,608	0	0	7,339	7,339	0	0
Lawyers and notaries	4,713	4,713	0	0	5,204	5,197	0	0
Librarians, authors, journalists	1,598	1,428	170	10.6	N.A.			
Musicians, music teachers	4,010	1,429	2,581	64.4	5,575	2,001	3,574	64.1
Physicians and surgeons	5,475	5,421	54	1	7,411	7,215	116	1.6
Professors, college principals	857	810	47	5.5	N.A.			
School teachers	39,476	8,606	30,870	78.2	42,286	8,223	34,063	80.6
Clerical workers	58,789	46,220	12,569	21.4	106,351	72,595	33,756	31.7
Managerial	N.A.				N.A.			
White-collar workers	N.A.				N.A.			
All occupations	1,792,832	1,554,883	237,949	13.3	2,723,634	2,358,813	364,821	13.4

Sources: Dominion Bureau of Statistics, Occupational Trends in Canada, 1891–1931 (Ottawa 1939), 20–8, Table 9; 1931–1961 (Ottawa 1963), 40–8, Tables 4, 5.
N.A.: Not available.

century, they were either excluded from or achieved only a token presence in the high-status middle-class occupations[10] (see Table 1).

Almost all these activities required post-elementary schooling, though it was certainly still possible to acquire middle-class status – particularly by rising through company ranks – without advanced educational training.[11] Increasingly, however, the chartered professions demanded from their members university credentials. While the specific processes through which professional training was integrated into universities varied from country to country, this development flowed from a set of circumstances that crossed national boundaries.

Professional employment expanded in response to the needs of a more complex market economy that placed an increasing premium on the importance of intellectual capital. Like large corporations, the more success a profession had in monopolizing control of the service it offered, the greater its importance and prestige.[12] Ironically, by eliminating com-

able 1 (continued)

1921	Men	Women		1931	Men	Women		1941	Men	Women	
Total	Men	No.	%	Total	Men	No.	%	Total	Men	No.	%
102,631	96,369	6,262	6.1	113,647	106,875	6,772	0.6	N.A.			
9,799	9,642	57	0.6	17,399	17,049	350	0.2	N.A.			
110,266	74,792	35,474	32	147,365	102,082	45,283	30.7	N.A.			
1,169	1,165	4	0.3	1,298	1,296	2	0.2	1,202	1,186	16	1.3
11,665	11,654	1	0.01	13,126	12,662	464	3.5	14,108	13,395	713	5
3,158	3,126	32	1	4,039	4,007	32	0.8	3,740	3,727	31	0.8
12,814	12,814	0	0	15,850	15,818	32	2	N.A.			
7,209	7,145	64	0.9	8,058	8,004	54	0.7	N.A.			
2,794	1,955	839	30	4,491	3,092	1,399	31.2	N.A.			
7,550	3,242	4,303	57	8,786	4,145	4,641	52.9	7,915	3,891	4,024	50.1
8,706	8,554	152	7.3	10,020	9,817	203	2	10,723	10,339	384	3.6
2,074	1,851	223	10.8	3,200	2,941	259	8.1	4,135	3,858	277	6.7
60,837	11,042	49,795	81.8	83,928	18,978	64,950	77.4	86,453	21,988	64,465	74.6
217,937	127,325	90,612	41.6	258,689	141,191	117,498	45.4	303,655	151,439	152,216	50.1
N.A.				219,753	209,101	10,652	4.8	225,242	208,937	16,305	7.2
N.A.				958,184	656,939	301,245	31.4	1,058,696	687,301	371,395	35
,173,169	2,683,019	490,019	15.4	3,927,230	3,261,371	665,859	17	4,195,951	3,363,111	832,840	19.8

petition in a competitive economy, both companies and professions enhanced their status.[13] Because they provided services as opposed to consumer goods and because their expertise flowed almost exclusively from the accumulation of advanced theoretical and technical knowledge, professionals needed to establish convincing criteria for proving their competence and maintaining their credibility in the markets they served.[14] Conveniently, the consolidation of their status and privilege was tied to their proclamation of an ethic of social service. The public, they claimed, could only be protected from pretenders and "quacks," also competing for consumer loyalty, by allowing the "genuine" experts the right to control access to various professions.[15] Employing complex technical language beyond the comprehension of most laymen, the most prestigious professions successfully cultivated a mystique around the services they provided, at once distancing themselves from the less educated while increasing public dependence on the professional's special skills. Following trends in Britain and the United States, government authorities in Canada provided chartered associations of doctors, pharmacists, dentists, and lawyers with exclusive authority to license practitioners and regulate their members' practices.[16]

At first training was conducted by the professions themselves either through apprenticeship or in proprietary schools run by professional organizations. But by the early twentieth century this method had become increasingly expensive, cumbersome, and impractical. The explosion of knowledge made it difficult for professional associations to remain current in the instruction they provided their students, including the requisite general education in arts and science. Nor could they adequately oversee both the training of and delivery of service by those whose professionalism and "expertise" were suspect. Situating the training of practitioners within universities enabled professional assocations to limit further the "destructive competition of an overcrowded ... marketplace" and, in a more efficient manner, to select candidates with the kinds of qualities and backgrounds considered appropriate for high-status occupations. While they surrendered some control to universities over curriculum and teaching, the elite professional associations retained authority to set licensing exams and certify practitioners.[17]

At the same time, universities found that their own prestige could be enhanced by establishing their relevance to an expanding industrial society. Engaged in the training of clergymen, the propagation of respectable culture, and the production of gentlemen scholars, universities found it more and more difficult to maintain and fund their programs. Beginning in 1868 in Ontario and 1872 in New Brunswick, denominational universities were denied access to provincial funds, and in Nova Scotia universities received no regular grants from the provincial government between 1881 and the 1940s. If student fees and support from sponsoring denominations could not sustain them financially, then religious colleges either closed, modernized their curricula, affiliated with non-denominational universities, or divested themselves of religious authority in order to receive public moneys. Then universities, particularly those with grand ambitions, like McGill, Toronto, Queen's, and Dalhousie, widened their student constituencies by broadening their programs to include extensive professional training. As Arthur Engel notes with respect to similar developments in England, the academic and professional worlds served their respective interests by responding collectively to the utilitarian demands of an industrial age:

With [the] development of university interest in the professions and, especially, as new degree programs were created, the professions themselves, especially the new aspiring ones, came to appreciate the traditional value of university degrees as external signs of "scientific status." It was the existence of university degrees which had given the church, the law and medicine the right to view themselves as "learned" professions. Universities played a crucial role in the creation of the ordered bodies of knowledge on which the claims of a profession to special expertise and to a unique position of dominance over the purchasers of their services had been based. Degrees were valuable, therefore, not only as ornamental symbols of status but as justifications for professional power and autonomy.[18]

Universities enhanced their social and economic relevance by engaging increasingly in scientific research, by providing degrees in such fields as agriculture, and by teaching business and commerce, the latter in nine Canadian universities by 1923. In the words of William Peterson, principal of McGill, writing in 1911, "It is in great measure the pressing demands of industrial and commercial life that are giving our colleges so intensely practical a turn at the present time" [1911].[19]

The size of universities and the number of professional schools depended in part upon the ability of the labour-market to absorb graduates and upon the degree of "surplus" capital available from government or the private sector for the expansion of higher education. These capacities in turn flowed from the extent of industrial-capitalist development in the society itself.[20] Where economies were more diversified, where the demand for professional manpower was strongest, where the "new" middle class was most numerous, and where private resources were most available (through such funding agencies as the Rockefeller and Carnegie foundations), as in the United States, higher education and professional training were most extensive.[21] Furthermore, the ability of professional associations both to foster a demand for their services and then to restrict access to schools by aspiring practitioners affected both the numbers of graduates and the incomes of professionals themselves. As we shall see in chapter 4, in the early twentieth century no profession succeeded better in this regard than medicine. Other professional associations – in such fields as law, engineering, social work, and agriculture – sought to emulate the medical example, achieving mixed results. Still, even the least elitist higher vocations achieved some status by associating with the culture of professionalism emanating from their dependence upon university training.

Owing to the generally unpredictable and unplanned nature of the economy, it was unlikely that there would be a precise fit between the demand for and supply of labour – including white-collar and professional labour. Shortages of trained personnel in good times and excesses of manpower in poor times tend to characterize labour-markets in undulating capitalist economies, to which educational and other training institutions respond, usually imperfectly.[22] Canadian economic and post-secondary educational growth fell far short of that in the United States at the beginning of the twentieth century, though, as we note later, the degree of Canadian development in university and professional education compared favourably with that in England and Germany.[23]

II

Despite its unmistakable and increasing importance, the extent of professional training in the early twentieth century should not be overstated, nor did the provision of professional degrees constitute the entire role of universities in that area. Between 1900 and 1930 over 50 per cent of full-time university students were enrolled in arts and science programs as opposed to the professions.[24] While extensive information on the fate of these graduates prior to the 1930s is limited, preliminary research suggests that male graduates who did not go on to professional training entered white-collar work in the public service or private sector.[25]

Indeed, a number of academics bristled at the notion of Canadian universities as mere centres of training. Professional education in the absence of moral and cultural teaching was, from this perspective, a betrayal of the university's responsibility. According to John McNaughton, a classics professor at McGill, "It will be a black shame to us if it can be said of an engineer in his epitaph that he was born a man, went through McGill University, and died a plumber."[26] In the mid-nineteenth century the university's commitment and duty had seemed clear: to provide future pastors with the appropriate doctrinal teachings and to ensure that other students, whatever their calling, would obtain the cultivation becoming well-bred citizens. According to the Bishop's College calendar in 1854, parents could be assured that their children's "moral conduct and discipline ... were carefully attended to by all Professors."[27] Courses in classics, religion, and moral philosophy steeped students in the pious values "respectable" society in mid-Victorian Canada, presumably meeting the approval of those who shared the concerns of John McNaughton.[28]

But under the pressures of religious diversity, secularization, scientific discoveries, and economic development, the "Christian" university faced new challenges. In pursuing more materialistic goals, had it lost its sense of righteousness and high purpose? Despite the claims of its critics, the Canadian university of the early twentieth century, including the non-denominational institution, did not abandon its commitment to moulding the character of its students. Instead it gradually re-formed its definition of the university's function in the hope of building a bridge between its traditional self-image and the pressures of modernity.

In its approach to the study of society, the arts curriculum was increasingly affected by new intellectual currents, embracing utilitarianism and empiricism over the previously dominant metaphysics and spiritualism.[29] None the less, for Canadian educators Christian idealism still had relevance. At Wesley College, the Methodist centre of higher learning in Winnipeg, on the encouragement of Principal J.H. Riddell the board of directors affirmed in 1925 that "the final end of education is character making, not the imparting of information. We believe that toward this end an invaluable contribution is being made by our Church through the maintenance of such institutions as Wesley College, where not only high standards of scholastic achievement are preserved but [so are] distinct assistance and impulse to Christian living."[30] Understandably, these commitments were particularly strong at other religious colleges and universities in both French- and English-speaking Canada, but they also found expression at non-denominational institutions such as the University of Toronto, where in his 1907 inaugural address President Robert Falconer claimed that "our people, being a Christian nation, will expect of a university that its influence will be favourable to the promotion of religion."[31] In subsequent years the appointment of several ordained ministers to the presidencies of non-denominational universities, admission policies restricting the numbers of non-Christians, the official requirement on some campuses that residence students attend chapel on Sundays, the active presence of religious student associations, and the influence of the social gospel helped to preserve – though less assuredly than in the past – a religious educational aura. Both denominational and non-denominational institutions still associated the character development of students with the Christian complexion of the country as a whole.[32]

This attempt by college authorities to temper an increasingly materialistic culture with righteous values by no means prevented universities from justifying their accelerating involvement in secular and utilitarian activities. Indeed, it was felt that there need be no contradiction between the university's training and civilizing functions. Well-taught professionals, grounded in the liberal arts and exposed to the influence of literate and virtuous teachers, would be effectively equipped to serve the nation as responsible moral leaders. Daniel Gordon, principal of Queen's and himself a clergyman, was fully committed to the integration of science into the university curriculum. He believed that balance could and should be attained between the "cultivated character and the dedicated specialist."[33] Similarly, Acadia University, a Baptist college with deep religious commitments and modest growth aspirations, included in its undergraduate program first- or second-year training in law, medicine, and engineering. G.J. Trueman, president of Mount Allison University, contended that the social gospel provided the moral context for the practical training in which his university engaged.[34] The provincial universities of Alberta and Saskatchewan were expected, too, both to serve the specific needs of the regional economy and to contribute to the moral development of the students.[35] While the University of British Columbia hoped to enhance the commercial and industrial development of the province, it sought in its first president "not merely a scholarly man with adminstrative ability but a scholarly man with executive ability and a noble character – a man who would leave the impression of his noble manhood on all the students of the University."[36] And in the words of McGill English professor Cyrus MacMillan, "The student who is sent up to college to-day is expected by his parents and those interested in his career to gain along three definite lines: he is to train and store his mind in the class-room and study; he is to gain from association with his fellows outside the class-room; he is to benefit from the influence of the college atmosphere on his point of view, his purpose in life, his habits of judgement. These three lines ... converge into one main idea – the making of a man."[37]

The university's promotion of "manhood," moral purpose, and modern technology all found further expression in the context of Canada's role within the British empire. The spread of organized campus sports helped to produce "muscular Christians" amid "international imperial rivalry among nations [where] it was all the more imperative to develop a healthy and vigorous citizenry."[38] In addition, many students, particularly women, participated in missionary activities on campus, later joining missions in Asia, where they served the poor and spread the gospels of Christianity and imperialism.[39] The creation of Officers' Training Corps on Canadian campuses, beginning at McGill in 1912, provided yet another outlet for physically active and idealistic men.[40] Finally, the eruption of war in 1914 provided an opportunity for English Canada to give full vent to the ideals of athleticism, militarism, imperialism, and Christianity. Universities answered the patriotic call by requiring military training for male students, by raising money and food for the troops overseas, by curbing campus social life, and, most critically, by providing several thousand soldiers at the front.[41] The war also demonstrated the critical contribution that scientific and technological development would play in protecting the nation from present and future enemies armed with increasingly sophisticated weaponry. The National Research Council, founded in 1916 in the midst of the war, facilitated the expansion of scientific research on Canadian campuses.[42]

Some continued to question these efforts by university authorities to reconcile the spiritual with the material, the intellectual with the practical, and the religious with the secular functions of contemporary higher education. Indeed, in the 1920s the process of secularization continued apace as universities, denominational and non-denominational alike, could not shelter students from the growing attractions of popular culture and utilitarian demand. A number of intellectuals, disillusioned by the war and dismayed by the spread of American commercialism and consumerism, searched in frustration for the ethical, academic, and moral bases of Canadian education.[43] Furthermore, in the 1930s, as we note in chapter 3, university officials worried that the liberal arts were in danger of losing their coherence and direction.

But these intellectual struggles over the state of the arts should not mystify the reality of what the university had by then become: an institution with social responsibilities that reflected the values and interests of its mostly middle-class constituency. With their devotion to developing skill and talent through extended education, their increasing belief in the value of hierarchically organized and specialized knowledge, their faith in expertise, their acceptance of a service ethic, and their quest for respectability and status in a competitive market, parents, students, and professors found in the university an appropriate, if imperfect, instrument through which to "prepare" youth "for life."[44] In more precise terms, Reverend H.J. Cody, president of the University of Toronto, defined the educated man as one able to use "the mother tongue correctly and precisely" and to demonstrate a "refinement of manners," having "the habit and power of reflection," the "ability to grow," and "the power to do or earn money in the workaday world."[45] Whether he was entering a profession or a less prestigious white-collar occupation, these qualities would mark the graduate as a worthy citizen with sound values, enviable education, prized, marketable skills, and the potential of sober and intelligent community leadership. Cultivating these attributes was the central mission of the Canadian university in the early twentieth century.

III

The challenging preparatory role of higher education was made more complex by the social phenomenon known, in retrospect, as the "discovery of adolescence." Industrialization speeded the process of urbanization, freeing more and more young people from the burden of farm labour and raising the question of how their time would be spent in the city. Compulsory public schooling (in every province but Quebec) occupied youth up to at least the age of fourteen by the mid-1920s, lengthening their years at home and delaying further their full-time entry into the work-force. In addition, the mechanization of factories and the growing influence of the "child-saving movement" diminished, without eliminating, the employment – and exploitation – of children and youth across the country. As the birth rate fell at the turn of the century, the average home contained older children whose physical and psychological dependence on the family had been extended. A more visible presence within society, adolescents thus became a public preoccupation – and a potential "problem."[46]

As in other aspects of social organization, "professionals" set out to influence the conduct of family life. Educators, psychologists, and social workers offered a steady stream of advice about how children and youth should be nurtured, reared, schooled, and conditioned. Peer relations, physical development, diet, even sexual habits were all the subject of commentary and counsel. Largely American in origin, these theories circulated widely in Canada. Mixing Social Darwinism, biological determinism, racial and class bias, sexual stereotyping, and Christian moralism, "experts" sought to reconcile youth's need for self-expression with society's insistence on behavioural restraint – the emphasis clearly focused on the latter.[47]

While all youth were touched by the "discovery" of adolescence, those in high schools and universities, whose emergence into adulthood was delayed the longest, attracted particular attention. Subjected to an extended period of institutional supervision but exposed at the same time to the potentially powerful influence of peer groups, students were closely scrutinized by parents and educational authorities seeking to manage the process of maturation. The school was surely the road to a productive life, but it was also considered a possible cesspool of temptation and sin. Even if they avoided the dreaded fate of juvenile delinquency, Canadian youth, according to its most nervous guardians, could be led astray by the latest fads: "unsupervised dances, disrespect for teachers, moral impropriety, the acquisition of undesirable habits, hip-flask drinking at student parties, and wild escapades in automobiles."[48] Incidents reflecting such behaviour were breathlessly exposed and forcefully condemned.

The Hollywood caricatures of "flaming youth," frivolous "flappers," and irreverent radicals distorted the reality of the typical student experience in both the United States and Canada. As studies of the campus environment at Regina College and McMaster University demonstrate, student life in the 1920s was more frequently characterized by seriousness, morality, intimacy, and compliance with authority. On the whole, students appear to have conformed to parental expectations and middle-class community standards.[49]

Still, the degree of deference – like the extent of rebellion – could be easily overstated. Canadian youth were neither as passive as the soothing rhetoric of university presidents suggested nor as haughty as popular portraits implied. An enduring theme in the history of youth is its struggle for greater autonomy from parental and institutional strictures. Young people on the verge of adulthood have always sought to expand their space and assert some control over their environment. The forms in which these contests have been engaged and the intensity of the challenges vary according to historical circumstances. Through the charivaris of the middle ages, the creation of fraternal associations in the nineteenth century, the student uprisings of the 1960s, and the contemporary struggles in China and Eastern Europe, youth has made its presence felt.[50] Sometimes evoking the sympathy of authorities, sometimes helping to foment revolution, youth can both reflect social convention and aid the cause of social change. Frequently, however, the behaviour of the young is misperceived by adult observers. Inclined to exaggerate and insensitive to the subtleties of the youth experience, anxious onlookers often simplify youth culture in a variety of ways: by denying its existence, by exaggerating its insurgent tendencies, or by proclaiming its utopian possibilities.[51] The study of the continuing process through which students assimilated the values while challenging the constraints of the Canadian campus demands an approach that is less vested, more empirical, and more attuned to the student voice.

While Canadian campuses of the mid-nineteenth century were evidently less raucous than those in the United States, episodes of student agitation were not unknown, an indication that the universities' official pious religiosity neither fully described the reality of campus life nor entirely satisfied students' needs. As recorded in the faculty minutes of Victoria University in the late 1840s, "the staff spent a great deal of time entering black marks, investigating and punishing misbehaviour, and lamenting neglect of their regulations."[52] Students asserted themselves with even greater vigour in the last part of the nineteenth century, in one case conducting a now-famous strike at the University of Toronto in 1895 and in another helping to drive from the University of New Brunswick a professor accused of "brutality and tyranny."[53]

Students could also behave in brutal ways, particularly through initiation rituals, which became common at the end of the nineteenth and continued through the early twentieth century. Through "hazes, hustles, scraps, and stunts," upper-year students imposed demanding physical tests on freshmen, engaged in sometimes bizarre ceremonies, and carried their disruptive activities into the streets, where they derailed trolley cars and invaded theatres.[54] While university authorities often attempted to eliminate the most extreme and violent of such incidents, they generally tolerated these student-run events. Initiations, after all, introduced new, frequently insecure students to campus culture and taught them the importance of fraternity, hierarchy, and conformity – values consistent with the emerging culture of professionalism. In addition, the competition, physical rigour, and indignities involved in initiation games highlighted the importance placed on "manly" virtues. Challenged by critics of the system in 1923, University of Toronto students voted overwhelmingly in favour of maintaining initiations on the grounds that they "fostered discipline, humility and loyalty to class and school."[55] Somewhat reminiscent of the "rites of misrule" carried on by European youth three centuries earlier, these activities could help to relieve tension and legitimize authority by exposing it temporarily to challenge and even ridicule.[56] Sustained and politically motivated rebellion, however, could not be tolerated, nor was it normally undertaken by students preparing for privileged professional careers. A sudden strike by students at Queen's University in 1928 over the enforcement of drinking and dancing regulations played itself out in twenty-four hours.[57]

If rebellion was not on the student agenda, political and social activism, largely inspired by religious commitment, did find a base on Canadian campuses, as it would throughout the twentieth century. Through the Young Men's and Women's Christian Associations, the Student Volunteer Movement, and later, the Student Christian Movement, students with a social conscience and an interest in world affairs campaigned energetically for "social improvement, without the overthrow of existing governments, through the working of the principle of divine unselfishness in the hearts of men."[58] Thus, while reinforcing the moral order of the campus and serving as a conservative force, the social gospel also inspired questioning among those determined to make Christianity a powerful instrument for social change in a world beset with greed, materialism, and war. For these students and their faculty sponsors, the privilege of higher education demanded service and community responsibility.

The most typical form in which students unleashed their considerable energy was through the creation of an organized extra-curriculum. Fraternities, literary societies, newspapers, and athletics increasingly complemented, and in some cases replaced, student involvement in religious activities. The rise of new professions, the broadening of the curriculum, and the growth of specialization were thus parallelled by the emergence of a more diverse, secular, and organized student culture.[59] Exclusive male clubs and teams arose in response to the presence of growing numbers of women on campus, perceived by many men as a threat to masculine values and privilege.[60] Though their extra-curricular sphere was more confined, women responded to this discriminatory treatment by forming separate societies better linked to their interests and social roles. Open only to women, these organizations provided freshettes with a more genteel introduction to campus life than that experienced by men.[61] Extra-curricular activities revolving around artistic, religious, or charitable work drew women who were also destined for middle-class lives, a minority as professionals, most as wives, mothers, and community volunteers.[62] Clubs, teams, and societies, of which there were more than forty at Toronto's University College by 1899, both served as popular outlets on campus and anticipated the social milieu that students would enter upon graduation.[63]

Thus, while Canadian students were customarily patronized, preached to, censured, and treated as something less than fully formed adults, they were not mere pawns of university authorities. In the 1920s, with or without official approval, they adopted the clothing styles, the cultural modes (including dancing and jazz), and the sometimes feisty deportment of their generation. Partly influenced by older and more worldly war veterans in their midst, students were known to drink alcohol, smoke cigarettes, skip chapel, and break residence rules. They sought greater freedom of expression even as they struggled with, accepted, and internalized the dominant social norms. In complex ways that their elders did not always understand, students participated actively in their own socialization to the middle-class values embraced by parents and teachers.[64]

The unexpected collapse of the North American stock markets and the outbreak of the Depression did not radically transform the mission of Canadian universities. But it did impose new challenges. Had economic realities not intervened, the universities would probably have continued to expand their enrolments, broaden their curricula, and extend professional education. Severe financial restraint made growth in these areas unlikely, if not impossible, as universities were forced to freeze their development, lower their expectations, and merely "mark time."[65]

Higher education carried on, but universities were now compelled to conduct and justify their activities in a world riven by deprivation and despair. Under these conditions, who would enrol in university courses? Who could afford to? What rationale could there be for sustaining the academic community in the face of competing social demands, and what did universities themselves offer to a restless, straitened society? How were university youth affected by the austerity and discord of the times? What social and cultural outlets did they choose, and what became of them? This book explores these students' links to the past, their place in the world around them, and their paths to the future. It paints a portrait of middle-class Canadians in the making.

CHAPTER TWO

Who Went
to University?

During the 1930s Canadian universities, like other institutions, trembled in the wake of economic depression. Unlike the economy's worst victims, however, the universities quavered without collapsing. They and their skittish but determined students were resolved to make the best of a bad situation. For some aspiring graduates, financial obstacles did indeed prove insurmountable, preventing them from enrolling or forcing them to drop out. Those fortunate enough to continue and complete their studies were realistic about their prospects. Modestly middle class in their social origins, most took neither security nor affluence for granted. They craved status and material comfort, though they recognized that in a depressed economy, even a university degree was no guarantee of success. What it did provide was a range of *potential* opportunities largely unavailable to less educated citizens. A combination of patience, diligent study, promising social connections, a conventional ethnic and religious identity, and plain good luck might still secure one a cherished position within the middle class. For students of the thirties the future was uncertain, not hopeless.

The financial state of higher education throughout the 1930s was far from enviable. University income, which had risen from $11.8 million in 1920 to $22 million in 1930, fell to $15.4 million in 1935 and "recovered" to $17.5 million by 1940, still well below the 1930 level. The darkest years were between 1932 and 1936, particularly in Quebec and western Canada. Deprived of adequate government and endowment support, universities secured an increasing proportion of their funds during the Depression from student fees. While full-time enrolment increased only 10 per cent between 1930 and 1940 (compared to a 28 per cent increase from 1925 to 1930), income derived from tuition fees rose 55 per cent, accounting for 15.1 per cent of total university revenues

Table 2

Full-time Enrolment in Canadian Universities, 1925–40

Year Beginning	Male		Female		Total
	1000s	%	1000s	%	1000s
1925	20.2	78.6	5.5	22.4	25.7
1930	25.1	76.3	7.8	23.7	32.9
1935	27.2	77.5	7.9	22.5	35.1
1940	27.9	76.9	8.4	23.1	36.3

Source: Statistics Canada, Historical Compendium of Education Statistics from Confederation to 1975 (Ottawa 1978), 208.

in 1930 and 29.3 per cent in 1940[1] (see Table 2).

The impact of these fiscal pressures on the operations of universities was considerable. While no institution was closed, building was postponed, selected programs were suspended, large deficits were incurred, and some inept or unlucky administrators floundered. Most institutions reduced salaries, and many laid off faculty, particularly from the ranks of part-time staff, teaching, and laboratory assistants.[2] For those professors who held on to their positions, however, salary cuts were offset by falling prices, which made the Depression endurable, if not exactly enjoyable. A survey of 1376 faculty at 17 universities in 1937 revealed that 73 per cent earned annual salaries of more than $2500, well above the 1935 average national wage of employed workers at $965.[3]

Who attended university during the 1930s? Although the school-leaving age had risen steadily through the first part of the twentieth century, the Canadian university was still the preserve of a minority of Canadian youth. In 1931 approximately 3 per cent of those between the ages of twenty and twenty-four were enrolled in post-secondary educational institutions, a rate far below that in the United States but above both the comparable British and German figures (see Table 3). While enrolments of full-time undergraduates levelled off during the Depression, graduate enrolment increased over the decade by 16 per cent, to 1569 students. Female students, constituting less than one-quarter of the student body, saw their proportion decline slightly during the 1930s.[4]

What is known about the backgrounds and social origins of these students? "Common" sense and historical impressionism have created a certain mythology about the class roots of students in the 1930s. Is it not logical to conclude that in the wake of the worst economic catastrophe in the country's history, only the very affluent could afford a

Table 3
Participation Rates of 20- to 24-Year-Olds in Higher Education, 1930

	%
Canada	2.8 (1931)
United States	11.3
Britain	1.9
Germany	2.6

Sources: Dominion Bureau of Statistics, Census of Canada, 1941, vol. 1 (Ottawa 1950), 314; Konrad Jarausch, "Higher Education and Social Change: Some Comparative Perspectives," in Jarausch, ed., The Transformation of Higher Learning, 1860–1930 (Chicago: University of Chicago Press 1983), 16.

university education? A British Columbia politician certainly took this view. In 1936 he claimed that the University of British Columbia was a "loafing place for rich men's sons."[5] Similarly, a class-conscious Kingston resident objected to hitchhiking by Queen's students on the grounds that in so doing they lowered themselves "to the level of the common herd [and] every-day bums." He also believed that hitchhiking was unnecessary since students were wealthy enough to travel by train.[6] Students who dressed fashionably, spent freely, and partied irreverently did little to alter these public perceptions.[7]

There is no question that the very poor found it harder than ever to attend, reinforcing the public's perception of the university as an institution with a well-endowed clientele. According to Carleton Stanley, president of Dalhousie (1934), "Canadian university students have always included a number of exceedingly poor boys, some of them even desperately poor. In the last two or three years all of the desperately poor have been obliged to desist altogether."[8] A spokesman for Queen's University agreed that as a result of the growing proportion of university costs covered by tuition fees, higher education was in danger of becoming "the privilege of the well-to-do only."[9] A number of observers pointed to the decline in the student population of those from rural areas of the country. At the University of Manitoba, the smaller size of the 1930 agricultural class, most of whose members came from farms, was attributed to the deterioration of family incomes arising from the "low prices of farm products."[10]

The difficulty that students had in obtaining part-time work in the depths of the Depression imposed even greater burdens on the poor, making it impossible for many to continue their education. The dean of women at the University of British Columbia noted that families who normally hired students to work as domestics in exchange for room and

Table 4

Occupations of Students' Fathers, 1935–36[11]

	Students' Fathers %	Canada 1931–41 Average %
Professional	27.1	6.4
Business	27.3	5.5
Supervisory	11.7	
White collar	10.0	24.8
Artisan/skilled	7.9	
Semi-skilled/unskilled	5.2	33.6 (skilled/unskilled)
Farming/fishing	10.8	27.3 (farming only)

These figures include students in all years registered at Dalhousie (totalling 707) and the University of Alberta (1437), first-year students only at the University of Toronto (1320), and first-year students in arts only at Queen's (218). Students not reporting their fathers' occupations were not counted. *Sources:* Department of Labour, *Occupational Trends in Canada, 1931–1961* (Ottawa 1963); Dominion Bureau of Statistics, *Census of Canada, 1941*, vols. 1, 7; Dominion Bureau of Statistics, *The Canada Year Book, 1934–35* (Ottawa 1935), Dalhousie University, Registration Book 1935–36, DUA; Queen's University, Registration Records 1935–36, QUA; University of Toronto, Registration Records 1935–36, UTA; University of Alberta, Report of the Board of Governors 1935–36, UAA. *Note:* Occupational categories used by the census and other studies drawing upon census material are not identical to those used in this study, but they are similar enough to make comparisons possible. A detailed occupational breakdown of the categories used here appears in Appendix B.

board were now able to employ in their place full-time maids for as little as eight dollars a month.[12]

These observations seem to be further sustained by quantitative data on the backgrounds and social origins of Canadian students. When university students registered, they were normally asked a variety of questions about their religion, nationality, career aspirations, and father's occupation. That such information should be solicited at all was evidence of the universities' concern about the social mix of their campus populations. Those convinced of the "privileged" class position of university youth could find statistical support for their claims. As Table 4 shows, more than one-quarter of a representative sample of Canadian students in 1935 came from "professional" families, though this group constituted one-fifteenth of the population as a whole in the 1930s. Similarly, while more than one-quarter of students' fathers were businessmen and managers, only one in twenty of the working population held such positions. More than one-quarter of Canadians were farmers during the 1930s, compared to one-tenth of the fathers of university students. And while one-third of Canadians were manual workers (skilled and unskilled), between one-seventh and one-eighth of Canadian students fell into this category. Thus there is no question that in terms of occupational back-grounds, university students were unrepresentative of the population as a whole. Generally, their fathers worked at jobs with greater prestige and higher salaries than those enjoyed by typical Canadians.

But to submit that Canadian students were relatively privileged by no means proves that they were uniformly affluent. To claim that they were, as many did, was a distortion. Understandably defensive, univer-sities themselves challenged those portraying students as idle offspring from the upper classes. According to the University of British Columbia, the diversity of parental occupations – which included bakers, barbers, bankers, journalists, and junk dealers – proved that the campus was no mere "playground for the rich."[13] The president of the University of Western Ontario went so far as to claim that the "the majority of our students are drawn from the families of moderate means and from the poor."[14] To the Kingstonian appalled by the spectacle of student hitch-hikers, the Queen's Journal responded indignantly that many simply had no money for more comfortable modes of transportation. "If [the complainant] knew the number of students who are forced to pay their fees in small instalments in order to scrape along at all, he would feel more charitable towards them."[15]

Beyond the rhetoric of editors and administrators, the evidence is strong that most students came from modest middle-class as opposed to exceptionally privileged upper-class families. While such class lines are never easy to draw and are inevitably challenged by those offering "purer" or more "scientific" models, the reality of social disparity with respect to occupation, income, and prestige, particularly in the Depres-sion, is incontrovertible and worthy of deeper exploration despite the diverse interpretative variations that might arise from the data (see Appendix A).

One approach, based on the directorships held by individuals in the 170 dominant Canadian corporations, led sociologist John Porter to conclude that in the 1950s, 985 residents constituted the Canadian "corporate elite."[16] If this group can be considered the upper class, and if it can safely be assumed that its size would have been smaller in the 1930s, it is evident that there were far too many Canadian students (more than 30,000 full time per year) to merit placement in this lofty category.

A more contemporary analysis was conducted by Leonard Marsh from McGill University and published in 1940. His model of social class combined factors of income, property ownership, occupation, and life-style. In the "well-to-do" category, which included those who earned more than $10,000 a year, there were some 10,000 persons, or 0.6 per cent of the Canadian population in 1931. These families would have to have had an average of three children – all in university – for the Canadian student body as a whole to qualify for membership in the upper class.[17] Clearly, this was not the case.

Within universities, the children of clergymen and teachers constituted a significant percentage of the student population. Yet they were hardly "well-to-do." In 1931 male teachers earned an average annual salary of $1127, and women only $917. Male clergymen earned $1527 in 1931, and women $1329. Doctors and engineers were also well represented among the parents of university youth. The former saw their average salaries decline from $3131 in 1931 to $2831 in 1941, while the latter earned an average of $2500 at the beginning of the decade and less at the end.[18]

Thus, while the children of professionals were over-represented at university and while they came from families with considerable social prestige, by Marsh's and Porter's standards they – and most other professional parents – could scarcely be considered upper class. Nor, of course, could the nearly one-quarter of the student population that came from the combination of white-collar, skilled, and unskilled labour categories (see Table 4). Male workers in Canada earned an average of $965 in 1935 and females only $782. At best Canadian students might aspire to rise to the upper class, since most did not originate there.[19]

Was anybody at Canadian universities rich? One British Columbia observer strained credulity by contending that the children of the well-to-do, whom he alleged attended university for purely social reasons, had been replaced completely by "serious-minded" students whose parents had to sacrifice to keep them in college during the Depression.[20] This was certainly an overstatement. There were upper-class youth attending university, though it is not clear precisely how many. As a case-study of Dalhousie University indicates, the very wealthy were likely to be found among the children of extremely successful businessmen. Data was available through Dun and Bradstreet business records for the 37 per cent of Dalhousie students in the 1930s who identified their fathers' occupation as "merchant." A total of 12.4 per cent of this group had assets of more than $50,000, including a small number with an "estimated pecuniary strength" of between $300,000 to $500,000. Offspring of the corporate elite could thus be found at Dalhousie and other Canadian universities.[21]

But even among businessmen, managers, proprietors, and merchants, the more modestly endowed predominated. Two-thirds of the Dalhousie sample had assets of under $20,000, and one-fifth under $5000. For the nation as a whole, as the Marsh study found, four-fifths of Canada's 125,003 retail-store owners, who were well-represented among the student population, were "single-store independents" (1931). More than one-third of these retail merchants operated businesses selling only $2000 worth of goods annually. A tiny minority, less than 0.1 per cent, sold goods valued at more than $4,000,000 annually.[22] Clearly, businessmen who avoided bankruptcy withstood the Depression more successfully than other groups, but the fabulously wealthy among them were a distinct minority. For example, even though Marjorie (Montgomery) Bowker's father was a successful Alberta businessmen, he could not afford to keep his two children in university at the same time. Marjorie was only able to enrol after her brother graduated in 1934.[23] There is evidence, too, that some upper-class families sent their children to university in Britain or the United States, further limiting their numbers in Canada.[24]

In addition, oral testimony reveals cases in which "middle-class" professionals and businessmen were forced to mortgage their homes in order to pay for their children's university education. Still others, "cut off at the knees by the Depression economy," were left with no property to mortgage yet witnessed their children struggling successfully through university on minimal resources.[25] While a middle-class background gave Canadian students a head start, for many, following the onset of the Depression, it was no guarantee of wealth or position. It was possible, if not the common experience of university students, to be both middle-class and poor during the 1930s.

That needy students continued to enrol at Canadian universities was proved by the hungry way in which they consumed the meagre funds available in scholarships, loans, and bursaries. A 1939 Dominion Bureau of Statistics study noted that financial aid across the country was inadequate, particularly in western Canada, where only 6.7 per cent of students held undergraduate scholarships, which were worth an average of $89 per year. This compared to 11.6 per cent in the Maritimes and 13.7 per cent in Ontario, with average annual values of $113 and $121 respectively. Britain, by contrast, provided almost three times as much scholarship money per student as Canada, and the United States, while offering awards of comparable value, furnished twenty-eight times the number of Canadian scholarships.[26]

Scholarships, of course, were generally directed to the best students, not necessarily the poorest; the latter were dependent on an equally inadequate variety of emergency loans, gifts, and promissory notes administered by universities. Everywhere the complaints during the 1930s were the same. Shrinking university investments reduced the amounts available to needy students. Loan funds were quickly exhausted and sometimes unredeemable from indigent student borrowers. According to the *McGill News*, "Many more students need assistance, students from the kind of families which have in the past sent their children to

University out of their own resources."[27] Universities hit hardest by the Depression improvised in order to retain students. Despite growing concern about their diminishing value, the University of Alberta accepted provincial savings certificates in lieu of cash for fees.[28] At Saskatchewan in 1934 promissory notes were received from six hundred students unable to pay their fees, representing one-third of the total student body.[29] Doug Cherry, the son of a laid-off farm-implements company manager, enrolled at the University of Saskatchewan in 1936. He received a fifty-dollar scholarship and was given permission by Walter Murray, the university president, to pay off the remaining forty-five dollars in fees over the following twenty-two months.[30] Similarly, Alice Johannsen, whose father's failed business forced the temporary break-up of her family for want of accommodation, was able to continue her studies at McGill only through part-time work and an "emergency" loan provided by the university.[31] There were numerous cases, too, of faculty members loaning or giving money to impoverished students. The dean of the University of British Columbia reported in 1935 that several students, unable to pay their graduation fees, were advanced the money by individual members of the senate.[32] Queen's University invited citizens to donate money to the university in the name of "nominated" students, whose fees would then be waived.[33] Thus, while their ranks in the university were depleted during the 1930s, poor students most assuredly did not disappear.

Their problems were exacerbated by rising tuition fees during the decade. Between 1929 and 1939 fees in arts increased by an average of 53 per cent at English Canadian universities. Where fee increases were the greatest, they were offset by a lowering of board and lodging costs as a way of "equalizing opportunity" betweeen students from the city and students from the country. By 1938, with arts tuition averaging $125 and residence fees $240, the total cost to students for a year of university away from home (taking into account books and equipment) was between $550 and $600. Students in professional programs spent more because of higher tuition fees.[34] With difficulty, large numbers of financially straitened students from all occupational categories persisted, survived, and graduated (see Table 4). There were at the same time many casualties. Carney Morris, the son of an Orillia bread saleseman, attended St Michael's College at the University of Toronto from 1932 to 1934 before being forced, along with twenty-five of his fellow students, to drop out for financial reasons.[35] The dean of law at the University of Alberta noted that, because "a large number of our students are self-supporting," failure to obtain summer employment prevented some from returning in the fall.[36] McGill University concurred. Shortage of funds would mean that "many very able students might be suddenly cut off from a university career, students of a class who cannot think of it as part of their normal expectations in life but who have to work for it, and who therefore appreciate their education."[37]

An option available to a small portion of the least affluent students was to study on a part-time basis. The adult-education movement had developed earlier in the century, and despite both severe funding restraints and lukewarm support from university officials after the First World War, it carried on through the 1930s with the determined support of organizations such as the Canadian Association for Adult Education, founded in 1935. According to the *Canada Year Book* of 1934–35, some fifty thousand students participated in post-secondary education though extra-mural, summer-session, or extended educational programs.[38] The best-known extension program, directed to fishermen, miners, farmers, and factory workers, was the co-operative Antigonish Movement, sponsored by St Francis Xavier University in Nova Scotia. In British Columbia, Alberta, and Saskatchewan the universities provided non-credit lectures, library services, and lantern slide shows that reached thousands of people in distant provincial communities. At Queen's and Western some students unable to afford to attend full-time were able to take summer-session courses towards an arts degree. According to one woman, whose father had died and whose mother earned less than $1000 a year as a factory inspector, "I should say that I never expected to attend University. The city where I lived was a workingman's city on the whole, and few parents, including mine, could afford to send their children to University." She attended summer courses at Western between 1931 and 1938, eventually qualifying as a high-school teacher in 1940, though because of her "inferior" part-time status on campus, she always considered herself a "non-student."[39]

Thus universities in the 1930s served a mainly middle-class constituency whose ranks ranged from the comfortable to the modest to the struggling. The upper class was certainly represented, but because it constituted such a tiny portion of Canadian society itself, it was not numerically dominant within universities. The working class also maintained a minority presence – far short of its proportion in the population as a whole. Most students felt the impact of the Depression economy, some far more severely than others.

Against this background, somewhat more carefully drawn than the caricatures of rich, carefree students, the recollections of alumni are instructive. The university was perceived by many as a class-leveller, characterized in hard times by a "curious kind of economic democracy."[40] Students' social backgrounds and current situations made austerity far less a source of embarrassment than a practical necessity, and ostentation was neither appreciated nor widely practised. One's wealthy classmates might be known by their expensive clothes, their modern cars, or their fraternity memberships, and they certainly could afford a fuller social life. Furthermore, on campuses such as McGill, situated in more affluent communities, class distinctions *were* greater, and, according to the *McGill Daily*, the rich were more inclined to "mix with other students from wealthy families."[41] But on the whole, either by choice or because of peer pressure, the "well-to-do" avoided overly pretentious displays. Student culture placed a high priority on campus unity, an environment that proved inhospitable to both the insufferable, snobbish elitist and the painfully shy pauper. While one Alberta student, the son of a poor farmer, recalled the presence of some "snooty fraternity" types, by and large, "you were accepted as you were."[42] A British Columbia youth, whose family was on relief following the collapse of its grocery-store business, agreed that the rich were not obviously distinguishable from the majority.[43] As we shall see, distinctions among students were made on other grounds, particularly gender and religion, but discrimination on the basis of wealth alone was less common. Most students "were not affluent," recalled the son of a Toronto minister; "we were living, we survived, and we did not starve."[44]

Many observers believed that within this predominantly middle-class community, women students came from more affluent families than did men.[45] Statistics from the University of Toronto tend to confirm this perception. While 64 per cent of first-year female students in 1935 came from professional or business backgrounds, 53 per cent of the men did. At the other end of the occupational scale, 16 per cent of men had fathers who were manual labourers, compared to 8.5 per cent of the women.[46] Because women found it far more difficult to find part-time work during the Depression (see chapter 5), they were more dependent on parental resources, particularly if they hoped to go away to school. Consequently, women had far less opportunity to attend university outside their home towns, and those who did were somewhat wealthier than their male counterparts. In the 1930s fewer than one-quarter of the male students at Dalhousie came from the city of Halifax, compared to two-fifths of the women.[47]

Canadian universities in general served primarily local and provincial constituencies, helping to foster regional consciousness among their faculty and students. "My parents were proud of the relatively 'new' local university," recalled Mary J. Wright, a student at the University of Western Ontario, who was raised in nearby Strathroy. "They regarded it as an achievement of great significance."[48] Through its publicity department the University of Alberta cultivated links with surrounding communities by providing local newspapers with information about accomplished students, a practice designed to pay political and financial dividends,

Table 5
National Origins of Canadian Students, 1935[49]

Birthplace	Canadian Students, 1935[1] %	Canada, 1931 %
Canada	76.4	82.5
British Isles	13	8.3
United States	7	2.7
Other	3.5	6.5

1 At Dalhousie, Toronto, and Alberta.
Sources: See n 48 and *Census of Canada, 1941*, vol. 1, 164.

especially necessary "in [economic] times like these."[50] Very few students in fact registered in universities in distant parts of the country. In 1934–35 more than nine-tenths of the students in western Canada attended universities in their home provinces, compared to four-fifths in Ontario and Quebec and two-thirds in New Brunswick and Nova Scotia. But if the Maritime catchment area is broadened to take in the entire Atlantic region, including Newfoundland, then universities in Nova Scotia drew more than four-fifths of their students from the area, and New Brunswick almost nine out of ten.[51]

Students residing outside of Canada rarely enrolled, though the percentage of those whose national origin was non-Canadian was more significant. In 1934–35 94 per cent of students had permanent addresses in Canada, compared to 4.7 per cent in the United Kingdom, 0.5 per cent in the United States, and 0.7 per cent in other parts of the world. Conscious of the composition of their student "stock," universities requested and often published information on the national origins and religions of their clientele. With some interesting variations, English Canadian universities were largely ethnically homogeneous institutions, slightly more so than Canadian society as a whole, as Table 5 indicates.[52]

As Table 6 shows, the religious affiliations of English Canadian universities mirrored those in Canadian society, with some important exceptions. United Churchmen and Jews were represented significantly beyond their numbers in the population, while Lutherans were under-represented. In addition, students, with some variations, tended to be drawn from the middle-class strata of their respective denominations. At the University of Toronto in 1935, 75 per cent of United Churchmen, more than 85 per cent of Anglicans, nearly 70 per cent of Presbyterians, and 67 per cent of Jewish students had fathers whose occupations were in the professional, business, or supervisory categories. (Jewish students' fathers were far more likely to be found in business than in the profes-

Table 6
Religious Denominations of Canadian University Students, 1930s (%)

Denomination	Dal.[1]	Tor.	UWO	Man.	Alb.	Canada, 1941
Anglican	22.6	21.6	15.2	16	14.8	15.2
Baptist	6.3	2.6	4.3	2.2	3.2	4.2
Jewish	11.3	7.2	1.9	11.4	4.2	1.5
Lutheran	.5	.5	2.5	2.4	1.2	3.5
Roman Catholic	15.1	14.7	20.2	10.3	9.1	43.4
Presbyterian	7.6	11.4	11.7	3.8	7.2	7.2
United Church	34.4	32.9	38.4	27.8	26.6	19.2
Protestant	.4	6.4	.4	17.7	26.6	.1
Other	1.8	2.7	5.4	8.4	7.1	5.8

1 Dalhousie figures include all students in the years 1930, 1935, 1939; Toronto figures, first-year students only in 1935; University of Western Ontario, all students in 1935; Manitoba, all students in 1939; and Alberta, all students in 1935. Summer-session students are excluded. The figures include students enrolled in affiliated religious colleges at Toronto, Western, and Manitoba. Many students at Alberta and Manitoba identified themselves as "Protestants" instead of by their specific denominations. Catholic students were more fully represented at French Canadian and at English-speaking Catholic universities and colleges.

sions.) In the Toronto sample, Catholics, Jews, and Baptists were more heavily represented among working-class students than were Presbyterians, Anglicans, and United Churchmen.[53] It is important to note too that Protestant religious colleges, such as McMaster in Hamilton and Acadia in Wolfville (both Baptist), increasingly enrolled students of various religious denominations. In the mid-1930s only one-quarter of McMaster's students were Baptist.[54] Thus, none of the major religious groups in Canada was excluded from Canadian universities, though Christians from middle-class backgrounds predominated among the student body.

Some universities were slightly less uniform than others in their student composition. The Maritime universities, particularly Dalhousie (at 15 per cent), had a relatively large contingent of students living in the United States in 1935. (The average throughout the region was 8.3 per cent). Of Canada's largest English Canadian universities, McGill attracted 11 per cent of its students from the United States and the University of Toronto only 1.7 per cent. The University of Western Ontario drew 12 per cent of its students from American locations. West of Ontario, however, only 21 of 8377 students lived in the United States (0.25 per cent), though considerably more were American by national origin.[55]

The Maritime link to the eastern seaboard and southwestern Ontario's historical connections to Michigan account for the comparatively large American constituencies in these regions' universities, though at denominational institutions, religious orientation also played an important role in luring Americans. When the University of Toronto made grade thirteen instead of grade twelve the basis for admission in 1931, its Catholic affiliate, St Michael's College, was threatened with the loss of its American contingent. It took the unorthodox step of enrolling these students officially at Assumption, a Catholic college affiliated with the University of Western Ontario in London (where grade thirteen was not required for university entrance). The following year the American students were "transferred" to St Michael's. In fact they had never actually left St Michael's, and in the transition year they were given the so-called Western course of instruction. If theological commitment inspired this arrangement, so too did financial exigency. According to historian Laurence Shook, "By 1931, the American students were numerically powerful and economically essential [at St Michael's] because they were in these depression years almost the only students still paying tuition.".[56] Saint Mary's University in Halifax, another Catholic college, also attracted a significant proportion of Americans, who made up some 10 per cent of the student body.

In another way religion accounted for the significant presence of American students at Dalhousie. For the years 1930, 1935, and 1939, four-fifths of the university's American students were Jewish. Barred from admission to "Ivy League" universities in the eastern states as the result of a rigid quota system, some Jewish-American students looked to Canada for post-secondary educational opportunities, especially in the professional faculties, and Dalhousie proved to be a particularly important outlet.[57] In 1935 alone (a year in which the proportion was, admittedly, unusually high) almost one-fifth of the student body was Jewish, and in 1939, 14 of the 36 graduates from the the medical school were Jews, all but one of whom were American. The University of Manitoba, too, was more ethnically diversified than most Canadian universities. Nearly 17 per cent of the student body in 1938–39 came from Europe. An additional 11 per cent of the students were "Hebrew," though there and elsewhere it was never made clear from what "nation" Jews or Hebrews originated.[58]

None of this should imply that Canadian universities were in general more receptive to racial and ethnic minorities than were educational institutions in other countries. Overwhelmingly white, Anglo-Celtic, Protestant, and to a lesser degree Catholic, English Canadian universities were determined to preserve their cultural mix. Like those administering immigration policy, university officials did this not by banning minority groups but by rigidly controlling their numbers. By virtue of the significant proportion who sought admission, Jews were perceived as a particular threat to the composition of the campus, and extraordinary actions were taken, similar to those in the United States, to limit, and in some cases reduce, their presence.

McGill University led the way on this front. In 1924–25 Jews constituted 24 per cent of the arts faculty, 15 per cent of medicine and 40 per cent of law. Reflecting both the increasing ethnic diversity of Montreal and the major emphasis placed on higher education by Jewish families, the growing presence of Jewish students roused the university administration to action. A major force behind the implementation of anti-Semitic admission policies was Ira MacKay, dean of the Faculty of Arts and formerly of the University of Saskatchewan, where he had participated in a faculty "revolt" in 1919.[59] In MacKay's view, "The simple obvious truth is that the Jewish people are of no use to us in this country. Almost all of them adopt one of the four following occupations, namely merchandising, money lending, medicine and law, and we have already far too many of our own people engaged in these occupations and professions at present." Claiming to have the "highest regard for the better class of Jews, some of whom are our best citizens," he concluded none the less that "as a race of men their traditions and practices do not fit in with a high civilisation in a very new country." In 1926 he advised McGill Principal Arthur Currie to limit the proportion of Jewish students in arts to 20 per cent, and in 1934 to reject appeals for the admission to the faculty of "displaced German scholars," many of whom were Jewish refugees. "There are very few questions upon which I am defiant," he stressed to Currie, "but this is one of them."[60]

The course followed by the university was, if anything, more restrictive than that recommended by MacKay. While he had suggested that Jewish high-school graduates be required to obtain averages of 70 per cent to qualify for admission, in fact at the end of the 1930s they needed 75 per cent. By contrast, gentile students achieving 60 per cent were permitted to enrol in the Faculty of Arts. Under the impact of such policies, applied with equal vigour to the professional schools, by 1939 Jewish representation had declined to 12 per cent in arts, less than 13 per cent in medicine, and 15 per cent in law.[61]

The University of Manitoba followed suit. According to the student author of a major report on campus life, "a racial problem does exist," the result of "the growth of a very definite anti-semitic sentiment on the part of the Anglo-Saxon majority." Practices in the Faculty of Medicine illustrate the point. In 1932 the university resolved to reduce the size of its first-year medical class from 64 to about 54, where it stood in 1944. The percentage of Jewish students in the class fell from 28 to 9 over this period, the result of systematic discrimination – applied as well to women and other ethnic minorities, including Ukranians, Poles, Dutch, Norwegians, Germans, Italians, and Mennonites. Each year applicants from these "non-preferred" categories were separated from a "preferred list," consisting of "Anglo-Saxons, French Canadians and Icelanders." Not more than one-quarter of those admitted would be chosen from the non-preferred groups (which represented 46 per cent of Manitoba's population). Anglo-Saxon students with lower grades (including some who had failed their last examinations) were regularly admitted over superior students from the minority groups. This quota system, said to be "in use in every medical college on the continent," was exposed in 1944 following an intensive investigation by the Avukah Zionist Society on the Manitoba campus. Presented to a select committee of the Manitoba legislature, the report led to a change in the Manitoba University Act, prohibiting the selection of students to the university on the basis of racial origin or religion.[62]

In the meantime, racial and ethnic prejudice pervaded Canadian universities throughout the 1930s, authorized institutionally and sustained informally in the campus and community culture.[63] While a small number of "coloured" youth from other Commonwealth countries were admitted to Canadian universities, this did not augur equality of treatment for racial minorities. City hospitals either denied or placed severe restrictions on the right of black doctors to take clinical training or to practice upon graduation, a prohibition that forced one Dalhousie student, unable to do his internship, to drop out of medical school.[64] Similarly, at the University of Toronto, Jewish women admitted to the physiotherapy program were not allowed to do their "required" clinical training at the Toronto General Hospital, creating a "knotty" problem for authorities.[65] Japanese-Canadian students in British Columbia carried the legacy of their historical mistreatment in that province, which reached tragic proportions with their internment during the Second World War. Forced to leave the University of British Columbia, some Japanese-Canadian students were able to complete their university educations elsewhere in Canada. But others were unceremoniously turned away.[66]

What inspired those students who successfully enrolled – from both minority and majority groups – to obtain a higher education? As in every era, college youth were convinced that university experience would improve their lives, but as always, the specific motives and the available opportunities arose from particular historical circumstances. In light of the emergence of professional education, which in the 1930s accounted for more than 40 per cent of university enrolment, many students aspired to specialized occupations, mainly in medicine, engineering, and agriculture. Theology, law, teaching, household science, dentistry, architecture, and library science also attracted students with specific vocational goals. Even if they were not enrolled in professional programs, students overwhelmingly saw themselves as ultimately working in professional fields, as evidenced by the stated career aspirations of the 1935–36 first-year class at the University of Toronto. The same was true of University of British Columbia graduates of 1930–31.[67] Clearly, students perceived university as a critical step to attaining, sustaining, or improving their position within the middle class.

This perception was, if anything, reinforced by the dismal Depression economy, which made employment upon graduation far from certain. As UBC alumnus Olga Volkhoff recalled, a university degree was "quite prestigious. If any job was open, your chances [of getting it] were improved tremendously."[68] In the view of *Managra*, the publication of the Manitoba Agricultural College, while current economic conditions might raise questions about the value of an agricultural degree, students should not despair. Not only were opportunities growing in agricultural service and research, but "good times will return by the time to-day's students are farming for themselves. A long time view is the only justifiable one."[69] Optimism and diligence would surely be rewarded.

Yet if most students expected to succeed in the long run, their immediate incentives and visions varied according to program and gender. Arts students in general were less sure of their direction and the possiblities open to them than were students engaged in professional training, a realistic perspective in light of the employment situation. As annual surveys reminded students, employers, however favourably they viewed a university degree, were neither eager nor able to hire arts graduates en masse.[70] When asked to state their intended occupations, only half of the men and one-third of the women in first-year arts at Queen's in 1935 were able to do so.[71] For other reasons too, jobs were not foremost in the minds of many. According to Grace Cullen, who received her BA from Queen's in 1931, "At that time, one had a different idea of education. You weren't going with the idea of making a living. You went for what you were going to get out of it, to enjoy it, to enjoy the courses ... and the friendships ... I wasn't thinking of making a living out of a degree at all, and I think that's true of a great many people at that time."[72] A 1938 survey of 167 female graduates from McGill, Queen's, and Toronto found that 149 favoured marriage over careers, and that the majority planned to abandon their jobs once they married.[73]

If the social side of university attracted some students, others – undoubtedly a minority – were motivated mainly by the love of learning. Mildred Nobles, another Queen's alumnus, who later became a renowned Canadian botanist, was inspired by her thirst for knowledge and her absorption in research. Similarly, Marion Cummer (BA Toronto 1933), was "a learner and thrilled to go." Gene (Morison) Hicks of Dalhousie and Jean Burnett of Toronto identified their heritage as a powerful force in shaping their perceptions of the university's importance. "My parents had the Scottish faith in education," recalled Professor Burnett. Hicks concurred. "My father and mother were both of Presbyterian Scottish background, and these people put a great emphasis on education. The idea of furthering your education was not strange at all in our family."[74] The traditional Scottish enthusiasm for higher learning is susceptible to a degree of myth-making, but claims for it are borne out by the experiences of numerous Canadian university youth. Other students with middle-class values or expectations also considered a university education to be a natural and necessary step to a successful and fulfilling adulthood. It was "always assumed," recalled Marjorie (Montgomery) Bowker, "that [the children in our family] were going to university."[75]

"Careerism," with its accompanying intensity and competition, played a more modest role in motivating students than it would after the Second World War.[76] In a less frenetic and more genteel atmosphere, the Canadian university was considered by the families who used it an appropriate place in which to prepare their sons and daughters for life. Along the way they would, it was hoped, accumulate cultural, social, and applied skills fitted to their middle-class aspirations and needs. Many students thus arrived at the campus unsure of what they would do, or even of what they wanted, but certain that they should be there. H.S. Ferns, whose father was a civil servant, recalled no doubts in his family about the merits of his attending the University of Manitoba. "The only question was whether they could afford to send me there ... As far as my parents were concerned they – and particularly my mother – conceived of a university education as a 'good thing' in a very generalized way but mainly as a means of 'getting on in the world,' of getting a better job than either of them had ever had. They had no specific ideas on this subject, and they never thought of me as becoming a lawyer or a doctor or an engineer or an agricultural scientist or an accountant. What I studied was left entirely to me."[77] The results of a major survey of University of British Columbia alumni – though conducted long after the fact – reinforce these perceptions of students' educational motives.[78]

If women were particularly inspired by the social or academic as opposed to the professional-training component of higher education, there was good reason. Their perceived and actual options were far more limited than were those of men. For a woman to aspire to a long-term career was neither impossible nor unprecedented. But it was rare. Even in the wake of the successful suffrage movement a generation earlier, women were still expected to become full-time wives and mothers, and they received little support and faced many barriers if they challenged this destiny. In the first two decades after the war, according to the Dominion Bureau of Statistics, "while a few [female students] appear[ed] in every branch of study," they made no significant inroads into male-dominated fields.[79] Not only were they subjected to quotas in professional schools, but if they became teachers or civil servants, they were forced to resign when they married. John and Catho (St Denis) Robbins, both of whom worked in the Education Branch of the Dominion Bureau of Statistics, kept their 1934 marriage a secret so that she could keep her job with the federal government.[80]

Aware of this "special" treatment, university women adapted both their expectations and their program choices to their environment. Fewer women than men even anticipated "careers."[81] Those who did – and most would have considered working for a brief period only following graduation – were confined to a few, mostly traditional possibilities, the main one being teaching. In Mary Alice Murray's circles (BA Queen's 1936), "Nobody had even thought of doing anything more daring than [teaching]."[82] For middle-class families, as Toronto graduate and future professor Jean Burnett noted, "teaching was the best career for women who didn't marry."[83]

While alternatives for women did appear, registration records and surveys generally bear out these oral testimonies. Of those who stated their ambitions, fully 70 per cent of Queen's women enrolled in arts in 1935–36 chose teaching, compared to 19 per cent of men. While the remaining men selected engineering, medicine, law, and business, most of the remaining women aspired to library work or journalism. Similarily, of UBC graduates in 1931, more than half of the women sought work in eduation or teaching, compared to four in ten men. While other choices for men included engineering, law, and medicine, the rest of the women considered librarianship, graduate school, or business.[84] Elsewhere, women aspired to nursing, secretarial work, social work, and household science.[85] If their "sphere" was somewhat broader than in previous generations, equality of opportunity and treatment, particularly in a depressed economy, still eluded female students.

University students in the 1930s, to be sure, were a select group. They constituted a small proportion of Canadian youth; they generally came from more "privileged" backgrounds than typical Canadians, and they hoped that university education would secure their place within the middle class. But in the main they were neither presumptuous nor ostentatious. While a minority among them were wealthy enough to be untouched by the devastation of a depressed economy, the majority lived in modest, frequently austere conditions, facing an uncertain future. If they were extraordinarily poor, ethnically or racially distinct, or female, they confronted special obstacles. Those students who survived and persisted would come to cherish their university experience, particularly the exciting social life it offered them. Their ever more serious professors hoped to imbue them with an equal devotion to higher learning.

CHAPTER THREE

Academic Culture

I

Nothing is more exalted than the lofty rhetoric of university presidents. Virtually on demand, they can turn convocations and businessmen's luncheons into grand celebrations of the university's historic and enduring importance. Facing a fickle public whose view of the university combines deference with scepticism, the effective president, like the trusted preacher, gently but earnestly proselytizes on behalf of a noble and righteous cause.

As paragons of social respectability, presidents and principals in the 1920s and 1930s attempted to cast universities in their own image. Whether they represented the large, multifaceted schools like McGill and Toronto, the "provincial" institutions like Saskatchewan and British Columbia, or the small denominational colleges like Acadia and Brandon, their messages were similar. They did not believe that university was for everyone, but the institution's exclusive constituency only enhanced its special importance and indispensability. For Leonard Klinck, the president of the University of British Columbia, the university was a place where "spontaneity and inward strength must be cultivated and a liberal and enlightened individualism encouraged."[1] "With a higher education," contended Robert Falconer, the president of the University of Toronto, "a distinctive attitude of mind is fostered. The educated man is supposed to sift ideas and search for and live the truth, to acquire a knowledge that will create a higher race."[2] His colleague Arthur Currie, principal of McGill, agreed. The university was obligated to "place in the plastic minds of the students the seeds of a courageous citizenship ... Let students always be devoted to duty."[3] These worthy goals could be accomplished even more effectively in a denominational college, according to R.J. Evans, the president of Brandon. "Because the Christian

College interprets education in terms of character and service, it is able to make an outstanding contribution to leadership. Because it aims to develop the moral fibre of its students, it is able to make a real contribution to the needs of civilization today."[4]

In the views of its official spokesmen the university was, in its ideal state, the house of high culture and the sanctuary of scholarship. It lured youth with character, spawned society's future leaders, and imbued them with civility, sound morals, and the spirit of patriotism. At its best it offered students the right combination of practical training and intellectual rigour. It served society without merely pandering to passing trends.[5]

In their social origins, training, and personae, the men who uttered these noble homilies set excellent examples. They were the kinds of individuals to whom middle-class parents could confidently entrust the guardianship of their sons and daughters. Unlike the sprawling mega-institutions of a later era, Canadian universities and colleges of the 1930s were relatively small, even intimate places, overseen by faculty familiar with the practice of educational paternalism. In the absence of an elaborate institutional bureaucracy, the respected president was the campus patriarch, who "ruled" the campus with benign authority. He took a custodial interest in the students, greeting the freshman class in the fall, sometimes interviewing every new registrant. When personal or disciplinary problems arose, he actively helped to solve them. A good part of his time was spent communicating with – and reassuring – parents and other citizens concerned about the performance or deportment of students.[6]

The values and public images of Canada's best-known university presidents were shaped by their backgrounds and breeding. Frequently raised in devout Christian settings, they were models of moral probity; religion mattered a great deal to the leaders of denominational and non-denominational universities alike. Both Robert Falconer, president of the University of Toronto from 1907 to 1931, and his successor, Henry John Cody (1932–44), were ordained ministers, of the Presbyterian and Anglican churches respectively. Robert Wallace, president of the University of Alberta from 1928 to 1936, and principal of Queen's from 1936 to 1951, was a United Churchman with a "strong sense of Christian duty …, puritanical in his distrust of emotion and display and in his standards of personal behaviour."[7] Saskatchewan's Walter Murray (president 1907–37), the son of a Presbyterian doctor, participated in the activities leading to the formation of the United Church in 1925.[8] The religious commitments of theological colleges, both Catholic and Protestant, were secured directly by official doctrine, as well as by the personal convictions of their presidents.[9]

But even in the "secular" universities, which eschewed religious ortho-doxy, Christianity's moral legacy, if not its sectarian particularities, had an assumed place. Admittedly, rigid religious codes were difficult to impose and sustain in the utilitarian climate of the modern world, but at the very least the sobriety and faith of the universities' leading figures should never become the subject of public suspicion.[10]

But the pious official pronouncements uttered by the university leaders, and favoured by equally earnest citizens, do not capture their entire perspective on the nature of higher education. Convocation speeches aside, a number of presidents (and other academics) were far less certain about the morality, quality, and depth of university intellectual life than their reassuring statements suggest. In fact, as they would admit to each other at university conferences, contemporary higher education left something to be desired.

In the wake of major developments in biological and physical science, the emergence of professional schooling, and the spread of a more secular and continental culture, some university officials in the 1930s wondered whether their high educational ideals could be realized. For J.S. Thomson, the president of the University of Saskatchewan and a particularly severe critic, higher education had simply lost its way. The unified and coherent curriculum of the late nineteenth century, which was rooted in moral philosophy and classical education, had been eroded by the insidious utilitarian forces of the marketplace. Scientists were increasingly "pre-occupied" with applied as opposed to pure research. Instead of providing students with the tools for "general cultural development," universities, in their quest for relevance, permitted and encouraged excessive spe-cialization in the arts as well as the sciences. "[We are] subdividing our subject-matter until the calendar becomes like a department store cat-alogue of offerings in the liberal arts."[11] There was too much "fact-cramming," too much emphasis on narrow professional training, too much John Dewey and too little Matthew Arnold.

Similar complaints were articulated in 1936 by Robert Hutchins, president of the University of Chicago, in his widely publicized book *The Higher Learning in America*.[12] Universities, according to Hutchins, reflected and perpetuated the shallow values of modern civilization. Expensive professional schools dominated many campuses, academic standards were too low, the classical curriculum was all but extinct, social life was over-emphasized, and students were obsessed with making a living instead of scholarly learning.

The National Conference of Canadian Universities, a forum through which university administrators could discuss academic issues, devoted considerable attention to Hutchins' book at its 1937 conference. Most commentators found his analysis stimulating and largely valid, but they questioned both the radicalism of his recommendations and their applicability to Canada. Hutchins called for the hiving-off of professional schools from universities, which should confine themselves to teaching the arts and sciences. President Cody of Toronto spoke for others when he rejected this proposal on the grounds that it would rob professional students of *any* exposure to culture and erudition. Furthermore, he believed that while the Canadian university had shortcomings, it had not "wandered as far afield as some in the United States. [In Canada] there [is] a healthy tendency to hold to a combination of theory and practice, of science and art."[13]

As Robert Wallace of Queen's noted, Canadian society had not embraced as fully as the United States the culture of acquisitive materialism. At the same time, he believed, Canadian universities risked alienating the public completely if they abandoned their commitment to professional and vocational training. Even as they served increasingly practical and technical demands, Canadian educators, in Wallace's opinion, still cherished moral and aesthetic values, which they believed flowed from the nation's British roots. Universities had not yet discarded the paramount aim of developing youth's "character." Nor should they.[14] From this perspective, the reconciliation of general and specialized education, of public and scholarly interests, and of pure and applied research, however challenging, was still possible and should be resolutely pursued.[15]

Educators acknowledged that such balance was difficult to achieve in a young, developing country facing the added burden of economic depression. In this environment universities were under considerable pressure to demonstrate their social utility. Often taxpayers, politicians, and businessmen showed minimal appreciation of the university's intellectual and moral role. Instead they wanted more immediate and serviceable results. As the governor general, Lord Tweedsmuir, said in 1938, "A university must fulfill a utilitarian purpose. Its work must serve some recognizable social needs. A smattering of general culture will be of little use to a young man if he is going to starve."[16] Quite simply, echoed the *Vancouver Sun* – a traditionally strong supporter of higher education – "we cannot yet afford in this province an educational institution that offers cultural facilities, as necessary as they may be, without offering parallel facilities for training those young men and women upon whose scientific abilities will depend the prosperity and growth of British Columbia."[17] In securing popular support and adequate funding for their institutions, university officials had to address this pervasive spirit of pragmatism and incorporate it into their philosophy of higher education. Administrators reconciled to the values of the modern world, like Robert Wallace and Walter Murray, found this easier to do than did traditionalists like J.S. Thomson and Carleton Stanley, president of Dalhousie.

Though they might emphasize different themes, and while some were more optimistic than others about the potential of higher education, Canadian university officials were largely in agreement about the goals they believed academic life should strive for. Denominational values might no longer be uniformly imposed, but universities could still serve as a moral and cultural anchor in a secular era. Graduates in arts, science, and the professions ideally would be intellectually rounded and spiritually unsullied. They would attain positions of respectability and community leadership. They would become both competent practitioners and estimable citizens.

What in fact went on in the classrooms of the nation? Were universities scholarly shrines or purveyors of low-brow popular culture, or some combination of the two? Did they successfully shape the characters and guide the destinies of their largely middle-class constituency, or were they foiled by insurmountable obstacles?

II

Canadian students of the early 1930s normally entered university through one of two streams. At least sixteen years of age, they would present to their chosen university either a junior or a senior matriculation certificate (or their equivalents). "Junior" matriculants had usually graduated from grade eleven of a Canadian secondary school, and senior matriculants from grade twelve, except in Ontario and British Columbia, where the last year of high school was grade thirteen. Students who had passed senior matriculation examinations could register in second year, while junior matriculants enrolled in first year, where they would attempt to complete senior matriculation requirements. In effect, the final year of secondary school was the curricular equivalent of the first year of university.

While there were significant variations in matriculation prescriptions, students were subject to qualifying examinations in a common range of disciplines. At Dalhousie, for example, all students, no matter what degree they were pursuing, needed eight matriculation credits in English, history, algebra, geometry, physics or chemistry, and two foreign languages, one of which had to be Latin or Greek. Bachelor of science students could escape the classical-language examination only by replacing it with an additional foreign language. In addition, all students took one elective.[18]

In western Canada there was somewhat less emphasis placed on the classics, for which matriculants could substitute a foreign language, usually French and less frequently German.[19] Another notable distinction arose in the first-year curriculum of denominational colleges, where students would be required to take at least one course in religion. Throughout the country students pursuing general or honours degrees would thus have acquired some grounding in the humanities (literature and languages) and the sciences (including mathematics). Apart from studying history, students would be introduced to the social sciences only after they had completed matriculation requirements and had begun to "concentrate" in particular fields.

Academic qualifications alone would not win students a place in university. As we saw in chapter 2, while they never openly admitted it, university officials took into account the factors of religion and race in admitting students to undergraduate and professional programs. University calendars, however, did acknowledge that a student's "personal characteristics" would affect his academic future. The University of Saskatchewan required successful applicants to be "of good moral character."[20] At St Francis Xavier, "candidates for admission, not personally known to some member of the Faculty," were "required to present a letter of recommendation from their Pastor, or from someone who is known to University authorities."[21] The president of the University of Western Ontario explained why "discrimination" in the selection of students was justified. "The laudable desire of our New World democracies to give everybody an opportunity to become educated needs to be tempered by recognition of the fact that all types of humanity cannot be educated unless discrimination is exercised as to differences in native gifts, aims in life, background, outlook and numerous other circumstances. Of course discrimination itself is nothing else than selectiveness."[22]

Thus, on the basis of official admission requirements, students were expected to have attained appropriate levels of both scholarship and character development (though the latter was admittedly harder to ensure). In a secular society, replete with the distractions of popular culture and feeling keenly the growing need for more narrowly trained specialists, universities still required entering students to have achieved a degree of academic breadth in the arts and sciences. So qualified, they would already have distinguished themselves from less refined commoners. Pursuing their education, university students, under careful guidance, could then enhance their cultural and intellectual worth.

Of course, scaling these heights was no small challenge, and it is clear that from matriculation to graduation, students achieved less than was expected by their academic overseers. The contest between high ideals and mundane reality pervaded academic life.

Critics lamented the impact of mass secondary-school education on the quality of teaching and learning that inevitably spilled into universities. Now that high schools were compelled to offer commercial, technical, and practical courses, the status of language and "literary" studies had been seriously compromised. Saskatchewan's J.F. Leddy noted the drastic decline in the percentage of Canadian high-school students studying Latin. In New Brunswick, 74 per cent of high-school students enrolled in Latin in 1933, compared to 45 per cent in 1943. While over half of Ontario high-school students continued to take Latin at the end of the 1930s, only 15 per cent of those in Alberta were still doing so, compared to 58 per cent in 1923.[23] For those educators convinced that a well-rounded liberal arts education required some exposure to the classics, this trend was an ominous portent, confirmed, as we note later, by the decline of interest among university students in Latin and Greek during the 1930s.

Despite its pretensions to coherence, the actual inconsistencies in matriculation standards and requirements elicited much consternation from university officials throughout the decade. According to the principal of Upper Canada College, instead of achieving through matriculation preparation a balanced and integrated education, students treated it as "a sort of jig-saw puzzle. Find the bits, fit them into the right holes, and lo! you are admitted to university ... We have compartmentalized our educational course to such a pitch, that the subject is now more important than the knowledge and thought of which it is only a minute part."[24] The inadequacy of educational facilities, particularly in rural areas, noted G.J. Trueman, the president of Mount Allison University, accounted for the presence in university of many students "with inadequate preparation, and without good methods of study, or worthwhile standards of judgement."[25]

Ill-equipped for university-level work, too many students quickly fell by the wayside long before completing a degree. According to the dean of arts at the University of Saskatchewan, "approximately 25 per cent of our students cannot meet the minimum requirements for satisfactory work."[26] At the University of British Columbia the failure rate among first- and second-year students in 1929–30 was considered "alarming."[27] At the University of Toronto failure rates among first-year students – those holding only junior matriculation – reached crisis proportions in 1930, when 50 per cent missed their year.[28] This led to a radical change in admission standards. Beginning in 1931 the university no longer admitted students without senior matriculation. This act, explained officials, "will mean that the idlers who have looked upon a year at the University as a natural reward for having obtained junior matriculation will no longer serve to waste the money expended by the government in educating them for that one year."[29] The impact was immediate. Failure rates of the 1931–32 class fell to below 20 per cent.[30]

University faculty elsewhere shared the concerns of their colleagues at Toronto, and in the interests of improving the status of their institutions, admission standards were raised incrementally at other campuses during the 1930s.[31] Regulations at most campuses forced students who had done particularly poorly in their first-year mid-term examinations to leave university – permanently in the most serious cases. For example, at McGill, first-year students who failed more than one-half or more of their interim tests were "dropped from the University and are not allowed to re-enter except with the consent of Faculty."[32] But Toronto's approach of excluding junior matriculants, however theoretically sound, was not universally popular in practice. A "Committee on Improvement of Students' Work" at Queen's contended that because senior matriculation courses were unavailable in poorer communities, where the secondary-school system was underdeveloped, their graduates would be disadvantaged by the University of Toronto "solution": "Toronto's plan is the result of local conditions rather than of a broadly conceived educational policy."[33] The Queen's committee worried as well about the depletion of the university's enrolments if it followed the Toronto lead, a loss that would prove very costly in the current economic climate. In defending its own refusal to bar junior matriculants, the University of Manitoba in 1936 echoed the rationale offered several years earlier by Queen's.[34] At Alberta, however, senior matriculation was required for entry to the university beginning in 1937.[35]

The various steps taken to tighten admission requirements led to less, not more, academic uniformity across the country by the end of the decade. Seeking to make a virtue of necessity, a commission appointed by the National Conference of Canadian Universities opted for flexibility in its approach to university entrance examinations. "Each province," it noted, "must be free to determine how its own needs can best be met. The needs of a western province with a mixed population are not those of a homogeneous eastern province ... The national interest is better served by diversity and experimentation than by fixed prescription and fixed procedures."[36]

Beyond matriculation, students pursued their undergraduate arts and science degrees through one of two routes: the pass (or general) courses and the honours programs. The purpose of the pass course, which normally required four years of study beyond junior matriculation, was to "afford some introduction to a series of subjects of which the educated man should not be ignorant ... It should contribute to orienting the student in the world which he finds himself by presenting him with some important part of the legacy of the past and showing him the use to which men have put and are putting it, and it should afford him, within the limits set by the degree of penetration into the subject, some genuine intellectual discipline."[37] Apart from requiring a minimum number of subjects in the general categories of languages, mathematics and science, humanities (English, philosophy, history, and fine arts), and the social sciences, universities generally allowed students considerable freedom to select their own courses, particularly in the third and fourth years. Observers noted that while this process exposed students to a broad range of disciplines, it provided too little integration between subject areas. According to University of Toronto English scholar A.S.P. Woodhouse,

the mere fulfilment of [compulsory matriculation and degree] requirements does not necessarily do very much to orient the student or help him to see the relation of one discipline to another ... For a young student to be compelled to attend a class in English literature from 9 to 10, followed by one in Latin from 10 to 11, is not necessarily in itself a particularly illuminating experience, especially if the English instructor never refers to the debt of English literature to the classics and the Latin instructor is sumberged in the details of syntax and translation, and if neither of them in dealing with his language ever calls in the other language to make his point clear. Nor will much be necessarily gained from the combination of subjects by the students going to philosophy or history from 11 to 12 and spending the afternoon dissecting a dead frog."[38]

In order to draw more intellectual coherence from this pot-pourri arrangement, some universities began to offer general introductory courses, though none went as far as Sir George Williams in requiring all students to take "pandemic" courses in the humanities, sciences, and social sciences that were both "broad and liberal."[39]

Honours students, who had generally achieved higher grades than pass students, concentrated in more specialized subject areas beginning in second or third year. In some cases (such as Toronto and Queen's) honours students required five years of study beyond junior matriculation. Elsewhere, while its requirements were more demanding than than those in the pass course, the honours degree could be completed in the same four-year period. Honours students represented the undergraduate elite and frequently found their way to graduate school or teaching careers. The most famous honours program, at the University of Toronto, was unique in several ways. Qualified students would choose to enter honours in first year, where they would be locked into a rigorous routine with a heavy load of compulsory courses throughout their undergraduate program. While fewer than 20 per cent of students were in honours programs in the rest of the country, at Toronto over 50 per cent of students were in the the honours stream. Determined to preserve the prestige of this program, the university devoted abundant faculty resources to its honours students. Consequently, this had "a depressing effect on the pass course, leaving it with few students of better than mediocre ability and application."[40] The heights that the university's reputation reached on the strength of the honours course were compromised by the downward pull of the inferior pass course, in which half the students were enrolled.[41]

If pass students suffered from too little concentration, honours students throughout the country faced the opposite problem. Academic depth was purchased at the expense of breadth and distribution. Humanities or social-science students might never take a science course beyond first year. Similarly, science students could generally avoid courses in the cultural and literary fields.[42]

While attempting to reduce the numbers of unqualified students, the universities could take some solace in the generally positive impact of hard economic times on the overall academic performance of university youth. Some faculty were positively effusive about the quality of their students. According to Frederick William Waters, a philosophy professor who returned to McMaster from Yale in 1936, "the calibre of students I have met and the character of the work [are] not at all below that of twenty-five years ago."[43] Historian Arthur Lower never "had more loyalty and stimulation" than from his students at Wesley (United) College in Winnipeg. "Brilliance" he recalled, "seemed literally to tumble forth" from Manitoba.[44] At Alberta, President Wallace noted in 1931 that honours students were "seeking increasingly the heavier disciplines, even at considerable financial sacrifice."[45] At Western the percentage of students who "cleared all their work" at final examinations rose from 61 in 1931 to 71 in 1936.[46] Everywhere students were found spending more time in the library. At Queen's, for example, eight hundred more books were borrowed in December 1936 than in December of the previous year.[47] While by no means pretending that studying was all that interested them (as we shall see in chapter 5), student writers, too, observed a greater degree of academic seriousness among their classmates. "There has been more time devoted to studies," concluded the McGill Daily in 1933. "Scholarship has improved."[48]

At the same time, there was no shortage of professors lamenting what they viewed as chronic mediocrity in the classroom. The ever acerbic Stephen Leacock, humourist and professor of political economy at McGill, complained that "universities are turning out keen young men for the day-to-day requirements of the business world, but we are turning out scholars nowhere."[49] Hamilton Fyfe, principal of Queen's, and Carleton Stanley, president of Dalhousie, used especially colourful prose to damn the intellectual level of the current generation. Steeped by background and bias in the Oxbridge myth, Fyfe believed that Canadian universities were "full of students who cannot appreciate the intellectual bill of fare." The academic program at Queen's, he submitted, "would not elevate a cow."[50] Stanley, too, regretted that students "have nothing like the mental equipment of Jusserand at their age. When they leave college they are not steeped in ancient philosophy and literature, they are not masters of any period of history, nor are they well grounded in science – that convenient alibi of our age to excuse ignorance of all other things."[51] Like J.F. Macdonald, an English professor at Toronto, he blamed the dismal state of public education on the plethora of poorly trained women teachers. Schooling would improve, contended Stanley, only if "the colleges take it as one of their chief practical duties, if not the chiefest of all, to send back some of the *very best male brains* into the school. After a certain age boys can be educated only by men."[52]

Yet such comments were based more on the authors' unhappiness with trends in contemporary North American culture – inevitably reflected in the university – than on proof that students of the thirties were particularly incompetent. Furthermore, as Frederick Gibson has observed, academics like Fyfe were insensitive to

the economic and social context of Canadian university education which distinguished it from the ambience of Oxford. University students in Canada, and more particularly at Queen's, did not enjoy the reassuring protection of inherited wealth and social position. They were, on the whole, people of modest means and uncertain prospects, drawn to university as the gateway to a career in the professions or business. Many of them, both men and women, were working their way through college and unable to devote their summers to reading and travel. Fyfe ... would have much preferred to see Queen's aim at graduating students of the Balliol type, ignoring the fact that the social foundations for such a type did not exist in Canada.[53]

In short, while the academic performance of Canadian students was by no means universally outstanding, neither was it entirely wretched. Judged against more realistic standards, free of extreme intolerance on the one hand and exaggerated ebullience on the other, the typical student of the 1930s appeared to perform tolerably well.

The undergraduate program reflected the growth of specialized knowledge in a secular world. Because religion and the classics could no longer provide the basis for a core curriculum, as it had in the mid- to late nineteenth century, universities sought intellectual coherence in other ways. The cultured student was expected to enter university having already been steeped in the moral and intellectual traditions of Western – particularly British North American – civilization. The matriculation courses would, ideally, provide this basis. Once enrolled in an arts or science program, students would find that their intellectual boundaries were broadened, incorporating the range of new knowledge that had swept through the early twentieth century. In pass courses students would sample this diversity, while honours students would explore one or two subjects in greater depth. Professional programs would demand yet a more extensive degree of technical training in more narrowly defined areas. By the 1930s, even students enrolled outside the professional stream, at small and large institutions alike, could major or concentrate in an unprecedented number of subjects. Those in honours could choose single or combined majors in some thirty programs at the University of Toronto, twenty-five at McGill, and twenty-four at the tiny University of New Brunswick.[54] Though they provided a less diverse curriculum and continued to require courses in religion throughout the undergraduate years, denominational colleges were also affected by these trends.

This cultural and academic transition elicited a range of responses from university officials and teachers – all trained in an older, more uniform system. Some were enthusiastic, most were accommodating, and a minority were outraged by modern intellectual currents. None was untouched by the external and internal influences that directed the course of higher education. The mission of universities had not changed dramatically. The successful institution would continue to produce respectable middle-class citizens, armed with a "disciplined intelligence" and ready to assume positions of professional and community responsibility. But the more complex environment in which this task was conducted challenged, and frequently frustrated, administrators and professors. They struck a bold pose, never hesitating to applaud the university's accomplishments, yet forced on other occasions to acknowledge the institution's academic limitations. The goal of a coherent, balanced liberal education with universally high standards remained entrenched in theory and elusive in practice.

III

Within this imperfect structure, educators strove to provide students with curriculum content considered essential for the cultured and well-trained citizen of the modern world. Yet as always the appropriate balance between these demands proved difficult to formulate and implement. The tension evident in the arts and sciences and the professional programs between proponents of intellectual depth on the one hand and advocates of serviceable schooling on the other expressed itself in the content of university courses, although optimists remained convinced that the elements could be successfully reconciled and combined. What, precisely, were students taught, and how well did their education suit their aspirations and future roles as middle-class workers and professionals in Canadian society?

As we have seen, the liberal arts curriculum, from secondary school through undergraduate higher education, no longer revolved around the teaching of the classical languages. The popularity and status of Latin and Greek were eroded both by students who used their post-matriculation freedom to choose other, less demanding subjects and by faculty who questioned the utility of the classics in the modern world.[55] Its demise notwithstanding, reports of the death of the classics in the 1930s were premature. Students in Catholic religious colleges like St Francis Xavier in Antigonish, St Michael's in Toronto, and St Paul's in Winnipeg received extensive exposure to Latin. In non-denominational universities, too, the classics still had their champions, including Maurice Hutton at Toronto, who trained an entire generation of classics scholars in Canada, and Carleton Stanley, president of Dalhousie, who succeeded in introducing a scholarship in classics and mathematics "for boys only" in 1932.[56] While Alberta's W.H. Alexander recognized the waning interest in his subject, he believed that the basis of classical learning might be saved if it were modernized. He initiated a course in classical civilizations based entirely on translated texts. Clearly striking a chord among students, the exploration of the literature and society of ancient Greece and Rome grew in popularity. By the end of the 1930s eight other universities provided such courses, representing a partial "victory" for classicists surrounded by an "unclassical generation."[57]

Despite the growing diversity of the curriculum, one subject – English – constituted the core of the liberal arts program, replacing religion and the classics as the nucleus of intellectual life for men and women of high culture. Virtually every university required students to study English beyond the matriculation year, exposing them to a common set of course options.[58] Surveys and specialized courses in literature, poetry, and drama from the medieval to the modern world almost guaranteed that students would have at least a passing familiarity with the literary icons of English civilization such as Chaucer, Milton, Shakespeare, and Tennyson. English literature most assuredly meant British writing, since American and Canadian authors occupied only a small corner of the curriculum. Though their popularity had grown steadily outside the university classroom, North American writers were largely kept at bay. Professor E.V. Knox of the University of Toronto complained that Canadian universities "were all too inclined to dismiss the literature of the United States as half-barbarous, because we know their movies are, in general, the antithesis of art, their magazines the apotheosis of bourgeois 'kulcher,' and their average novel the product of a perverted romanticism, and because we feel that culturally they are decidedly inferior to Englishmen." The author failed to understand how such writers as Emerson, Poe, Longfellow, Whitman, Sinclair Lewis, and Robert Frost could be dismissed so lightly. In Canadian universities, however, they were, as literary tradition prevailed.[59] Despite being influenced by continental trends in other areas, of twenty-eight English courses, the University of Western Ontario, typically, offered only one course in Canadian and American literature.[60] As Patricia Jasen notes, the prestigious place of English literature and composition aroused little opposition, as most academics could accept both the cultural and practical value of the subject. "Humanists were generally grateful for any guarantee that students would have some exposure to culture. [Scholars] in social sciences, sciences and the professions were willing to concede that some kind of cultural influence was beneficial, and they could always hope that an English course would teach their students how to write if nothing else."[61] Courses in composition, rhetoric, and "the forms of public address" provided English students with skills that might also be applied to other disciplines.[62]

History, too, had earned a more than respectable position in the liberal arts curriculum. Like English, it bridged, to a degree, traditional and modern intellectual currents. Once the domain of romantics and "literary amateurs" who were absorbed with epic and spiritual events on the one hand and historical ephemera on the other, the study of history became more specialized and professional by the early twentieth century. Like other social scientists enthusiastic about the application of the scientific method to social affairs, historians increasingly derived status from their "expert" use of evidence in reconstructing the past.[63] Yet they were hardly mere technicians. George Wrong, the most influential Canadian historian of his generation, believed that while historians should be politically impartial, they were also obliged to draw "moral judgments" from their measured study of society's development.[64] Though he retired from the University of Toronto in 1927, Wrong left in his wake scholars and teachers increasingly adept at research, but persuaded still of the important role that historical knowledge might play in humanizing and ordering the community.

The teaching of history in the 1930s reflected these dimensions. European and British history predominated, and it was hoped that Canadian students exposed to these subjects would come to an appreciation of their social heritage. But with the growth of Canadian nationalism following the First World War, some influential historians looked more to North America and less to Britain for the sources of Canada's identity and character. Harold Innis and Arthur Lower, for example, who studied at Chicago and Harvard respectively, returned to Canada to write and teach about the economic and geographical – as well as the political –

origins of Canadian society. They and some two dozen fellow academics wrote a multi-volume series on Canadian-American relations (sponsored by the Carnegie Endowment for International Peace), which was conceived by its editor, J.T. Shotwell, as one instrument for preserving good relations between the two countries, an association that could set an example for the whole world. "The history of Canadian-American relations became a model of how nations might live together peacefully if only the correct lessons were followed."[65] Anglophiles suspicious of the United States might draw from the historical record different conclusions from those stressing the virtue of closer ties with America, but neither imperialists nor continentalists doubted the applied cultural value of learning from the past. Historians – even the "specialists" among them using the tools of modern social science – could still offer moral and political guidance to students and the public. Indeed, the mere exercise of studying the past, whatever the lessons elicited, helped to preserve the high purpose of the liberal arts, and history's significant position within the humanities was thus secured.

Proponents of the humanities also assigned an important place to the study of modern languages, though here too there was debate over the question of whether language teaching served primarily cultural or utilitarian functions. A 1928 report on modern-language instruction in Canada contended that it should do both. Not only should students be technically proficient in writing and speech, but in studying foreign civilizations they should enhance their "literary and artistic appreciation."[66] One critic, however, claimed that in the classroom the humanists were being overwhelmed by what he contemptuously called the "mathematico-psychologists," who believed that language study should be subjected to the scientific method. Employing "word counts, frequency tests, and composition scales," they had sought to turn the schoolroom into a "laboratory," where the teacher would "treat the student like a guinea-pig and count his squeaks on an adding-machine."[67] He admitted, however, that these insidious modern techniques, which robbed foreign languages of their aesthetics and integrity, were more popular in the United States than in Canada. At the University of British Columbia, first-year French students continued to study Molière, La Fontaine, and La Bruyère, and a German professor at Toronto still compelled his students to "sharpen their wisdom teeth" on the First Part of Faust.[68] Academic purists firmly bound to tradition also lamented the failure of language teaching to attract large numbers of male students. According to the 1928 report, beyond the first year, women in these courses outnumbered men by a ratio of five to one, a pattern that diminished the status of the discipline. "The right-thinking young man was encouraged to seek success and a career in business; economics and history were thought to be more in his line." Males evidently avoided courses that required "exercises and children's stories and grammar tests and long hours of translation – translation – translation. The Modern Langauge departments have frequently not attracted men students because they have not deserved to attract them."[69] The distinct sexual bias aside, such judgments seem overly harsh. Courses in French, German, and Spanish grew in popularity during the 1930s, indicating that many students had more ecumenical cultural interests than their severest critics implied.[70]

Students studying philosophy also rode the wave of shifting intellectual tides. From the 1870s to the 1920s the dominant figure in Canadian philosophy was John Watson of Queen's, an "idealist" who attempted to reconcile Christianity with "the advance of science, the theory of evolution, the new biblical criticism, and an aggressive enlightenment."[71] He and his followers faced the secular world with the belief that once anchored in Christian faith, students could safely confront a complex world with rationality and civility. Despite the numerous challenges, it was still possible for students, particularly those steeped in the thought of the towering thinkers of western civilization, to live moral and useful lives.[72] In their own way the prominent university philosophers who lectured students in the 1920s and 1930s maintained the mission of accommodating ethical values with practical experience, though in their teaching and writing, religion *per se* diminished in importance. Philosophical idealism yielded gradually, but less uniformly than in the United States, to various forms of realism and pragmatism, approaches that sought truth less through metaphyscial speculation than through logic and empirical analysis.[73]

Perhaps the most influential academic philosopher was George Brett, who in 1926 was appointed head of the department of philosophy at Toronto's University College, which eventually became one of the largest philosophy departments in the world.[74] Brett's "contribution to philosophy was characterized by a profound and comprehensive scholarship, an unceasing use of the historical method, and an abiding confidence in the function of reason."[75] He attempted to demonstrate the "unity of civilization" and the "historical relationships between philosophical ideas and other great systems of ideas in science, politics, and religion."[76] Like others, he deplored the rise of irrationality that had culminated in war and dangerous mass movements. Reason, above all, would restore equilibrium and sanity to the world.

His colleague at Dalhousie, Herbert L. Stewart, expounded a similar philosophy both in the classroom and through regular radio broadcasts on the CBC. A Nietzche scholar and an editor of the *Dalhousie Review*, his analysis of world affairs flowed from the careful exploration of conflicting values that underlay national and international antagonisms. He, too, appealed to moderation, reason, and fastidious attention to history in the conduct of public affairs, though his ideology became noticeably more conservative towards the end of his career.[77]

Working amid the harsh realities of a pioneering region, some leading philosophers in western Canada focused even more on the problems of social and community organization. Rupert Lodge of the University of Manitoba believed that "philosophy is a practical activity. It seeks to produce coherent ways of confronting the tasks of life and its motivations are, in any case, basically practical ... In the end it does not so much solve problems as inform life. It enables the man who insists upon reflecting to develop a policy. But it cannot finally decide that policy."[78] Lodge described his teaching method:

We begin teaching undergraduate students in their second year of Arts, introducing them to critical self-reflection by having them write a large number of essays upon the moral and intellectual problems arising out of their own development to maturity. These essays are discussed in class, and in connection with these discussions an outline of systematic thinking on ethics, logic, theory of knowledge, and metaphysics is presented in such a way as to show the students how to make practical application (both to life-problems and to their problems as students of arts and science).[79]

If, as Leslie Armour and Elizabeth Trott note, Lodge did not successfully reconcile idealism, pragmatism, and realism in his eclectic writing, his courses and those of other philosophers around the country exposed students to a wide range of philosophical thought, from Plato to John Dewey.[80] Ideologically, Canadian philosophers generally eschewed both dogmatism and radicalism. Students, for example, would have been introduced to the ideas of Marxism, but there were no advocates of this theory in the mainstream of philosophical teaching. Neither were philosophy classes overburdened by preachy conservatism. Whatever distinguished them from each other, Canadian philosophers were more pluralistic than their European counterparts, and less drawn by the technological models of thought current in the United States.[81]

Despite growing competition from other disciplines and despite the reservations of old-school academics, the humanities were hardly manifestations of intellectual and cultural barbarism. Undoubtedly falling short of some lofty (and probably unattainable) classical, romantic, or Victorian ideal, the curriculum attempted to provide students with the intellectual discipline considered appropriate to the respectable middle-class lives they were destined to lead. While the quality of their work varied, students studying languages, literature, history, and philosophy (along with theology and fine arts) learned something of tradition, literacy, and moral order.[82]

This approach was accompanied in the arts curriculum by courses stressing the social utility and problem-solving capacity of knowledge. Having opened the door to the wonders of scientific inquiry, scholars in the late nineteenth century soon found their academic sanctuaries filled with the spirit of modernity. As a number of historians have found, the unity of thought and experience, once built on a religious foundation, was recast in the early twentieth century by intellectuals hoping to harmonize spiritual values with the practical requirements of a secular, industrial society.[83]

By the 1920s and 1930s practical training was itself idealized as the university's claim to high purpose was tied increasingly to the principle of public service. From this perspective, respectable culture, embodied in the teaching of the humanities, would be strengthened – not diminished – by applied skills derived from the social sciences and the professions.[84] The emergence of academic psychology, economics, commerce, politics, and sociology best typified these trends in the liberal arts prior to the Second World War.

"The history of psychology falls into two great divisions," observed a contributor to Queen's Quarterly, "the study of the soul and the study of behaviour without the soul."[85] In its former embodiment, psychology, seeking the sources of human motivation, followed the lead and was taught under the rubric of philosophy. But like the adolescents they "discovered" and studied at the beginning of the twentieth century, psychologists sought greater autonomy from their aging, traditional parents. Convinced that human actions could be explored and explained scientifically, contemporary researchers, inspired by John B. Watson of Johns Hopkins University, pursued a "form of 'behaviorism' which eschewed psychology's traditional links with philosophy and metaphysics."[86] Applied and clinical research in the United States and Canada led to extensive studies of child-rearing, educational training, juvenile delinquency, and the adjustment of war veterans to civilian life.[87] Intrigued by the possibilities of social engineering, academics developed specialties in experimental psychology, educational psychology, social psychology, animal psychology, and abnormal psychology, though Freudian psychoanalysis aroused a good deal of scepticism in Canada. But in the view of its most enthusiastic proponents, there was no limit to the practical utility of the new discipline. According to William Tait of McGill, medicine, education, business, social work, physical education, and human relations were all its potential beneficiaries.[88]

While some academics, particularly George Brett at the University of

Toronto, resisted the separation of psychology from philosophy, denouncing the "fragmentation" and "desperate positivism" of the new discipline at the expense of "introspective study of the conscious, individual life," the times were receptive to the new currents.[89] Enrolments grew in psychology between the wars, and at most universities the break with philosophy was achieved in practice if not completely in theory. At Manitoba it was noted that "that there has been a growing demand on the part of students for special work in Psychology beyond the regular Fourth year course, principally in preparation for professional work in fields such as the various branches of social service, nursing, medicine and teaching."[90] Separate psychology departments were created at McGill and Toronto in the 1920s, and elsewhere, even where the "marriage" of the two disciplines endured, they led independent intellectual lives. The American enthusiasm for intelligence measurement and testing was in evidence at a number of campuses, including Western, where in 1937 the university required a psychological examination for all first-year students.[91]

Also reflecting American trends was the deep impact that psychology had on teacher-training programs across the country. Courses in educational psychology were intended to bring a scientific perspective to the study of the motivation and behaviour of children and adolescents. The "science of psychology" was introduced to education students through such texts as Peter Sandiford's *Educational Psychology* (1928), and addressed such problems as "inherited human characteristics, motivation, individual differences, adaptation to environment, control of environment, efficiency in learning, the laws underlying certain accepted methods of teaching, discipline, intelligent behaviour, habits and their development, transfer of training, infancy, childhood and adolescence, and character and personality."[92]

While psychology's relevance and utility appealed to career-bound students, at least one Alberta graduate believed that specialization within the discipline had gone too far. A typical textbook, he noted, contained "much on the measurement of intelligence but nothing on thought; half the book deals with learning but perception is struck out ... Whereas in the early days of the century educators studied psychology and did not know how to apply it, now they apply it and do not know how to study it."[93]

Despite such reservations, the enthusiasm for applied research and training persisted in the social sciences. There was certainly no shortage of problems to which academics might fruitfully devote their attention in the period following the First World War. Urban settlement, rural depopulation, labour-management relations, federal-provincial conflict, and Canada's place within the British empire and on the continent elicited a body of scholarship that found its way into university classrooms. While their interests and emphases varied, scholars grappled with the challenge of "increas[ing] the efficiency of the capitalist system in Canada," a mission rendered particularly onerous by the sudden eruption of the Depression.[94]

Of all the social sciences, the subject of economics, frequently taught within departments of "political economy," achieved greatest prominence in this period.[95] More than forty monographs in Canadian political economy were published during the 1920s, surpassing the total of the entire previous century, and in the 1930s the publication rate tripled.[96] The prestige and professionalism of the discipline are indicated by the fact that the University of Toronto hired nineteen economists between 1922 and 1937, compared to two political scientists and one sociologist.[97] Many of the books used in Canadian courses embraced the neoclassical approach to the study of capitalism, as refined by Alfred Marshall, in which the forces of supply and demand were perceived to function in symphonic harmony, largely free of government intervention.[98] Some academics, like W.J. Waines of the University of Manitoba, were positively reverential in their respect for free-market economics, while others, like Waine's colleague Archibald Brown Clark, W.R. Maxwell at Dalhousie, and J.C. Hemmeon at McGill, allowed "opportunities for argument and the consideration of alternatives to [Marshallian] authoritative pronouncements."[99] Furthermore, Canadian academics such as W.A. Mackintosh and Harold Innis added a unique dimension to the classical analysis by stressing the importance of Canadian economic history, through which state involvement (in such areas as resource exploitation, agriculture, and transportation) had played an important developmental and stabilizing role in the emerging market system.[100]

The Depression affected the practice of economic science in two ways. It undermined comfortable assumptions about the market forces driving the economy, and it drew university professors into direct public service as "expert" advisers to government policy-makers. The publication of John Maynard Keynes's *General Theory of Employment, Interest and Money* in 1936 diminished the credibility of those who believed dogmatically in the "self-correcting" capacity of the depressed capitalist economy. For Keynes, shaking the system out of its paralysis required the stimulation of investment and consumption by governments themselves. Canadian economists by no means became proponents of radical economic thought, let alone uncritical followers of Keynes, nor did they abandon their essential faith in capitalism. But according to Doug Owram, a growing "professional" consensus emerged during the 1930s around the need for selective "ameliorative" actions by government to restructure and co-ordinate the economy. Canadian economists, unlike bankers, favoured the creation of a central bank, which was accomplished in 1934, though the academics remained conservative on the question of deficit financing.[101] Unlike the small minority of political economists associated with the socialist League for Social Reconstruction, mainstream economists continued to believe in "fiscal conservatism," although the Second World War inspired some exceptional, if temporary, forms of economic planning.[102]

By the late 1930s typical programs in political economy, such as that at the University of British Columbia, included courses on the principles of economics, economic history, money and banking, government finance, international trade, corporation economics, labour problems, transportation, and statistics.[103] Modified classical economics (which acknowledged without necessarily celebrating the ideas of Keynes) and, where the literature permitted, the institutional and historical particularities of Canadian economic life constituted the course content. While far from oblivious to new currents in economic analysis, the discipline, in W.H. Alexander's somewhat cynical view, remained ideologically "safe."[104]

Economists and other social scientists were given unprecedented opportunity to affect public events by virtue of their extensive work for federal and provincial governments. At a time when "the academic pursuit of reason and the scientist's pursuit of truth were ... thought to be reconcilable with activity in government," social scientists answered the call of politicians requiring expertise in a variety of policy areas.[105] Though some professors, like Harold Innis, objected to the potentially compromising position in which this placed the scholar, most felt that contracted academics – both as researchers and as civil servants – could fulfil their "social-citizenship" role without being politically partisan. In addition, from a less idealistic point of view, the supplementary income generated by this work in hard economic times was not easy to turn down.[106] The participation of academics in public affairs reached new heights with the work of the Royal Commission on Federal-Provincial Relations (1937–40). Twelve of the commission's sixteen research reports were written by university scholars, as were several of the provincial submissions.[107] These activities both reinforced the utilitarian orientation of higher education and enhanced government service as an attractive and prestigious career option for university graduates with marketable skills.

Students anxious to advance within the private sector enrolled increasingly in commerce and business administration courses, which had evolved into degree programs in a number of universities by the Second World War. Between 1937 and 1941, 1065 students received commerce degrees, compared to 334 between 1922 and 1926. In addition, a large (though undetermined) number took individual courses in this field as part of their liberal arts training.

Proponents of commerce education contended that universities were obliged to meet the demands both of the business community, which required managers with specialized skills, and of students seeking responsible positions in the corporate world.[108] The example of the prestigious Harvard Business School, which the University of Western Ontario explicitly attempted to emulate, demonstrated the potential benefits flowing to universities able to mount reputable business programs.[109] Although commerce students enrolled in technical courses such as accounting, statistics, and marketing, and, in the case of Western, secretarial science, they were expected to develop far more sophistication than business students in high school and private colleges. Most degree programs required students to complete a range of courses in the liberal arts before concentrating in commerce and finance in their upper years. As the *Queen's Journal* noted, "The new and better path lies in the application of the professional spirit and professional methods in business ... The task insofar as it can be performed by education is one which only the university can perform."[110] Gilbert Jackson, professor of political economy at the University of Toronto, claimed that mathematical and accounting courses were "tools" requiring disciplined thinking of "adult minds," no less than that demanded by "the logic of Hegel" or "the dialectic of Plato."[111]

Critics were unconvinced, dismissing such claims as mere rationalization. Classicist Charles Cochrane of the University of Toronto charged that commerce courses attracted students "who had no real interest in cultural pursuits"; further, the excessively narrow training offered in these programs bore no relationship to "the critical examination of methods" characteristic of true science.[112] In historian Frank Underhill's opinion, commerce courses attracted inferior students who would simply add to the population of "polished, well-behaved young Babbitts who are already so drearily a familiar sight on any big University Campus."[113]

Some universities, including Toronto and Manitoba, sought to forge connections in the business community by inviting corporate officials to participate in the planning and implementation of commerce programs.[114] But businessmen themselves were not all persuaded of the value of such training in universities. Dismal economic conditions limited employment opportunities for graduating students during the 1930s, but even where positions were available, applicants frequently found "an inherent prejudice against university trained men and women."[115] A spokesmen for the British Columbia Telephone Company reported on conversations he had held with Vancouver businessmen on the subject of college graduates. Students aspiring to corporate life were perceived to have unrealistic expectations. They were unwilling to start at the bottom of the company ladder; they would try "to reform the whole business"; they would not "take orders readily and they lacked patience."[116]

Some of these perceptions were confirmed in letters received by the president of the University of Alberta, who in 1935 appealed directly to Alberta businessmen to hire university graduates. Many responded positively or promised to consider graduates if positions opened in the future. Small businessmen who had employed students in previous summers with favourable results were especially enthusiastic about the benefits of hiring graduates. But larger institutions, particularly insurance companies and banks, were more sceptical. Banks generally chose to hire graduates directly out of high school, while the insurance industry sought mature family men who were at least twenty-five years old and had some sales experience. University graduates, with or without business degrees, were considered less likely to make long-term commitments to these institutions.[117]

In general, commerce education did not necessarily disadvantage students seeking business careers, and as we shall see in chapter 7, a significant proportion of university graduates eventually succeeded in the private sector. None the less, business executives continued to place a great premium on the value of having employees – whatever their educational backgrounds – work their way up through corporate ranks from positions of minimal status. Rather than over-emphasizing their degrees, ambitious graduates meeting prospective employers were advised to demonstrate appropriate "attitudes," such as "confidence, initiative, personality and cheerfulness."[118] While college-based business training had achieved a high priority in the United States by the 1920s and 1930s, this developed north of the border only after the Second World War, owing, in all probability, to Canada's comparative lag in economic development and industrial diversification.[119] Thus, the efforts made earlier by universities to provide prestigious commercial education elicited mixed responses within both the academic and business communities.

If psychology and economics headed the social science "family," political science and sociology were its poor relations between the wars.[120] Typically, at the University of Alberta in 1935, of 18 courses offered in the Department of Political Economy, 17 focused on economic themes and only one on politics.[121] At Western only 6 of the 27 courses in the Department of Economics and Political Science dealt primarily with political themes.[122] J.A. Corry, hired to teach political science at Queen's in 1936, had "no formal qualifications" in the subject. "All I knew of consequence," he recalled, "was self-taught."[123] Because "there were not more than four or five persons in Canada professionally trained to teach" political science in the mid 1930s, students were usually instructed by those for whom the subject was a secondary vocation – economists, historians, lawyers, and philosophers.[124]

Unlike economics, which approached the study of market relations on the basis of "a fairly exact body of principles," political science, having "a more amorphous subject matter," appeared less capable of problem solving – and thus had less status as a social science – in the utilitarian academic climate.[125] Scholars had yet to explore systematically such issues as the operation of political parties, the process of policy formation, or the political behaviour of voters – topics that would consume the interests of a future generation of political science researchers.[126] Instead, as the discipline struggled to assert its territorial integrity, teaching and research focused on historical and constitutional developments that recounted the evolution of Canada's "dominion status." Academics such as Corry, W.P.M. Kennedy, R.A. Mackay, R.M. MacIver, and R. McGregor Dawson produced a collection of enduring monographs that documented the British roots of Canadian political institutions. Augmented by legal and constitutional texts emanating from England, the political science curriculum in its embryonic phase thus stressed the ordered, civilized growth of Canadian society, a theme not inconsistent with the predominant ideological orientation of the liberal arts.[127]

Somewhat more intellectually adventurous were the handful of scholars who introduced Canadian students to the subject of sociology. Initiated by theologians, moral reformers, and social workers who strove for harmony and efficiency in a problem-infested world, sociology courses, in the few institutions that offered them before the First World War, had a utilitarian as opposed to an academic or theoretical orientation. In 1914 the University of Toronto established a Department of Social Service, described by Professor R.M. MacIver as embracing "the sphere of Applied Social Science, the study of the conditions on which social welfare begins."[128] McGill followed with the founding of a Department of Social Study and Training in 1918, designed for students seeking careers in welfare agencies, hospitals, prisons, and the clergy.[129]

In an effort to strengthen the program's academic content, McGill hired J.W. Dawson, a graduate of the Acadia divinity program and the University of Chicago's Department of Sociology, to head what would become Canada's first department of sociology in 1926. Dawson inspired teaching and graduate work that were based on the theory of "human ecology" (developed by Chicago's Robert Park), which analysed the community as a complex organism thriving on the interdependence of the individual and the environment.[130] Focusing on urban problems such as

prostitution, delinquency, child dependency, and communications systems, Dawson and his students stressed the critical importance of empirical, scientific research, laying the basis for a professional sociology with
a distinct intellectual terrain.

In the 1930s Dawson turned his attention to western Canada, and
along with several Canadian academics published the nine-volume Fron-
tiers of Settlement series, which explored the establishment and adjustment of immigrant and farming communities to Canadian life.[131] With
the aid of a grant from the Rockefeller foundation, Dawson's colleague
at McGill, Leonard Marsh, headed the Social Science Reseach Project,
which produced a number of studies on the social conditions of Montreal
and culminated in an extensive investigation of employment and social
class called Canadians In and Out of Work.[132]

These promising developments, however, represented less the vitality
than the limits of sociology between the wars. Most universities recognized the emergence of the discipline but continued to offer only a
few sociology courses, usually under the rubric of political economy.
For both intellectual and ideological reasons, sociology was not yet an
entirely respectable subject. R.J. Urwick, the head of political economy
at Toronto, both feared the tendency of sociology to fragment the liberal
arts curriculum further and doubted the ability of its practitioners to
remain scientifically objective when exploring "human behaviour."[133]
Other critics questioned the theoretical foundation and breadth of the
discipline in its contemporary mode.[134] The conservative governors of
McGill, traditionally supportive of "useful" academic knowledge, none
the less found fault with the particular orientation of applied sociology.
They were preoccupied with what they viewed as the leftist politics of
Leonard Marsh and his students, whose investigation of the urban under-
life implied the need for interventionist, non-market approaches to the
social problems of the Depression. When funding for the Social Science
Research Project evaporated, Marsh and his left-of-centre colleague
Eugene Forsey were released from the faculty for what historians have
since determined were clearly ideological reasons.[135] In light of this
unenthusiastic reception, sociology at McGill and elsewhere survived
but languished until it was revived in Canadian universities in the
1960s.[136] Thus, sociologists between the wars first enjoyed the fruits
and then, to their dismay, encountered the limits of academic pluralism
in the liberal arts curriculum.

In the 1930s the tensions between traditionalists and "modernists,"
specialists and generalists, proponents of high culture and practitioners
of applied scholarship found expression within the undergraduate curriculum. Indeed, if the academic rhetoric of the time were to be taken

entirely at face value, and if higher education were to be examined exclusively as a problem in intellectual history, then it would be tempting to conclude, as some have, that universities were sustaining an academic cold war, with the dark forces of utilitarianism perched on the edge of victory.[137] A broader perspective, however, leads to a less dramatic, more qualified judgment. The struggle was somewhat less titanic than the protagonists' debate implied.

As a result of shifting social demands and new intellectual currents, the curriculum now offered students a wider variety of course options. Without question, this led to a greater degree of program fragmentation and specialization. Not all students were brilliant, and not all faculty were comfortable with or fully prepared to embrace the new trends. Yet the university's *raison d'être* was neither the production of genius nor the achievement of curricular uniformity for its own sake, though these were admirable and frequently espoused ideals. Instead, the university was expected and undertook to equip graduates with the kinds of skills and values that would prepare them for professional and middle-class lives. However much they mistrusted each other, humanities and social science teachers contributed collectively, and in a complementary way, to this end. The former exposed students to the culture of Western and especially British civilization. The latter both introduced them to contemporary intellectual currents, including those emanating from the United States, and stressed the value of applied learning. The successful graduates were expected to be literate, respectful of tradition, organized, patriotic, inquisitive without being radical, and able to hold responsible positions in the community. The curriculum as a whole contributed to the cultivation of these characteristics. Professors could vigorously debate the appropriate mix of subjects, or lament the emptiness of modern culture, but had students taken more Latin or less psychology, it is difficult to see how this would have altered either their world-views or the role of the university in girding them for the future. The attention devoted to professional training, as we shall demonstrate in the next chapter, reinforced this social mission of the Canadian university.

CHAPTER FOUR

Professional Culture

Professionalism entrenched itself in the halls of higher learning at the end of the nineteenth century. As we noted in chapter 1, this development arose from a combination of economic and social pressures that led to both the broadening of the university's training function and the middle-class search for new means to ensure status and respectability. Traditionally, scholars have portrayed the emergence of professionalism as an organized and efficent process through which specialized talent was provided to consumers in a complex industrial society.[1] Revolutionary changes in science and technology, according to this view, required well-educated experts to absorb and sort through intricate information and deliver needed services to a more demanding public. Told in these terms, the story is a comforting one, filled with the spirit of enlightenment and reflecting in its rendering the whiggish enthusiasm for the spread and delivery of schooling to growing numbers of education-hungry youth in Canada, the United States, and Europe.[2]

Without denying the significance of technologically driven change or the virtue of society's providing more accessible public schooling, other observers take a less benign and less idealistic view of the rise and extension of professionalism in this era.[3] Unquestionably, doctors, dentists, lawyers, and engineers found themselves confronted with a vast new range of intellectual and social problems requiring more education and training, particularly in light of the rapid growth of urban centres fuelled by massive immigration to North America. For practising and aspiring professionals, this posed an opportunity as well as a challenge.

As the scope of professional practice broadened, growing numbers of "experts" with varied backgrounds and experience were able to claim authority and achieve some success in the intense contest for clients. On the one hand, this was legitimate in a free-enterprise economy, to which professionals remained committed, but on the other hand, unrestrained rivarly was potentially damaging to the private interests and collective images of the professions as a whole. The unregulated expansion of private proprietary schools, and of individuals using professional titles, undermined the credibility of these groups at the end of nineteenth century. This was perceived to be a particular problem in the United States, and in response the medical, legal, and engineering professions took steps to bring order to the training and certifying processes. On the whole they successfully salvaged and then enhanced their reputations and positions.

In Canada, too, professionals followed the example of doctors in attempting to protect themselves from excessive competition. While they tackled this problem with different strategies, amid considerable internal conflict and with varying degrees of success, professional associations agreed that their special social standing required training and certifying systems that were more rigidly controlled. Locating professional training within universities served this end. While the utility of higher education was doubted by some established professionals, it served in the long run to strengthen their positions. The numbers of potential graduates admitted and the qualifications required of them could be more effectively regulated and standardized in the universities, where students were exposed, both directly and indirectly, to the dominant ideas and values of professional culture. In an era when the faith in science and expertise had reached unprecedented if not mystical proportions, practitioners with improved academic qualifications earned both greater public deference and higher financial benefits. They strengthened their legitimacy by exalting the ideal of public service and by developing codes of ethics. The most successful among them were thus able "to translate one order of scarce resources – special knowledge and skills – into another – social and economic rewards."[4]

In an effort to understand how these processes shaped the academic lives of students, we shall examine and compare professional culture and education in the fields of medicine, engineering, law, dentistry, and agriculture. The unique – and more confining – experience of female students aspiring to professional careers is also examined. The chapter ends with a discussion of student views of teaching and training methods.

I

Between 1900 and 1940 both the training of students and the practice of medicine underwent an important transition in North America. Concerned about the flood of practitioners on to the market, the uneven quality of medical education, and the lack of uniform standards, the American Council of Medical Education sponsored an investigation of

Table 7
Courses of Study at Canadian Universities, 1935
(Full-time Enrolments)

	Students	Women	
Courses	%	No.	%
Arts and science	54.0	18,085	30.4
Engineering, applied science	10.8	3,618	.8
Medicine	9.0	3,037	4.2
Religion and theology	7.9	2,643	.9
Agriculture	3.3	1,008	1.8
Law	3.0	1,005	2.3
Education	2.5	857	52.2
Commerce and business	2.3	786	13.0
Household science	2.1	688	100.0
Pharmacy	1.4	484	8.0
Dentistry	1.3	439	.7
Nursing	1.1	372	100.0
Veterinary medicine	.7	245	0.0
Fine and applied arts	.5	155	83.9
Total	100	33,522	22.4

Source: Adapted from Statistics Canada, Historical Compendium of Educational Statistics (Ottawa 1975), 216.

the state of medical training in the United States and Canada. Written by Abraham Flexner of the Carnegie Foundation for the Advancement of Teaching and published in 1910, the report contended that the profession would be best served by the closing of medical schools that lacked intellectual rigour and adequate training facilities. The American Medical Association's Council on Medical Education, whose approval medical schools across the continent required in order to maintain credibility, supported the Flexner Report's findings, and the number of American medical schools declined from 131 in 1910 to 76 in 1920.[5] While Canadian medical schools by no means escaped criticism – Western's program was reproached for being "as bad as anything on this side of the line" – none of the eight facilities north of the border was compelled to close. Already affiliated with individual universities, Canadian medical schools were less exposed to the type of criticism directed at entrepreneurial training institutions in the United States, many of which had undertaken questionable – and in some cases overly innovative – training practices.[6]

In the wake of the Flexner Report, admission standards were tightened, laboratory and clinical facilities were gradually improved, and, after 1912, all Canadian graduates were compelled to pass examinations required by the (Canadian) Council of Medical Education before being licensed. Two new medical schools were founded at Alberta (1913) and British Columbia (1923), bringing the total number of schools to ten. (One of these, Saskatchewan did not offer a full training program until the 1950s.)

Having secured a monopoly in the training and certifying of doctors, the medical profession enhanced its prestige by increasing its application of the scientific method to the treatment of illness. Around the turn of the century, research in bacteriology, immunology, and biochemistry had led to major advances in medical understanding of the nature and causes of communicable diseases such as cholera, diphtheria, dysentry, tetanus, and typhoid.[7] The discovery of insulin by Banting, Best, Collip, and Macleod at the University of Toronto in 1921–22 heightened the status of medicine even more, as did the innovative use in the 1930s of protonsil and sulfanilamide in the treatment of infections.[8]

Despite these impressive advances, doctors knew only too well that there was a limit to their actual healing powers. During the 1930s, for example, pneumonia, tuberculosis, and polio continued to kill or cripple thousands of North Americans, and general practitioners, particularly those in poorly equipped country practices, found themselves confined to treating symptoms or temporarily relieving pain. Awe-struck patients who survived, however, exaggerated the significance of these therapies and medications, and physicians chose not to disabuse them of their illusions. As one general practitioner recalled, "More important than the symptomatic treatment and the medications was the doctor's presence, his reassuring voice and manner, and his soothing hand."[9]

But medicine's successes, more than its failures and frustrations, gripped the public imagination, and to a greater degree than ever medicine became widely associated with the ideals of progress, objectivity, and altruism. The fame and "heroism" of Frederick Banting, for example, which endured into the 1930s and beyond, was, in Mary Vipond's words, the "product ... of the mystique of the healing physician, fused with the new glamour of scientific research as the progenitor of future progress."[10] The status that medicine men, faith-healers, and priests had achieved through mysticism and religion in earlier eras was, in the early twentieth century, inherited by doctors steeped in modern medical practice. The image of the profession thus rose with the public's faith "in the power of scientific medicine to protect [them] from pestilence, whether foreign or domestic; to discover and remove the causes of disease within and around their homes, and to promote the general health of communities."[11]

As beneficiaries of these cultural, technological, and organizational changes, general practitioners had become models of social respectability. But like the science they practised, their position was not immutable. Gradually their status was challenged from within the profession by the growth of medical specialization, yet a further consequence of the engagement in scientific medicine. In the face of a growing population, advances in such areas as bacteriology, pathology, and radiography, and the use of more sophisticated equipment for the performance of surgery and obstetrics, more and more doctors undertook their practice within hospitals. No longer a charitable institution where the ailing poor were sent to die, the hospital became a workshop for the "highest type of professional practice, and the physician was being brought into a more intricate relationship with this institutionalized collective enterprise."[12] Increasingly perceived to be the true expert, the hospital-associated specialist more than the general practitioner, now burdened with traditional equipment and a folksy image, rose quickly in the medical hierarchy and became the new symbol of supreme accomplishment. The newer specialties – pediatrics, neurology, internal medicine, and surgery – were in turn divided into numerous sub-branches such as psychiatry, orthopaedics, plastic surgery, and proctology. By 1935 one-third of all Canadian physicians had become specialists.[13] Reflecting North American trends, 36 per cent of University of Toronto medical students were engaged in specialist training.[14]

While part of the impetus to specialization could be accounted for by the more sophisticated application of new medical knowledge, this was not the whole explanation for the phenomenon. According to the prestigious Commission on Medical Education, which was formed by the Association of American Medical Colleges, and reported in 1932, the self-interest of doctors combined with the exaggerated faith of the public in technological expertise to enhance the position of the specialist. "The tendency has arisen partly out of the eagerness of physicians to provide up-to-date medical care, sometimes without realizing the limitations as well as the value of special laboratory, x-ray, and 'expert' services, and partly from the demands of patients and relatives who think that X-ray and laboratory examinations, specialists, expensive hospital accomodations, consultants, and special nurses are necessary to insure adequate care in all instances."[15]

In the view of the commission, the potential for the efficient, less costly treatment of patients should have been enhanced by specialist practice in clinics or hospitals, but the reverse was too often the real result. "To specialism must be credited no small part of the advances which have occurred in medical knowledge and practice in recent years. It is recognized, however, that many specialists are self-named; many are not fully trained even in their limited field and still less well equipped in the broad fundamentals of medicine; some are frankly commercial."[16] Doctors frequently yielded to the "temptation to require more examinations and consultations than are necessary" and were known to engage in the unethical practice of "fee-splitting." In addition, as many observers, including the dean of McGill's medical faculty, complained, excessive specialization encouraged doctors, fascinated by the intricacies of science and technology, to treat the "disease and not the patient."[17] "Because the efforts are often confined to a single phase of medicine, the specialist looks too frequently upon the problem of the patient solely from the aspect of his specialty, rather than from the needs of the patient as a whole."[18]

Thus, while specialization enhanced the image of medicine as a lofty and increasingly exact science, and while it accounted for acknowledged advances in the treatment of certain maladies, it had other less admirable consequences for the culture in which aspiring doctors were steeped. It furthered professional hierarchy, eroded the status of general practitioners, contributed to the depersonalization of medical treatment, and revived competitive entrepreneurialism within the profession.

Given these organizational and political developments, students who aspired to the relatively lucrative and secure practice of medicine, particularly in urban communities, required more than up-to-date technical training to achieve success. In a study of the "Informal Organization of the Medical Profession," Canadian sociologist Oswald Hall explored the complex network of "sponsorship and contacts" that doctors in training were pressured to participate in during the 1930s and 1940s. Because one's admission to medical school, to internship programs, to specialized training, and to private practice, both within and outside hospitals, depended to a considerable degree upon support and references from established, influential practitioners, it was important for the students to learn the system's dynamics. According to one veteran practising in the United States, "When a doctor gets into a position of head of a department over at the big hospital he can do a great deal for his young friends ... For example take Dr. Y who is sharing my practice now. I met him at a Medical Association dinner. He had gone from here to McGill Medical School [and] I was impressed by his character. He mentioned that he would like an internship at our large hospital. I was helping the internship committee, so it was easily arranged."[19] A fellow practitioner agreed: "Doctors can practice only on the invitation of the men already on the staffs. Hence the doctors holding the positions of importance in the dominant hospitals of the community wield a peculiarly important type of power. Moreover the newcomer entering medicine is extremely dependent on the selection policy of those in positions of authority."[20]

To secure such opportunities within the professional medical "fraternity," students and young doctors often felt compelled to cultivate appropriate social skills and to adhere to unwritten codes of behaviour. "I think a strong factor of loyalty runs through all the practice of medicine," noted one doctor; "there is a guild sense in the profession."[21] Since graduating students were assumed to have roughly equivalent technical qualifications, distinctions among them were made on the basis of other, more personal, criteria, consistent with the profession's values and self-image. Ideally, medical schools sought students with strong character, "personality, industry, native ability, alertness, devotion, thoroughness, judgment, [studiousness], and good health."[22]

In practice, one's "ability to mix well, to be humble to the correct degree to superiors, and to act the dignified but definitely superior part towards patients" could enhance the medical student's opportunties for advancement.[23] According to the dean of medicine at the University of Alberta, students experienced these pressures during the "annual scramble for internships ... beginning in the autumn term and lasting well into February."[24] Nor did the need to forge social connections diminish in the years that followed. "You want to know how a doctor gets a practice? Well, when a doctor comes into a community he usually sends cards to all the other doctors to solicit their good will. They will help him where they can, though they may be very critical of him."[25]

At the same time, inappropriate backgrounds and behaviour might well limit one's prospects. According to a number of individuals interviewed by Hall, young Jewish doctors were mistrusted and frequently excluded from inner professional circles, thus perpetuating the kind of social prejudices reflected in medical-school admission policies (discussed in chapter 2).[26] Physicians from minority ethnic backgrounds who did gain entry thus tended to begin and even confine their practices to the religious and cultural communities in which they were accepted. In addition, "trouble-makers" who questioned conventional practices, "just like these labour agitators," could find themselves thwarted in the competition for promotions and patient referrals.[27] Women, too, faced special obstacles. According to a contributor to the *University of Toronto Medical Journal*:

On approaching graduation, one finds that a remarkably small number of worthwhile internships are available for women graduates. This is not entirely the fault of the hospital staffs, since we, as women physicians, have been unable to break down completely the traditional antipathy of many patients. When a woman doctor makes a mistake, she is often crticized doubly; once for her mistake, and once for being a woman ... It has been said by many people that woman doctors lack self-confidence. Would it be any wonder if we did? Complete and justifiable self-confidence can come only with experience, responsibility, and a sense of achievement.[28]

Through such informal networks, concluded Oswald Hall, "rights to position, status, and power become recognized and upheld; mechanisms of legitimate succession and patterns of recruitment become established."[29]

Students were exposed to the professional medical culture early on in their training. Medical fraternities at Canadian universities both promoted themselves and were perceived by others as the elite campus associations. They held social and cultural events designed to foster a distinct and appropriate professional consciousness. In 1938–39, the Queen's Medical Society sponsored a number of lectures, including one on the ranking of the university as one of the continent's "best medical schools," another by a respected physician who had been one of Queen's "most brilliant graduates," and a third by the internationally renowned neurosurgeon and scholar Wilder Penfield, of the Montreal Neurological Institute.[30] Annual medical fraternity banquets (at Queen's, McGill, and Western) provided opportunities for celebration, ribaldry, and social bonding.[31] The 1937 graduating class at Western was told by a local physician that professional medical associations were of critical importance to their futures. "A man is known by the company he keeps. Make sure you are in good company. You will find it in your medical society."[32]

Students were informed as well of current political and bureaucratic developments that affected both the conduct of medical practice and the economic standing of practitioners. Given the increasing costs of running a practice, doctors sought new ways of organizing and attending to their business affairs. In 1935 a magazine devoted entirely to such matters was founded and distributed free to doctors, hospitals, and medical fraternities. The *Canadian Doctor* provided its readers with financial and investment advice, discussed various business problems, and provided a forum for the airing of controversial subjects.

No topic was more widely discussed than the problem of state-run health insurance. Britain had already introduced such a scheme, and doctors anticipated a similar development throughout Canada, particularly in light of the tabling of a draft health-insurance plan in the legislature of British Columbia in 1935.[33] Ideologically, the Canadian medical establishment opposed any scheme that threatened the autonomy of individual doctors and their self-governing medical associations. Government-administered fee scales were seen by many, including contributors to the *Canadian Doctor*, as the first step down the slippery slope towards professional servitude and state socialism. According to one writer, "Doctors' ills are many and find voice in countless individual plaints. They are likely to increase with the trend evidenced in social legislation of all kinds."[34] Another speaker told University of Western Ontario medical students that doctors would suffer from the impact of state-run health insurance "unless the medical profession is united and able to make itself felt in the framing of any health insurance law."[35]

Yet during the Depression, as a number of studies confirmed, Canadian doctors faced a serious erosion of their incomes as a result of indigence among their patients.[36] State-funded medical insurance, which would both eliminate the need for doctors to collect fees privately and provide them with greater income security in hard times, had some clear practical advantages. Recognizing the growing popularity of public health insurance, the Canadian Medical Association in 1934 proposed a scheme that embraced the concept for low-income Canadians but insisted on a central role for doctors in the administration and operation of any such system – something they later claimed was denied in the British Columbia proposal.[37] Limited subsidies were provided by some provinces, most notably Ontario, to municipal medical-relief plans, from which doctors derived a degree of financial benefit, but nation-wide such aid to the ailing poor was inadequately and unevenly distributed.[38]

While the war interrupted plans to implement public medical-insurance programs (except in Saskatchewan, which introduced a plan in 1944), students in the 1930s, like practitioners, debated the appropriateness of this form of health-care delivery. Most published opinion on the subject reflected current thinking within the profession itself. Student writers worried about the impact that state control would have on their status, though they recognized the immediate financial advantages both to doctors and to the impoverished. While the editor of the *McGill Medical Undergraduate Journal* acknowledged that in England the poor fared better under socialized medicine than before its implementation, the social costs to class-conscious doctors were, from his point of view, severe. "Under our present economic system anyone who is not engaged in some form of individual effort occupies one of the lower berths of the social scale. Socialized medicine presupposes support by universal taxation, which places the doctor, intrinsically one of the most important figures in any community and hence deserving of some prestige, in the position of the clerk who sorts the mails, lower indeed than the haughty customs official, since all will be paid from the same source."[39] Like the professionals they aspired to become, typical students appear to have favoured actions by the state that would protect or enhance doctors' status and independence, and to have opposed anything that threatened them. Students learned to cherish and hoped to inherit doctors' admired public image, enviable professional autonomy, realtively comfortable life-styles (despite recent pressures), and advanced technical expertise (particularly of the specialist).

However much they idealized medical "professionalism," student and faculty critics found much to debate about the nature and effectiveness of medical education. As with undergraduate training in the arts and sciences, some university officals spoke glowingly of the improved quality of Canadian medical training. Combining the best of British tradition and American innovation, the medical course at the University of Toronto, according to President R.A. Falconer, offered the right mix of cultural breadth and technical depth in the 1930s. The "Edinburgh" model, introduced to Canada (at McGill) by William Osler in the 1880s, stressed the importance of clinical training and "bedside teaching," an approach later complemented by an American-inspired emphasis on academic and theoretical science, which was strongly encouraged by Abraham Flexner in his 1910 report for the Carnegie Foundation. By the 1930s the length of the medical training program had been extended to a norm of six years beyond senior matriculation. These generally comprised two years in basic arts and science, two years of lectures and laboratory work in the basic medical sciences, and two years of clinical and hospital ward work – including an internship, which had by then become institutionalized in North American medical training.[40] At Toronto, as Falconer noted in 1931, "apart from slight modifications, this course has been in existence for ten years and the faculty has seen no reason for radical change."[41]

Others – at Toronto and elsewhere – were not so sanguine. By far the most common complaint, particularly among students, concerned the rigid system of rote learning, which required endless memorization, countless examinations, and too little independent or critical thinking. As one writer noted, "the demand for licences to practice is unques-tionably the most important factor governing the teaching system. It stamps the course in a fixed mold prescribed by our educational masters." Students dutifully followed lectures, "word for word ... copying their laboratory results from previously copied results, and preparing for the almighty examination by extensive synopses."[42]

The report of the 1932 American Commission on Medical Education concurred. "The dependence upon sheer memory tends to defeat the development of a scientific attitude and point of view. This makes the application of sound educational methods almost impossible, for the intellectual development of students can not occur in a breathless, hur-ried, pressing schedule of assigned exercises."[43] The limitations of this approach were evident during the internship term, where students placed

in "inferior" settings were either given too much independent responsiblity without adequate preparation or were compelled to perform
menial tasks that served hospital work schedules more than they
enhanced the individual's medical skills.[44]

With the emphasis on the mere accumulation of facts and details – a
pedagogical approach that accelerated with specialist training – students,
to the dismay of some, were not encouraged to think broadly about the
social context of medical practice. They spent almost no time discussing
such issues as workmen's compensation, public health, mental health,
preventive medicine, and the uneven distribution of health resources.[45]
Culturally, too, according to critics of the system, medical training left
enormous gaps in students' educational training. Despite the affiliation
of medical schools with universities, the influence of the latter "was
usually limited to improving the teaching of science. The humanistic
values of the liberals arts seldom affected either educators or their students."[46] One doctor lamented the contemporary emphasis on technical
competence and material rewards over the spiritual values that he claimed
animated the Greek ideal of medical training.[47]

But such lofty concerns could be over-emphasized, in the view of one
writer, who urged medical educators to take a more realistic account of
the world around them. If anything, medical training should take less
time, be more practical, and keep course requirements in the arts to a
bare minimum. After all, "life is short and the pockets of parents and
guardians at present are shorter still."[48] Medical training, like university
education as a whole, was, in the end, shaped by such mundane material
pressures and considerations.

Despite its acknowledged imperfections, there were few alterations
made in the medical training programs during the 1930s, though in the
interests of ensuring greater selectivity – and discrimination – in the
choice of applicants, a number of Canadian medical schools, as we saw
in chapter 2, reduced the size of their entering classes.[49] The McGill
medical faculty introduced additional reforms in 1936. Inspired by the
severe criticisms uttered for years by its retiring dean, C.F. Martin,
McGill modified its program by shortening its training period by one
year. But because the annual academic session was lengthened from seven
and a half to nine months, students received almost as many classroom
and clinical hours as in the past. In addition, preference would now be
given to "appliants who have had a full academic course [preferably a
bachelor of arts or science] in which the humanistic studies have not
been sacrificed to a narrow scientific specialization."[50] To encourage
more "self-reliance," students in the early years were allowed a greater
degree of flexibility in choosing their courses.[51] Though inaugurated
with great fanfare, these changes proved far from substantial, and the

traditional program, as elsewhere, remained largely intact.[52]

Like their counterparts in the humanities and social sciences, those associated with medical training were not blind to the system's deficiencies, but neither were they moved to alter it significantly. Gaps remained between the high ideals of the profession and the reality of both educational training and medical practice. While doctors were admired for their technical expertise, their educational training was based on a narrow, positivist pedagogy. The social respectability that students craved and physicians enjoyed was accompanied by displays of self-interestedness and professional jealousy between specialists and general practitioners. While altruistic, cultured doctors were idealized, they and their less well-rounded colleagues emerged from a schooling process that paid too little heed to the broader medical and health needs of Canadian society. It was a system that rewarded those who learned to cultivate the right connections, and stifled the advancement of women and those with unpopular ethnic backgrounds. The practice of medicine and the training of its students thus embraced the scientific advances, the special economic opportunities, and the social biases offered up by the middle-class communities from which future doctors generally originated.

II

Medicine was not the only career choice for students proficient in the study of science. Engineering also attracted those who sought to build their futures in the world of applied technology. There were important parallels in the social and economic circumstances surrounding both professional development and academic training in these two fields. Significant as well were the differences in the challenges faced by aspiring doctors and engineers seeking professional status and security during the 1930s.

As with medicine, those engaged in the practice of engineering in the early twentieth century confronted economic conditions that simultaneously broadened working opportunities and threatened to erode the engineer's relatively comfortable social standing. Since the middle of the nineteenth century the profession had been dominated by civil engineers, who, as independent, self-employed consultants, designed the country's enormous complex of canals and railways. Frequently self-taught, or more commonly trained through apprenticeships, they were in the intellectual vanguard of a society riveted by the wonders and potential of science and technology.[53] Perceiving themselves as cultured "gentlemen" equipped with indispensable skills, they straddled two worlds. On the one hand they embraced the rationalist and technical thinking characteristic of the new industrial age. On the other they were profoundly conservative – almost aristocratic – in their views of politics and social organization. Pro-imperialist, suspicious of unions, sceptical about the relentless spread of democratic practices, and uncomfortable with the impersonality of large corporate and commercial enterprises, many engineers felt professionally diminished by the impact of the Industrial Revolution.[54]

And the impact on the profession was considerable. The rapid and remarkable technological developments accompanying the process of industrialization required both more engineers and a greater variety of specialized skills. The exploitation of hydroelectric power, the expansion of the mineral, pulp and paper, and automobile industries, of commercial and residential building, of town planning and local transportation networks, all provided work to some fourteen thousand Canadian engineers by 1931.[55] Civil engineers, now joined by specialists in chemical, electrical, mining, and metallurgical engineering, touched virtually all aspects of "everyday life."[56]

No one doubted their social and economic importance, yet engineers were gripped with insecurity and steeped in conflict over the issue of their relative professional standing. Cherishing the autonomy that once enhanced his prestige, the modern engineer found it more difficult than ever to earn his living as an independent "entrepreneur." As the journal of the Engineering Institute of Canada observed in the early 1930s, "A much smaller proportion of our members than heretofore are now engaged in consulting work, and a greater number are in the employ of large organizations ... This change has been accompanied by more detailed specialization, so much so that in many cases an engineer finds himself occupied continuously with problems of substantially the same kind, his work thus giving him no opportunity for broad experience."[57] While doctors and lawyers also felt the effects of specialization and the growth of larger, more "bureaucratic" institutions, they were better able than engineers to preserve their professional autonomy. Rather than contracting engineers on a fee-for-service basis, as was normally the case for elite professionals, major companies now hired them on as salaried staff. If they seldom occupied the bottom rung on the corporate ladder, only in rare cases – usually as successful capitalists – were they able to rise to the top. Instead, much like educated civil servants, they occupied middle-management positions, where they supervised and performed important technical tasks but lacked overall authority and decision-making responsiblity within their respective enterprises.[58]

The status of "professional" engineers was affected as well by their inability to monopolize their practice. By the early 1920s engineering associations had, like those in medicine and law, obtained licensing and regulation powers from government authorities in most provinces.[59] While strengthening their position as professionals by enabling them to exclude others from their associational ranks, provincial charters for engineers had less weight than those secured by doctors and lawyers, who wielded greater political influence. One could both obtain work in the field of engineering and call oneself an engineer without belonging to the chartered organizations. Nor was there an engineering equivalent of the bar admission or Medical Council licensing examinations. Professional engineers thus found themselves competing with less-educated, lower-paid technicians for commercial and industrial employment opportunities.[60]

Furthermore, because so many engineers were employed by private corporations, their occupational fate, more so than that of other professionals, was bound directly to fluctuations in the business cycle. Salaries and employment rates rose with market conditions in a prospering economy and diminished in hard times. A Dominion Bureau of Statistics study noted that for the period 1936–38, the "percentage of losing time" – that is, weeks of work lost due to economic conditions – was higher for engineers than for other professionals.[61] This was reflected too in annual wage earnings. During the 1930s civil engineers and surveyors earned an average of $2448 each annually, compared to $5506 for judges, $3034 for lawyers, and $2972 for physicians and surgeons. Compared to teachers, clergymen, social workers, veterinarians, and dentists, however, engineers fared well in terms of average annual earnings.[62]

The prestige of engineers, as compared to that of doctors, was limited further by the nature – and public perception – of their work. While few laymen grasped the scientific and technical complexities of the engineer's or the doctor's craft, there was a greater mystique – and thus more status – associated with those professionals who worked with "people and their troubles ... as opposed to materials and their utilization."[63] The very precision of the engineer's work in the form of a completed building or bridge thus exposed it to quick and simple judgments from consumers and observers. The structure might stand or fall, induce efficiency or confusion, be aesthetically pleasing or not, rendering the reputation of the "professional" designer vulnerable to assessment by the non-expert. Because the outsider perceived fewer absolutes in the delivery of health care, and because the inability to cure a patient was seldom seen as anyone's fault, the professional prestige of doctors was more secure. They were admired for their successes and excused for their – and the profession's – limitations.

Occupying a lower position than others in the professional hierarchy, engineers sought to improve both their corporate image and their material benefits, but there were differences between veteran and modern practitioners over how this might best be achieved. The conflict involved such questions as the purpose of professional associations, entry qualifications, ethics, and engineering education. These debates rippled throughout the profession during the 1920s and 1930s, permeating the culture into which aspiring practitioners were drawn.

The traditional perspective was represented by the leaders of the Engineering Institute of Canada (EIC), an organization founded in 1897 as the Canadian Society of Civil Engineers and renamed in 1918 in an effort to reflect and represent the interests of all branches of engineering. While recognizing both the new economic realities and the greater priority attached to professional certification, the EIC still perceived itself primarily as an educational forum, fostering the exchange of information, ideas, and "professional knowledge." It continued to promote the ideal of the inquisitive, cultured engineer, and included in its ranks self-taught "amateurs," or "affiliates," whose working experience and intellectual enthusiasm compensated for what they lacked in formal educational credentials. While this conventional view faced growing challenges from within the organization, the EIC retained an elitist, "gentlemanly" aura, controlled until the end of the First World War by a Montreal "clique" of influential businessmen and high-ranking civil servants.[64] Its structure was hierarchical: full membership rights were available only to those who were at least thirty-five years of age and had twelve years of professional working experience. Something less than equal privileges were then granted, in descending order of rank, to associates, juniors, and students.[65]

Provincial engineering associations, which represented more fully the interests of the new middle class of salaried "organization men," placed more emphasis than the EIC on pragmatic professional matters. Though provincial regulations varied throughout the country, engineers without "appropriate" educational certificates were generally excluded from the associations, though a hierarchical membership system was retained.[66] Unlike their seasoned colleagues, who were wary of new trends, contemporary engineers favoured "bureaucratic functionalism and the exact techniques of social management. They were singularly dedicated to the attainment of economy and efficiency for their own sake and impatient to bring the world into conformity with their values. They fostered the notion that society could be 'engineered'; that science, not common sense, should determine social policy and, above all, that experts, not popularly elected amateurs, should manage the new urban-industrial order."[67] As a 1932 report to the EIC noted, the "average" engineer in Canada now expected "something more from the organization than a mere means of interchange of knowledge – he has the right to expect that membership will give him some prestige."[68] From this point of view, the creation of a "stronger professional consciousness and esprit de corps among engineers comparable to that existing in other professions" depended upon the ability of engineering associations to secure better material benefits.[69]

Yet throughout the 1930s organizational unity eluded the profession. Concerted efforts were made by the EIC to strengthen its position as an effective nation-wide umbrella association by enlisting the membership of provincial engineering bodies and their individual constituents. Despite extended conferences and several major committee reports, the membership of the EIC, including affiliates and students, totalled only 4091 by 1936. Furthermore, 500 members of provincial associations had refused to join the EIC, and 1500 engineers belonging to the EIC had never taken out membership in the provincial organizations. Intra-professional competition was exacerbated by the existence of other engineering associations, including the Canadian Institute of Mining and Metallurgy, the newly created Dominion Council of Engineers, and a variety of American organizations in which Canadians enlisted.[70]

The decade-long campaign for professional co-ordination achieved only token success with an agreement for common membership between the EIC and the Association of Professional Engineers of Nova Scotia in 1938; owing to philosophical differences and organizational jealousies, the co-operative effort foundered at every other level.[71] According to a Saskatchewan delegate, the defeat of the consolidation proposals arose from the unhappiness of many engineers with the institute's ability to do "very little to further the professional interests of members."[72]

Engineers thus shared the culture and aspirations of doctors and lawyers without achieving the same degree of influence, prestige, monopolistic powers, or material rewards. Seeking to exclude those considered unworthy, they were unable to achieve consensus about exactly where professional membership lines should be drawn or how jurisdictional powers should be allocated. Convinced that engineering fulfilled the definition of a "learned profession," they craved recognition as something more than well-educated tradesmen. As middle-range employees for whom the "entrepreneurial route was [largely] closed off," they lacked the authority that came with more independent status and more powerful, legally sanctioned corporate charters.[73] Still, in comparison to less affluent professionals and less educated workers, engineers, whatever their collective or individual insecurities, were a relatively privileged, middle-class group.

The debates about the orientation and quality of professional life were reflected in the thrust of engineering education during the 1930s, by which time all of Canada's major universities offered courses leading to applied science and engineering degrees. Few significant changes were made in the teaching of engineering between 1920 and 1940, though at most universities the degree programs were extended by one year, eventually requiring a norm of four years beyond senior matriculation.[74] In light of the impact of economic conditions on both university resources and employment opportunities, the number of engineering and applied-science graduates nation-wide reached a steady state during the 1930s, peaking at 642 in 1935 and falling to 629 in 1939. Furthermore, engineering faculties remained exclusive male preserves. From 1930 to 1939, only 9 women graduated with applied science or engineering degrees from Canadian universities.[75]

While calendar rhetoric was rather more lofty, the engineering curriculum remained specialized and narrow. According to the University of British Columbia, the program was intended to "train students in exact and fertile thinking, and to give them sound knowledge of natural laws and of the means of utilizing natural forces and natural products ... The undergraduate course is made broad and general."[76] Students were required to take English composition in their first three years and a foreign language in first year, but beyond that they were bound almost exclusively to courses in science and engineering specialties, though options in engineering economics and contract law were also available.

Like their counterparts elsewhere, British Columbia students were required to combine their academic course with practical work in the field, where they were exposed directly to the realities of professional life. The calendar advised them to "register with the Association of Professional Engineers of British Columbia in third year, and to associate with the appropriate engineering societies." Furthermore, before graduating the student had to "satisfy the Department that he has done at least four months practical work related to his chosen profession," and he was expected to find summer employment in the field as well.[77]

The universities' focus on technical training aroused considerable discussion in academic circles about the limitations of the applied-science curriculum. Few were as extreme in their criticism as Toronto historian Frank Underhill, who claimed that engineering schools "do the work that they profess to do well, and they do not profess to do anything more than turn out barbarians who can build bridges."[78] Even within the profession, concerns were expressed about the lack of the curriculum's intellectual breadth and the consequent effect on the profession as a whole. According to the Committee on Engineering Education of the EIC, "the reason the engineer does not occupy the position as a professional man that is accorded to other professions lies largely in our present curricula and the fact a cultural background is not provided." Its call for an additional two years in the engineering course that would include additional cultural studies went unheeded.[79] A contributor to the *Journal of Engineering Education* advised engineering faculties to counteract society's pervasive materialism and its "exalted ostentation, extravagance and unfair trade practices" with teaching programs that stressed the engineer's "social obligations." Teachers with mere technical proficiency were inadequate. They should also be "decent, inspiring, upright, and promising leaders of youth" – essential qualities for turbulent times.[80] "At the present time," echoed another writer, "many of the students are leaving their alma maters without information, other than technical, as to their duties as citizens and professional men."[81]

Few would have challenged such noble sentiments, but implementing such recommendations was not a high priority. Significantly, the profession itself provided little guidance. Following considerable debate within the organization, the EIC failed to revise or strengthen its "unenforcable" code of ethics. While convinced of the "instinctive" morality of the majority of its members and while allowing for the expulsion of those who were guilty of "felony, embezzlement, larceny, misdemeanour, or any other offence which in the opinion of the council renders him unfit to be a member," the professional associations virtually never acted upon such codes, thus "nullifying" their value and, in the view of some, diminishing the profession's image. Nor was much attention devoted to the question of ethics in engineering curricula.[82]

In an effort to expand its students' horizons, McGill University in the early 1930s began a series of lectures on the general history of science, gave greater attention to English and economics, and offered its students a course in public speaking.[83] But there as elsewhere, scheduling problems combined with pragmatic professional interests to prevent – or at least limit – more extensive curriculum reform. Engineering students worked very hard, as a former University of Toronto student and future professor recalled. "The school days were long – at least from 9 a.m. to 5 p.m five days a week and from 9 to 12 noon on Saturday with usually three lab reports to write each week ... Electives were rare and the curriculum did not provide any opportunity to take courses in the humanities or social science in other parts of the university."[84]

To the degree that curriculum revisions were supported, many teachers and practitioners felt that a closer integration of science with business would benefit both students and the economy. According to one company president, corporations required engineers with a "broad[er] knowledge of business" and an ability to adapt efficiently to the complexities of large corporate organizations in which engineering practice was increasingly conducted.[85] In this context, courses in economics, business management, marketing, and social science – all retaining a strong utilitarian purpose – could provide engineers with a greater ability to regulate and manage human affairs both inside and outside corporations. According to the University of Toronto calendar, "As the future engineer is vitally concerned with the development of the country, it is essential that he be instructed in the rudiments of economics, administration, and business, which with his scientific training will enable him to increase his usefulness to the full."[86]

To the extent that students participated in these discussions, they appear to have shared the perspective of their professors and future employers. A paper on the teaching of engineering, submitted in an essay competition to the Engineering Institute of Canada, called for more effective technical education and practical training and for even less emphasis on "irrelevant" subjects in the humanities and social sciences. "The dead languages, psychology, political economy, English literature should not be included in an engineering curriculum." Another career-conscious student argued that the graduate who "is trained how to think, rather than what to think ... is the more useful in his profession, and the more capable of future success." The same student believed, however, that this skill would best be provided not through the liberal arts but through courses in "economics, business administration, accounting, public speaking and psychology."[87]

Thus, while the universities acknowledged the need for a more balanced engineering curriculum and made minor adjustments, the academic program, as with medical training, remained technically oriented, highly specialized, and bound to the pragmatic demands of professional and economic life. Upon graduation its young practitioners – assuming they could find work – entered a middle-class professional community that emulated the values, without entirely achieving the social status, of their counterparts in medicine.

III

The debate over appropriate training methods was engaged with special vigour within the legal profession, particularly in Ontario. Until the late nineteenth century one qualified to practice law by apprenticing with a law firm, usually for five years, though university degree-holders were required to "article" for only three years. Upon completion of examinations set by law societies, graduates would be called to the bar.

For a variety of reasons, however, this procedure was reformed, though by no means abandoned. Conscious of the enhanced prestige that accompanied professions that required academic as well as practical training, legal communities throughout the country (over the strong reservations of some members) acknowledged the need for regular classroom instruction. Influenced as well by the innovative "case-study" method of legal education, introduced at Harvard and other American schools in the

1870s, Canadian law societies hoped that a systematic and scientific approach to the study of law would produce more cultured professionals with more respectable credentials. At the same time the legal associations jealously guarded their prerogatives to examine and admit graduates to the inner professional circles. Academic reform would not be permitted to strip the profession of its cherished autonomy.[88]

The greatest potential threat to this autonomy came from universities, which, responding to utilitarian demands, began to include legal training in their curricula. By 1890 fifteeen universities were offering instruction in law, though with the exception of the well-respected course at Dalhousie the teaching programs were generally of inferior quality and confined largely to the periodic setting of examinations and granting of degrees. Several law faculties were also established in western Canada after 1900, but throughout the country few curricular innovations were introduced over the next quarter-century. Canada's largest law school, Osgoode Hall, established permanently in 1889, was operated independently in Toronto by the Law Society of Upper Canada and refused (until the 1950s) to "grant any credit for the legal studies offered at the University of Toronto," which had initiated its own faculty of law in 1930.[89] Between 1889 and 1924 Osgoode graduated some 2500 lawyers.[90] By the mid 1930s must provincial law associations conceded that aspiring lawyers should have completed at least two years of post-secondary education (including senior matriculation), but resolutely they continued to require several years of articling before admitting students to the bar.

Throughout the period, lawyers, academics, and students conducted a sustained debate over what constituted the appropriate balance between academic and practical training. Academic critics of the system lamented what they perceived to be a stale, unimaginative approach to both the study and practice of law. F.R. Scott, a law professor at McGill, denounced the profession for being "notoriously conservative." Preoccupied with the skills required to "hold his own in the professional struggle for existence," the student was taught law "as it is ... and not enough if anything, about the science of law and the sociological approach to law."[91] Practitioners were both irresponsible and out of step with the times, echoed Osgoode professor Cecil Wright, in their belief that law could be successfully taught as "a collection of skills and rules that had to be learned by rote and applied precisely in practice."[92] He characterized the law instead as "a living thing rather than the stagnant well of technicalities which it has always seemed to the man in the street."[93] Lawyers and law schools needed to address themselves to the complexities of modern society by honing students' intellects and thus raising the standards of professional practice. As Sidney Smith, the dean of Dalhousie, noted, "We must believe and practise that law is not merely a set of rules for the adjudicating of disputes between x and y but that it is a social instrument through which Canada may be made a finer land in which to live."[94]

In a limited way, legal training as it evolved in the 1930s did reflect the new institutional and social realities of Canadian society. Stimulated by the growth of government and the public sector, courses in administrative and public law were introduced at Saskatchewan, Dalhousie, and the University of Toronto. Constitutional and international law were also offered for the first time at a number of institutions. Under the direction of political scientist W.P.M. Kennedy, the University of Toronto law course supplemented these subjects with offerings in Roman law, the history of English law, labour law, and jurisprudence. Bora Laskin, a Toronto student and future chief justice of the Supreme Court of Canada, was stimulated and impressed by this effort to treat legal education as "part of the social sciences and humanities," particularly in comparison with other law courses, such as that at Osgoode Hall, which offered a "very narrow professionalism."[95]

However they attempted to modernize and sophisticate their curricula, law faculties faced the protective, pragmatic sensibilities of provincial law societies and veteran practitioners. One contributor to the *Canadian Bar Review* dismissed as unrealistic those academics who were "infatuated with law as an art."[96] From this perspective, nothing could surpass the 'education' one received as a young working apprentice in a law office. Academic training had its place, but it should never be permitted to interfere with or attain higher priority than hands-on experience. Nor should the course of study be overwhelmed by high-falutin, subjects of questionable utility in the practice of law. As one Toronto lawyer put it, 'In order that a man may attain the position, in society, that his profession commands, with as little delay as possible, all but the most essential academic studies should be eliminated.'[97]

Nowhere were lines drawn more sharply than in Ontario at Osgoode Hall Law School, where students asserted themselves in this debate with exceptional boldness. As the instrument of the Law Society, Osgoode had eschewed innovation in legal training, stressing the traditional bias within the profession in favour of the articling experience. But under the influence of a more progressive dean, John Falconbridge, who was hired in 1923, a number of changes were made over the next several years. Two new full-time professors were hired; admission standards were raised (now requiring two years of university); the number of lecture hours was increased; the case-study method was more widely adopted, and more Canadian content was introduced into the curriculum.[98]

   With the outbreak of the Depression, however, the law school reverted
to traditional training practices. While other professional schools
responded to the glut of practitioners on the market by raising admission
standards and cutting back on enrolments, in 1931 Osgoode moved in
precisely the opposite direction by once again requiring from applicants
only one year of university training – an action criticized both by the
Canadian Bar Association and by other Canadian law faculties. Justifying this policy on the grounds that higher admission standards dis-
criminated against the economically disadvantaged, the Law Society's
self-proclaimed altruism rang rather hollow. The following year the
society imposed even greater burdens on the poor by doubling articling
fees to $100 and increasing tuition fees by 50 per cent to $150, suggesting
that the real motivation behind the lowering of entry qualifications had
been to replenish the Law Society's diminished financial coffers.[99]
   The mediocre state of legal education at Osgoode elicited criticism
not only from frustrated, reform-oriented academics, like Professor Cecil
Wright, but also from the school's students. In a report to the Law
Society's Legal Education Committee in 1934, a representative committee of students issued a sweeping condemnation of the Osgoode
training program.[100] Lectures, they contended, were "conducted, generally speaking, in a very elementary manner," and little effort was made
to encourage students to "think for themselves." Furthermore, with the
return to lower admission standards the quality of students had noticeably deteriorated. Before the change 89 per cent of entering students
had had university degrees, compared to 49 per cent after the reversion,
the results of which were evident in the classroom, which many students
attended unprepared, only to burden the instructor with "foolish questions." Because law was now the among the easiest of professions to
enter in Ontario, it attracted ill-equipped students who, it was argued,
would eventually lower the image of the profession as a whole.
   The impact of these questionable standards was aggravated by the
"concurrent" teaching program, by which students were required to
attend lectures twice a day, at 9 a.m and 4:40 p.m., while articling in
a law office during the remaining hours. "Torn between two masters,"
their performance suffered on both counts.[101] If they were lucky enough
to obtain articling positions, they were frequently treated as glorified
office boys and assigned only menial work. They were paid as little as
ten dollars a week – some even worked for nothing in the hope of securing
experience and cultivating contacts for employment after graduation. In
a depressed economy, the report noted, "young barristers are a drug on
the legal market and their services can be procured at a very small
wage."
   Seeking professional respectability, these student critics held the school
and its supporters responsible for demeaning the legal training process.

Indifferent teaching methods, combined with inefficient resource allocation and overcrowded market conditions, provoked legitimate questions about the "ethical standards" of the entire legal profession. Neither the academic nor the practical sides of law stressed sufficiently the lawyer's "obligation to the community in which he lives." If acceptable professional practices – let alone higher ideals – were to be achieved, major changes were necessary. The students called for the concurrent legal education to be replaced by a "consecutive" training system, such as that employed in Alberta and Nova Scotia, where three years of full-time classroom instruction would be followed by one year of full-time articling. Students also favoured higher admission standards, scholarships for the poor, and a number of new courses relevant to current legal problems.

Despite such challenges from students and dissatisfied faculty, the Law Society of Upper Canada proved entirely unresponsive to these and other criticisms, as traditional teaching practices, with minor revisions, prevailed. According to the head of the Legal Education Committee, those who sought to emphasize academic education at the expense of practical training ignored the realities of Canadian society. The school could best serve its students' long-term interests not by emulating the "methods of Harvard or Oxford" but by helping them to forge links with potential employers. Osgoode, after all, was a "small, poorly endowed" school whose graduates would find it challenging enough to secure "humble positions." Over-extending itself in the pursuit of unrealistic academic and cultural ideals would serve neither its future graduates nor the profession itself.[102]

Similar debates over the appropriate road to professionalism were conducted elsewhere in the country, though Osgoode stood largely alone in the determined manner with which it resisted even moderate educational reform until well into the 1950s. In general, throughout the 1930s the Canadian legal profession preserved its licensing monopoly, offered technical and utilitarian education with a slightly more rigorous intellectual component, and preferred values that reinforced the social and ideological norms of the professionally trained middle class. Students who spoke out were critical less of the profession's goals than of the inexpedient and muddled manner in which they were sometimes pursued. Aspiring lawyers sought to cultivate both the skills and the esteemed images befitting those expecting to hold positions of relative social and occupational privilege.

IV

Canadian universities offered a variety of other courses that were intended to fit graduates for specialist careers, though for a number of reasons students proceeded through such programs with a less inflated professional consciousness and more modest employment prospects than those discussed above.

By 1930, like their fellow students in medicine, those enrolled in Canada's five dental schools required two years of pre-dental education (including senior matriculation or its equivalent) plus four years of specialist training in order to graduate. A report on the state of dental education in Canada and the United States, issued by the Carnegie Commission in 1926, had emphasized the need to broaden the scientific and cultural backgrounds of dental students if the profession hoped to enhance its status. While its recommendations for higher educational standards were subsequently implemented, the dental profession as a whole was particularly hard hit by the Depression, and languished during the 1930s. Enrolments in Canadian dental schools dropped from a peak of 1200 in 1920–21 to below 400 in 1930–31, increasing only marginally during the decade.[103]

Practising dentists, furthermore, earned considerably less than doctors, lawyers, engineers, and architects (under $2000 annually on average), and according to a historian of the profession, many were the victims of economic indigence within their communities. More so than in medicine, "in dental practice, the most regrettable result was neglect – patients put off treatment rather than build up a debt which could not be paid."[104] In 1930–31 there were dentists known to be on relief, and many were compensated – if at all – in kind, not in dollars, particularly in rural areas.[105] In 1930 the president of the Ontario Dental Association also expressed concern about the unethical practices of some dentists, which was reflected in the widespread use of tasteless, glossy advertising. "There is an element of commercialism which creeps into our profession here and there, like a thief in the night. It robs the profession of that high ideal for which we exist and creates in the public mind a wrong and unpleasant attitude toward us, as members."[106] All of this made it difficult for the profession to secure the kind of public esteem and material well-being it sought, thus reducing its attractiveness to those seeking professional positions. Still, those veteran and novice practitioners who were able to work in affluent urban areas enjoyed enviable living standards.

The preoccupation of some observers with the dynamics of urban and industrial life by no means rendered the problems of rural communities irrelevant or insignificant during the 1930s. Canadian universities, particularly (but not exclusively) in the west, placed considerable emphasis on the value of agricultural education. Degree, diploma, and extension programs in this field were available at British Columbia, Alberta, Saskatchewan, Manitoba, the Ontario Agricultural College (in Guelph),

McGill, and Laval. While more demanding entry requirements and the introduction of graduate work in agriculture reflected "growing stress on the scientific as distinct from the practical aspects of agriculture," few university programs were as down-to-earth in the courses they offered.[107] The University of Saskatchewan, for example, taught field husbandry, poultry breeding, dairy inspection, and horticulture.[108] A University of British Columbia graduate, working as an assistant in the department of dairying, taught an accredited course in butter-making. She recalled, "there was a little cheese factory on the campus [where] I used to teach the butter making, and I gave the lectures on cheese making, while the cheese maker taught the actual production."[109] Even though "Aggies" were steeped in more technical training and manual labour than most students, university degrees provided them with an important, if modest, symbol of professional standing. Many found work in government departments, the farm press, and marketing agencies.

However university courses in agricultural might benefit the individual student, they were of critical importance to the public image of western Canadian universities as a whole. As Sidney Smith, president of the University of Manitoba, noted in 1936, "In this agricultural province, support for the University in the Legislative Assembly depends in no small degree upon the good will and interest of the representatives from the rural constituencies. That good will and that interest can be developed through this Faculty. This is a selfish view which I do not emphasize and I hasten to assert that as the Provincial University we are duty bound to offer sound courses in agriculture and to carry on investigations of the problems that are confronting that industry."[110]

And the problems of western farmers during the Depression were legion. Universities knew that in the competition for scarce public resources they would fare especially poorly if they were perceived as distant, elitist, and irrelevant by struggling citizens. They therefore highlighted the important agricultural research and services performed by faculty and students, always regretting that in the midst of the Depression they could not do more.

Through their service to rural constituents, as well as in their broader corporate activities, universities in the Canadian west were sources of both community pride and social mobility for a small percentage of the region's youth. As R.C. Wallace, president of the University of Alberta from 1928 to 1936, noted in an article entitled "The Function of the Universities in Western Canada," higher education was perceived as one of the few vehicles through which students who were not necessarily wealthy might obtain professional careers. The institutions hoped to imbue these future graduates with sound "permanent values" and a respect for their local and regional roots.[111]

The priority that these institutions assigned to utilitarian – particularly agricultural – education frequently elicited condescension from those with a more traditional view of the university's role, but such attitudes were somewhat insensitive to the realities of life in the prairie west. The survival of specialist education there spoke to a willingness of a young – and in the 1930s, impoverished – region to sustain, without indulging, the universities in difficult times – a commitment that reflected not disrespect but an enduring regard for the importance of higher education. For the links it helped to forge with the community and the positive results it was expected to produce in the form of applied research services and well-trained "professional" technicians, Saskatchewan's president, W.C. Murray, considered the institution's college of agriculture "the sheet anchor of the University."[112] His successor, James S. Thomson, concurred. "We had become so accustomed to the complete integration of agricultural science with the life of the University ... agriculture was no poor relative to be relegated to the some obscure corner, either physically or academically."[113] Agriculture degree-holders – even those who obtained work during the Depression – may well have lacked the polish and pretension of McGill's doctors and Osgoode's lawyers, but they found their own route to middle-class respectability within the communities that spawned them.[114]

Degree programs in pharmacy, forestry, and veterinary medicine kept alive continuing debates about the university's proper role. On the one hand their place in the curriculum elicited some tough intellectual questions from classicists, general educationalists, and other proponents of high culture, who were forever suspicious of creeping vocationalism.[115] On the other, their presence highlighted the actual function of the modern university: to provide a small portion of Canadian youth with useful and relatively prestigious occupations sustained by the appropriate social values that an advanced and proper education might best provide.[116]

v

Women were not excluded from these possibilities, but as we noted in chapter 2, their career expectations and options were far more limited and confining than those afforded men. Barred for generations from a number of "male" professions, women had by the 1930s gained the right to enrol and practice in virtually all such fields, though their numbers remained small and quotas limiting their access were still employed. None the less, asserted the president of the University of Alberta, "if co-eds want to take up engineering, law, medicine or whatever other professions they have a mind to, it's their own business ... I think the whole of life should be open to women."[117] These are days, enthused a Toronto *Globe* editorial, "made bright by the girl graduates ... The world is glad to greet her as she steps up to receive her diploma."[118]

Such liberal sentiments, however, reflected neither consensus nor reality. Many academics openly bemoaned the growing presence of women in bachelor of education programs, the one traditional area in which they had achieved numerical equity with men. As J.F. Macdonald, a Toronto English professor, told the 1930 meeting of the National Conference of Canadian Universities (NCCU), the mere fact that the profession of teaching was "rapidly becoming in this country to be regarded as a woman's occupation" lowered its "social standing," a sentiment reiterated both by Robert Falconer, the president of the University of Toronto, and Carleton Stanley, president of Dalhousie.[119] Lamenting the pervasive presence of women in undergraduate arts programs, the ever-opinionated Frank Underhill told the NCCU that "no university teacher wants to be condemned to teaching women. He knows that that means an old age of pedantry or empty, meaningless aestheticism."[120] No one challenged such views; indeed, no women were present at the NCCU meeting.

Academic preconceptions about the mental ability and emotional fitness of women for professional life could have an enormous impact on the future of female students. A University of Western Ontario alumnus recalled a conversation with the dean of arts. "I explained to him that because I was doing well and had a strong penchant for medicine, I would like to transfer from the Arts College to the medical school. He was a likeable man, truly interested in all of his students, but he bristled at that and said he really would advise against such a move. 'After all,' he said, 'you wouldn't get the use out of such a career, as you'll probably be a wife and a mother soon after graduation.'" The student finished her arts degree and joined the nursing class at a London hospital in 1940. But when she became engaged, she was dismissed from the course because the program barred women planning to marry. Subsequently, she had five children and was never employed outside the home, though she undertook extensive volunteer and community work.[121]

Even for women who completed non-traditional courses, entrenched gender bias limited their professional opportunities. An unnamed science professor at the University of British Columbia claimed that "women do not make as good scientists as men. They are much better laboratory technicians, but they do not have the male's larger grasp of scientific problems and trends." His colleagues also "preferred women for the routine drudgery of lab work, but required men for the carrying out of more advanced experiments." The majority of women in science at UBC specialized in biology or bacteriology, but upon graduation they found themselves confined to nursing or laboratory work. "It is a pretty dull outlook for a woman who feels she would like to follow scientific work," noted one professor. "These places just swarm with girls, and they get paid next to nothing for doing the work for which men would have to be highly paid."[122]

A practising British Columbia lawyer described her experience to a UBC class. She admitted that opportunities for female lawyers were "really not very wide as yet. For some reason the public has no confidence in women. In obtaining and holding legal positions in competition with men, a women must be far better to get the same recognition."[123]

Comparative salary levels in law and other professions gave quantitative expression to these sentiments. While male lawyers earned an average of more than $3000 annually during the 1930s, women earned $1725. Male doctors averaged $2972, compared to $1741 for women, and while the earnings of the former fell 10 per cent between 1931 and 1941, those of the latter fell 42 per cent. Female dentists were paid $1302 annually, compared to $1961 for their male counterparts. The incomes of female engineers declined a remarkable 65 per cent over the decade, compared to 13 per cent among males.[124]

It is not surprising, then, that professionally oriented women usually chose courses of study in which their gender was viewed as an asset, not a liability, though even in these areas – such as teaching, and library and social work – men earned more than women.[125] But in fields such as household science, library science, nursing, and social work, the university culture reinforced instead of demeaning the female student's choices and aspirations. Indeed, that these courses were now accepted as legitimate university subjects was in part a testimony to the efforts of a previous generation of female activists to force academic recognition of women's interests.[126] By 1940 ten institutions offered degree or diploma courses in household science, a program that reflected the growing belief that domestic life would prosper from the application of more systematic and scientifically based skills and management. While graduates frequently became home economics teachers in elementary and secondary schools, others found work in the new specialties of nutrition, dietetics, hygiene, and child care. Hospitals, large restaurants, private clubs, and tourist camps frequently employed dietitians.[127]

Still, the social and cultural utility of such courses was considered as vital as the occupational preparation that they offered. Conventional perceptions about women's "proper" place were hardly dislodged by university training. In campaigning for the reintroduction of a home economics program at the University of British Columbia, which was withdrawn in 1932 as a result of funding cut-backs, advocates told the university board of governors that "there ha[s] long been a demand for a course of high cultural and practical value to all women students, both as training for their most essential function in society, that of home making, and for many women's vocations."[128] Undoubtedly, contended a Manitoba student journal, "Science and household economy applied in the home would do much to increase the happiness, health and well being of the homes of our country. Why should the greatest institution, the home, suffer from the lack of the use of modern study and science, when these are being applied in all other phases of human activity?"[129] Ironically, according to James Struthers, the profession of social work, which offered employment outside the home to well-educated women, supported as "a principal objective" the "crusade to reduce infant mortality and to enhance family life ... by keeping women in the home."[130] Writing in the *University of Toronto Monthly* in defence of higher education for women, alumnus Margaret Ray argued that librarianship was a profession particularly suited to females because it drew upon "peculiarly feminine attributes such as sympathy, intuition, patience in research, thoroughness in detail and a tendency to stress the human side of library work." University training in general strengthened the woman's ability to contribute to family life, she added. "It develops her inherent qualities, and as a result has made her a more intelligent and more understanding wife and mother."[131]

Thus science, technology, and urban growth had assigned greater value to the kinds of professional work for which women were considered uniquely fit, but the Depression years neither provided nor even promised equality of professional opportunity to female students. Those bold enough to enter male-dominated occupations learned to endure professional pressures without achieving the same employment, financial, or social rewards as men. As we shall see in the next chapter, educated women were expected to follow a different path to middle-class respectability.

VI

Because Canadian students sought to reap the rewards of a university curriculum stressing the importance of "useful" knowledge and applied professional training, they raised few objections to the content of their courses. Some, in fact, hoped for an even hastier retreat of "irrelevant" subjects, such as the classics. But on the question of teaching methods, students were far more vocal and critical. Throughout the 1930s the student press devoted considerable space to commentary on pedagogical processes considered either too restrictive or simply ineffective. Compulsory attendance rules, tedious lecturing by dull professors, and excessive use of examinations elicited a combination of sober and sarcastic responses.

Typical academic regulations, such as those at McGill, required students to attend seven-eighths of their lectures or labs in each course. Professors were supposed to take attendance, and chronic absenteeism could lead to grade penalties or even failure. Most undergraduate classes – at McGill and elsewhere – were taught through lectures, though class enrolments were sometimes low enough to permit discussion between the professor and his audience. Small tutorial groups were normally confined to selected upper-year or honours classes. Considerable emphasis was placed on mid-term Christmas examinations, which, if badly botched, could lead to the student's eviction from university. Final examinations at the end of the spring term were considered a dramatic and possibly frightening ordeal – an academic rite of passage with enormous implications for the student's future.

Some viewed the rigid, rote-like nature of the process as the antithesis of "higher" education. "Babies," perhaps, but not responsible adults aspiring to professional careers, should be forced to attend classes, declared the *McGill Daily*.[132] In 1933 Queen's students in applied science submitted a petition to the dean calling for an end to compulsory classes in the final year of the program, and two years later the student body as a whole voted 521 to 94 for a freedom-of-choice rule for all but first-year students. Freshmen were not to be trusted with such independence, not even by other students.[133]

Such agitation yielded fruit. The applied sciences students at Queen's achieved their goal, and at other campuses attendance rules were also liberalized. "We have the feeling," explained R.C. Wallace, president of the University of Alberta, "that compulsory attendance is not advisable in senior work but that it is not yet advisable to make attendance optional in junior classes."[134]

Students gained some sympathy, too, though fewer actual results, when they challenged the pervasiveness of examinations. President Sidney Smith agreed with Manitoba students who denounced the way in which examinations rewarded memory-work over "original thinking." "Universities, colleges and schools on this continent have unduly accentuated in their programmes the importance of passing examinations. Any change that could represent to the students a shift in educational processes from a mulitiplicity of tests to the engendering of a genuine thirst for knowledge and a burning anxiety to develop mental power is desirable."[135] While University of British Columbia students praised the institution's increasing use of essay writing as a means of measuring ability and progress, there is little evidence from elsewhere across the country of reform in the regular cycle of formal campus tests.[136]

Bearing the burden of boring professors did not, it appears, dampen the wit of some outspoken students. A Dalhousie writer defined the lecture system as a "process by which the notes of the lecturer are transferred to the notebook of the student without ever passing through the minds of either."[137] "Most of us can sleep in class almost as well as in bed," moaned an Alberta critic,[138] while Manitobans sought "to avoid a relationship between teacher and taught which is symbolized by the image of the pump and the bucket; a pump that discharges a stream of cold … information, and a bucket that receives it passively and without enthusiasm, and only desires to retain it until the Professor, turned into examiner, asks for it again."[139] A national student conference in Winnipeg in 1937 called for university lecturing to be supplemented by more tutorial instruction, which would better cultivate the skills of critical reading and thinking.[140]

While poor faculty communicators were unappreciated, as in every era, students had nothing but praise and fond memories for the best classroom performers. A recent survey of 318 University of Saskatchewan students who graduated betwen 1914 and 1935 found that the "approachable," "interesting," and "dedicated" teachers earned far greater plaudits than those who were merely in command of their subject. Those who "lacked empathy," lectured prosaically, or behaved with "haughtiness" were ranked poorly.[141]

For his wit and irreverence, if not his wisdom, humourist and political economist Stephen Leacock made a great impression on students when he embarked on a national speaking tour in 1936, following his forced retirement from McGill. Using academic sacred cows as his foil, Leacock communed with budding middle-class professionals who admired the qualities of poise, panache, and verbal adroitness. Student newspapers were filled with the writings of wisecracking wordsmiths who mocked convention with pointed quips and endless puns, and no one so excelled at this as the aging bard of Mariposa. By tweaking the academic establishment, Leacock the entertainer, unlike Leacock the (more restrained) professor, invited his student audiences to join his insolent but largely harmless satirical conspiracy. "Entry into the professions must be certified by technical examinations," he announced, "and while it is difficult to see why a horse-doctor must pass in Latin, it is not illogical when one realizes that after mastering the intricacies of Latin Grammar, the insides of a horse present no difficulties."[142]

One Albertan student's lengthy "summary" of his academic career was worthy of the best from the Canadian master of satire:

Four years ago I entered the University, and since then I have spent a little short of 28 months come this April, within its walls. What have I done?

Well to begin, I smoked 17,000 cigarettes, drank 740 cups of coffee, and 650 glasses of beer. I bought 65 books, 40 of which I subsequently resold, and went to 450 lectures, 350 of which were not worth listening to. I came into personal contact with 10 professors, 3 of whom were teachers in the best sense and 5 of whom I considered more stupid than myself. Three of my 20 courses I passed by learning the notes of a friend taken more than 5 years previously. The professors had not improved or changed their lectures by as much as a single word; 300 examination questions were set before me of which I was able to regurgitate a nauseous mass of partly-digested lecture notes.

More valuable and vastly more interesting were the 100 "bull sessions" I took part in. In the course of these I argued for communism 50 times, for a controlled capitalism 50 times, proved there is no God 79 times, and made also 300 very wise remarks concerning women.

From the library I drew 300 books, of which 60 were reference books and the rest chosen with the selective care a magpie might use in a five-and-ten-cent store. I resolved to read the reference books, go to lectures, and thereby make high marks to please my parents 68 times ... On 5,633 occasions I worried about the future.[143]

Despite the criticisms of those students who chose irreverence over deference, the teaching environment remained rather formal and paternalistic. University officials allowed students – within limits, as we shall see later – to use the campus press as an outlet for their cleverness, but the classroom was normally a serious place. At a number of campuses, students were required to wear gowns to lectures. At the very least, men wore jackets and ties, women wore skirts and sweaters, never slacks. Students were addressed as Mr or Miss, and professors, if questioned, were seldom contested. Frequently, however, students, especially those in upper years, were invited to their professors' homes for tea or dinner, and while the atmosphere retained an aura of sententiousness, it did offer the prospect of greater faculty-student familiarity.[144]

While students occasionally demanded release from the staid academic environment, even fault-finders shared the university's vision. Like their contemporaries at Osgoode, undergraduates elsewhere reproached their institutions for not being vigilant enough in the pursuit of professional ideals. A lengthy examination of academic life at the University of Manitoba by a student commission called for professors and teachers to be better trained, for the creation of a degree program in business, and for more applied research that might earn the university greater community support. At the same time it questioned the effect on the university's image of its provision of mere diploma courses. "A 'Diploma' savours too much of the specialized High School course, private, or correspondence school, or business college ... The standards demanded should be in keeping with the prestige and dignity of the degree which a University bestows."[145] The message was clear: the university should not trifle with the future of its class-conscious students.

CHAPTER FIVE

Associational Life: The Extra-curriculum

In the university of the 1930s learning was not merely an academic exercise. Values and culture considered essential for the full development of the Canadian student found expression in the pervasive and varied extra-curriculum. Students cherished these activities and poured enormous energy into sustaining them. While periodically forced to rein in extreme manifestations of student recreation, university officials were fully aware of the purpose and merits of campus associational life. Conflict between students and faculty periodically erupted, and the potential for confrontation was always present. But it was limited by a number of factors, not the least of which was the Depression itself, which, perhaps ironically, diminished students' inclination to rebel. Rules and discipline helped to maintain order on campus, but more than anything else a rich extracurricular life provided university youth with an outlet for their abundant physical and social energies. Through it students augmented their academic training with activities viewed by them and by university officials as essential to their growth, maturation, and successful integration into the community.

I

Academics in every era complain that students play far harder than they study. Fads and frivolity, it would appear, forever divert the attention of youth from serious academic pursuits. For university presidents such as Carleton Stanley of Dalhousie this problem seemed to have intensified in the early twentieth century. "In no generation," he complained in 1936, "have there been such stunning distractions from study" as "movies, comic strips, jazz music and other alleged amusements."[1] What Stanley disliked was the continuing tendency of education to cater to the physical, emotional, and social development of growing adolescents.

As they spent longer in school preparing themselves for urban living, students observed, consumed, and brought to the campus the newest manifestations of North American popular culture. For those who shared Stanley's views, the university resembled more a youthful playground than a sanctuary of scholarship. Everything conspired, it appeared, to soil the high purpose of higher education.

All university officials admitted the danger of student over-indulgence in extra-curricular activities, but most did not share Stanley's anxiety about the nature of campus life. For Sidney Smith, the president of the University of Manitoba, social activities were not only legitimate but necessary. Students were multidimensional in their needs and potential, and the university ignored this reality at its – and society's – peril. "It is sometimes declared that the task of a university is to develop the intellectual capacity of the students who register for its courses. I hasten to add that the improvement of their physical, social and moral qualities are not one whit less important. Particularly in these days of shifting ideas and changing ideals a university should seek to inform and to strengthen the individual student, and at the same time, it should endeavour to inculcate in him or her a deep sense of social obligation, and to infuse a yearning to lead and to follow wisely."[2]

Students needed no convincing about the value of participating in campus social life. The milieux in which they moved and to which they aspired upon graduation greeted the pure intellectual with suspicion and condescension. "Do not allow yourself to become a bookworm," the *Queen's Journal* always advised incoming freshman. "A judicious mixture of all activities ... has an intangible asset which cannot be measured but which is of inestimably greater use than the extrabook learning which could have been acquired in the time devoted to these endeavours. It prepares the student against the day when he will be inevitably cast out into the hard realities of a world which is more accustomed to smile at the erudite learning of the college graduate than to accord him honor."[3]

But even students acknowledged the risks of excessive socializing. Campus editors became defensive when students were attacked by parents and politicians for being undisciplined, selfish, immoral, and obsessed with football and partying.[4] These negative public perceptions arose largely from exaggerated cinematic portraits of the freewheeling "collegiate" life in American universities during the 1920s.[5] Canadian students disliked being cast in this mould. As much as they craved and valued the extra-curriculum, they sought to assure observers that campus life was restrained and that students were responsible. To be equated with American stereotypes was demeaning and inaccurate. Typical was this comment by a University of Alberta editor: "The American rah-rah college boy type has been a subject of derision in Canadian universities.

The coonskin coat and the do-or-die for Alma Mater spirit has never been prevalent here, and in fact the side of college life it represents seems to be waning rather than increasing."[6] If students had been more carefree in the previous decade, the Depression was perceived to have restored an equilibrium between study and leisure. Even on the drought-stricken prairies, hard times engendered neither despair nor irresponsible behaviour among university students. According to the University of Saskatchewan *Sheaf*, "Instead of being dismayed or demoralized or recriminating or lethargic, [students] have summoned up initiative and energy as if determined to make the most of a bad bargain."[7] Canadian students would have accepted Vincent Massey's assessment that a "well-balanced academic and social activity is the characteristic quality of Canadian Universities."[8]

Such descriptions, reassuring and self-serving as they were, fairly reflected the quality of campus life. A veritable smorgasbord of campus clubs and societies helped to make the routine of lectures, papers, and exams tolerable. The diversity of the extra-curriculum was a continental phenomenon that owed its origins in the late nineteenth century to a shift in the traditional process through which students proceeded through university. Once bound to a single class with a common curriculum, students would cultivate social contacts and develop group loyalties in the context of the academic setting. But with the rise of electives, specialties, and a more varied set of course offerings, unity in both the curriculum and the composition of the class began to break down. It was still possible – and remained so in the 1930s – for medical students or engineers to forge a cohesive group consciousness, but arts and science students no longer interacted in the classroom on a regular basis. The growth of the "extra-curriculum" thus offered new forums for students with common social interests throughout the university to connect and associate.[9]

In its embryonic phase "collegiate life" could be raucous, unregulated, and a vehicle for student rebellion. University authorities came to understand that students would find extra-curricular outlets whether they were "permitted" to or not. The challenge was to channel collegiate life into socially acceptable modes and to prevent pandemonium. Student associational life was thus legitimized and institutionalized as part of the campus routine, and the pursuit of "balance" in the conduct of student life was more systematically engaged.

Student activities were overseen on most campuses by an elected student government, which distributed funds to recognized campus clubs, approved the annual schedule of social events, promoted "school spirit," and provided acknowledged student leaders with a forum to develop their political, managerial, and accounting skills. Annual elections were elaborate affairs, mimicking democratic parliamentary procedures. While controversial issues sometimes animated the election campaigns, they were contested largely on matters of administrative style, personality, and leadership. As the University of British Columbia student newspaper noted in 1935, "The principal requirements [for student council president] are natural ability to lead his fellows, sound judgement, tact, previous experience, and preferably ability as a public speaker."[10] The limited autonomy attained by students through their elected councils was counterbalanced by the ultimate authority held by university officials over student affairs. As Sherwood Fox, the president of the University of Western Ontario noted, campus youth were adults in the making, but they had not yet emerged. The "educative effect of self-government upon students ... during the days when their minds are yet plastic cannot but be the best preparation for the duties of citizenship, notably the duty of sharing in the responsibilities of governing their country."[11]

The range of student activities was enormous – a marketplace of events and organizations that responded to the physical, social, and material interests of Canadian youth aspiring to success and social respectability. Inter-university and interfaculty athletics; drama, music, and literary societies; fraternities, religious and debating societies, yearbooks and newspapers, military training, and political discussion groups rounded out the options. Students could thus test their physical skills in manly (and womanly) sports, refine their artistic tastes, improve their writing and public-speaking talents, extend their knowledge of world affairs, or improve their images by gaining admission to the organizations with high status. Where dances were permitted, students looked forward to the annual round of formal balls where men dated and courted women and where the socially successful publicly distinguished themselves from the uninvited and excluded.[12] In the clothes they wore, the friends they made, the diverse talents they displayed, and the images they projected, the most admired students set a cultural standard considered certain to maintain their campus status and ensure their future success.

II

If citizens judged university youth on the basis of what they witnessed at the beginning of each fall term, they could be forgiven for questioning how well universities were being run and how civilly students behaved. The annual cycle of student activities began with the initiation ceremony, a custom reaching back to the nineteenth century – further in American and European institutions – in which "freshmen" were introduced to and integrated into campus life. The initiation ritual had been particularly uproarious in Canadian universities during the 1920s, but it remained an encounter that bold students greeted with enthusiasm and the timid viewed with terror. Both student types were the targets of experienced, cocky sophomores, who, having survived the ordeal, relished the opportunity to turn the tables. They were permitted to inflict on incoming students both petty indignities and brutal "hazing." At its most extreme initiation was a form of sanctioned ritual violence, defended by student leaders and tacitly approved by university authorities.

Initiation rites served a number of purposes, most of which were consistent with the university's role of developing the character of students while coping with youthful exuberance. Aspiring to elite and professional careers, which were characterized by codes, ethics, and a group consciousness, first-year students were informed in a playful but rigorous manner of their potentially special status. Entry was not automatic – there would be bridges to cross and trials to endure. Surviving these tests brought its own reward. As Keith Walden has noted, the university "provided something of a corporate sensibility, and initiation symbolized the entry of freshmen into a privileged circle."[13] According to the *Queen's Journal*, "Initation rules taken in the right spirit, will tend quickly to bring about a real college loyalty, which here at Queen's is especially intense and binding."[14]

Loyalty to the school served its broad corporate cause, and loyalty to the class gave first-year students an immediate identity in a novel and sometimes intimidating social world. One could lack physical prowess, good looks, and social graces, but as a member of the freshman group one was neither overlooked nor permitted to hide. Everyone was forced to participate, and however objectionable some found this, they could at least hope to forge new friendships through such encounters. While initiation rituals demeaned the class as a whole, they temporarily created an equality within it – unrelated to academic standing – where the country bumpkin was as important, or as inferior, as the "uppish," confident sophisticate. A regular justification for initiation was the supposedly valuable role it played in putting such "self-important" individuals in their place. Athough students were engaged in a rite of passage with many historical precedents, most did not preoccupy themselves with the hidden psychological meaning and social significance of initiation. It simply afforded them a legitimate method for expending energy and carving out a valued niche within their peer group.[15]

Typical initiation rules required freshmen to wear the campus-coloured tam, to yield seats on buses to upperclassmen, to repeat a college yell on demand, and to attend all major football and hockey games. Women might be prevented from wearing make-up or forced to dress in absurd costumes. At one campus at least, male freshmen were bound to the no "fussing" rule, which prohibited them from being seen in the company of individual women for the entire first term. These "mild" forms of initiation were accompanied by more physical trials to which men, generally not women, were subject. These included hair-cutting, assaults with tomatoes and eggs, baths in molasses and castor oil, and sporting contests that deteriorated into violent confrontations. In addition, ritual "snake" parades into cities frequently turned disruptive. Freshmen and others used these occasions to escape from the line and wreak havoc in the community. They continued tradition by antagonizing merchants, theatre proprietors, and home-owners – invading their premises or trashing their streets. Throughout the country, displacing trolley cars from their tracks was still a favourite student prank.[16]

When complaints were made to university authorities about damaged property, apologies were usually forthcoming, and student councils took some responsibility by conducting "trials," fining the culprits if they could be found and reimbursing the victims.[17] This strategy of using peer pressure to maintain order and impose discipline freed administrators of the need to act in authoritarian ways. It tested the skills of budding lawyers, stressed the value of "ethics" and self-control, and underlined the need for students to uphold the image of the university. At McGill "the students [of the Students' Society] helped with discipline ... They consulted the Principal and he very often consulted them. Discipline was apt to be informal but the system worked, quietly and efficiently."[18] Authoritarian means, however, were used by faculty-controlled discipline committees as a last resort. As the University of Saskatchewan calendar warned, "Students conducting themselves in an improper manner may be admonished, fined, suspended, dismissed or expelled from the University."[19] These were not simply idle threats. Three Wesley College students caught consuming liquor and causing a disturbance were expelled in 1934.[20]

Students were thus expected to deport themselves responsibly. But in practice it was clear in the early 1930s that unruly conduct was not always cause for great concern. When it erupted, university officials sought to appease the public while seeking their tolerance for the aggressive behaviour of youth, which was sometimes difficult to contain. University spokesmen might even deny that their students were responsible for annoying the community. It was rare, in any event, for hazing and property damage to continue beyond the initiation period or to turn into a serious challenge to authority. In response to a letter from a distraught citizen, Robert Wallace, president of the University of Alberta, wrote: "I must say that your reaction does not seem to be the reaction of some men with whom I have talked ... in that a certain amount of freedom not disturbing to other people has generally been considered not unreasonable as part of the initiation proceedings. Personally, I would prefer that there be nothing at all of the kind but I feel it unwise to make such a ruling until or unless by discussing the matter with the students in responsibility, the sound public opinion in the student body prevails in that direction."[21] In 1939 the president of Dalhousie University thanked the police chief of Halifax for dealing "leniently" with a number of students caught damaging residential property. "You have been very human and tolerant about the pranks of young blood," he wrote, "and we have tried to see to it that you will have few pranks to overlook."[22] In small religious colleges, too, university officials could see the advantage of dealing tolerantly with rowdy behaviour. Two students at Brandon College who dropped a water "bomb" on the president of the college were summoned to his office for disciplinary action. They were undoubtedly relieved when the president sent the perpetrators away with the "laconic" comment: "Old stuff, it's been done before."[23]

While student provocations and university responses followed these patterns for much of the decade, complacency about the degree of initiation violence was shattered in 1932 following a widely publicized incident at the University of Alberta. Following his subjugation to hazing rituals, Charles A. Powlett, an arts and law student, suffered a nervous breakdown and spent time in a sanatorium. He and his father sued the university and received a court award of $50,000 plus costs. On appeal, the decision in favour of the plaintiff was upheld, though the award was reduced to $15,000.[24] The appeal court transcript provides a vivid account of the brutality and humiliations to which Powlett and others were subjected. The victim was "skin-assed," or beaten and dragged down the hall on his bare buttocks; "hot-handed," or strapped on the hands with a shingle while blindfolded; and "tubbed," or dunked in cold water.[25] Powlett was also forced to eat lunch in the cafeteria with the name "R.B. Bennett" (Canada's prime minister) painted on his forehead in india ink. The next day, found visibly incapable of functioning, he was taken to hospital and placed in the psychiatric ward.

The university contended that Powlett was particularly high-strung, inordinately worried about hazing, but forced to endure no trials out of the ordinary. It was argued that he was not of sound mind before the incident and that the university should therefore not be held responsible for his psychological injuries. The court disagreed, finding the complainant to be "an excellent type of boy, physically and mentally healthy with the same number of so-called faults" as others. In reviewing the testimony of the psychiatrists, the judge concluded that Powlett's mental illness was "caused by the proceedings of the initiation to which he was subjected." The university had a "contractual" relationship with the student to take every effort to ensure his physical safety and psychological well-being. Instead, it was guilty of negligence, for despite being aware of the risks involved in these activities, it gave "tacit approval and permitted [hazing] to be carried on without proper supervision."[26]

The Powlett incident led to concerted efforts by administrations and student councils alike to control hazing throughout the country. Fearing public rebuke and legal and financial liability, many campuses officially banned initiations involving physical force or personal humiliation, an approach endorsed by the National Federation of Canadian University Students. Violent initiation rituals thus diminished, though they did not disappear, and at a number of locations were resurrected in the last half of the decade, sometimes in defiance of student council regulations.[27] Universities thus continued to face the challenge of simultaneously preserving an image of respectability, coping with the feistiness of youth, and facilitating the socialization of freshmen to the dominant campus culture.

Fraternities and sororities were another important instrument for the promotion of school spirit, behavioural conformity, new friendships, and campus hierarchy. Rooted in the creation of secret societies in eighteenth-century Europe, where young men forged social and political bonds, frequently challenging established authority, they spread to the United States in the early nineteenth century, where they sustained a post-revolutionary oppositional culture and helped to keep chaos alive in American universities. Always a source of potential rowdiness, they gradually set new standards for social achievement in an increasingly secular society. They developed codes of behaviour that students, aspiring to success in the business and professional worlds, felt obliged to follow. Infused with class bias, they placed great emphasis on a student's social background, appearance, athletic prowess, and ability to mix smoothly in the proper circles. Academic distinction alone, however, was more a liablity than an asset and would not gain the student entry into the privileged fraternity circle. Like professions themselves, fraternities enhanced their importance by strictly guarding access through their gates. As American universities became larger and more fragmented, the number of fraternities grew, competing for status and increasingly dominating campus extra-curricular life. By 1930 there were 3900 fraternity and sorority chapters in the United States, owning property worth $90,000,000.[28]

To the degree that as university youth they shared an interest in a broader campus culture, and as Canadians were inclined to look south for examples of material success and social advancement, some students eagerly embraced fraternity life by establishing "branch-plant" chapters (headquartered in the United States) in the 1910s and 1920s. But because Canadian campuses were generally smaller, more intimate, and less diffuse than those in the United States and because most university administrations refused initially to approve the formation of these associations, the fraternity craze did not immediately sweep Canada. By 1928 there were twenty associations each at the two largest campuses in Canada, McGill and the University of Toronto, though only a handful elsewhere in the country. They found little favour at religious colleges, where authorities worried about their effect on the moral tone of the campus, already surrounded by secular distractions. At Queen's University, a nondenominational institution, fraternities were banned following an intense campaign and referendum in 1934. Students and faculty agreed that the Greek-letter societies would "jeopardize the student unity and spirit which are the envy of other Canadian universities." As one student leader put it, fraternities were unnecessary because Queen's was already "one large fraternity." From an academic and cultural perspective, the other arguments against fraternity life seemed compelling. American studies showed that fraternity students achieved lower grades than nonfraternity members; they indulged in drinking, gambling, and rowdy behaviour; they imposed and maintained invidious distinctions among students based on race and social class, and they dominated campus social life.[29]

Despite these historic deficiencies, fraternities did spread throughout Canada in the 1930s at most non-denominational campuses. Student advocates in these centres petitioned regularly for the right to form local chapters, finally breaking down the resistance of sceptical university officials. At Alberta, for example, the requirement that students pledge on registration forms never to join a "secret society" was withdrawn in 1929. According to the dean of arts, "I believe the prohibition against [fraternities] to be no longer tenable. We may as well face the situation with good grace."[30] Students argued that fraternities added to the quality of campus life by cultivating "the development of personality and character, group contacts and discriminate social activities."[31] Arthur Currie, the principal of McGill, acknowledged earlier that in an era when religion no longer provided university youth with a powerful basis for sustaining "eternal brotherhood," fraternities helped to fill that gap by stressing the importance of "service and loyalty."[32] However convincing such arguments, the decision to allow fraternity organization was easier for authorities to justify on practical grounds. Fraternities performed a vital service to Canadian universities in terrible economic times by providing students with off-campus housing that was otherwise difficult to obtain. It was simply impossible to find the funds for adequate residential space on campus, and university officials had to admit the attractiveness of this student-made solution.[33] While complete figures are not available, institutional examples indicate that on campuses where they thrived, one-fifth to one-quarter of students belonged to fraternities and sororities in the 1930s.[34]

Official recognition gave universities an opportunity to oversee and temper fraternity activities; administrators believed that the excesses of American fraternity life could be avoided in Canada. Every year the University of Western Ontario evaluated the grades of fraternity members and usually found them acceptable.[35] Normally, firm regulations were imposed on the process of fraternity and sorority "rushes," through which new members were invited to join these select circles. Freshmen could only be recruited at the end of the year, pending their successful academic performance. Fraternity constitutions forbade or at least promised to control gambling and alchol consumption on unsupervised fraternity-house premises. Conscious of the importance of maintaining a respectable image, fraternities pledged loyalty to the British Empire, to Canada, and to the university. They resolved to contribute fully and enthusiastically to the creation of "good fellowship" and the conduct of student life.[36] The elite societies reflected community standards and fraternity tradition in another way by excluding from their numbers non-whites and Jews, a practice that seemed never to elicit criticism from university officials. Jewish students responded to this discrimination not by petitioning for admission but by forming their own fraternities.[37] Access to fraternities and sororities was also limited by membership costs. Students of especially modest means neither expected to join nor succeeded in participating in these select, some claimed "snobbish," associations.

By being restrained and co-operative, fraternities earned the tolerance, if not the love, of university officials. They engaged in their share of high jinks (typically rebuked without being taken terribly seriously), but unlike fraternities at American colleges and universities, they kept a relatively low profile and were not perceived to dominate campus life. At their best they engaged in genial rivalries, fostered their own code of excellence, and produced some renowned campus leaders. All of this faculty and adminstrators could admire. Their social and cultural potential was identified in a letter from an Alberta professor endorsing the recognition of a Pi Beta Phi sorority at another university. "The families from which these girls come represent an excellent cross-section of the best features of our Canadian life in the west. That assures you of the soundness of their social background – surely a very important factor in influencing your decision. They are distinctly well connected in all branches of business and professional life."[38]

Thus fraternities and sororities were created and endured for three reasons: students demanded them; they provided off-campus housing in hard economic times; and both in the way the students ran them and the way the universities oversaw their activities, they were considered no serious threat to the culture and civility of the campus.

In their scrutiny of student residence life, university officials also had to balance the quest for greater student autonomy with the role of adult guardianship. Residence women, far more than men, were subject to rules, regulations, and restrictions. Men dominated and set the tone of campus social life, and university authorities, playing the role of substitute parents, felt obliged to uphold the virtue and morality of the women in their charge. The rules governing dormitory living were elaborate and frequently petty. Annesley Hall at the University of Toronto required women to seek permission to hire a car, to drive home, to go tobogganing, skiing, or boating. Week-night check-in time was 10:30, later on weekends and on special occasions. Men were allowed to visit the residence reception hall from 7:30 p.m. to 10:30 p.m. on weekends only; of course, they were prohibited from calling on women in their rooms.[39] Breaking curfew earned violators loss of privileges or fines or worse. Wallingford Hall at McMaster charged late-comers two cents a minute for the first ten minutes of their absence and five cents a minute beyond that. A University of Alberta woman "shocked and disturbed the whole residence" when she sneaked into her room after curfew by scaling the building and climbing through an upper window. Consequently, she was confined to the campus for fourteen days, fined two dollars, and prevented from attending any formal dance at the university for the remainder of the year.[40]

Some universities, like Dalhousie, required all out-of-town women to live in residence, a rule rationalized on moral grounds and reinforced by financial exigency. Shirreff Hall, the women's dormitory, was chronically burdened by excess capacity, a problem exacerbated by the levelling-off of enrolment during the Depression. Elsewhere, women who either chose or were compelled to live off campus had their premises inspected and approved by university officials.[41]

Life in male residences was freer: alcohol was forbidden, as were excessive noise and rowdiness, but curfews were less frequent than for women. While the rules governing religious colleges were more stringent than those of other institutions, men generally came and went as they pleased; off campus they lived in boarding houses of their own choosing, without requiring official approval. Although they were treated paternalistically – and in the case of women, governed by a "warden" – students endured dormitory conditions that were far from prison-like. As with initiations and fraternities, the numerous rules were offset by an animated community of peers, who socialized, partied, and tested authority, all of which was anticipated, overseen, and sometimes overlooked.[42] Even rule-breaking was expected to be a learning experience:

student-run residence committees were normally responsible for assigning duties, enforcing regulations, and dispensing "justice." In the opinion of its advocates, residence living was thus expected to round out one's education. A spirit of camaraderie, which commuter students often found difficult to penetrate or emulate, infused residence life. With his tongue only slightly in check, Stephen Leacock contended that the residential experience provided even more valuable instruction than classroom teaching. "Students must live together and eat together, talk and smoke together. Experience shows that this is how their minds really grow ... If a student is to get from his College what it ought to give him, a college dormitory with the life in common that it brings, is his absolute right. A university that fails to give it to him is cheating him."[43]

III

Whether or not they lived in residence, students showed great enthusiasm for inter-university sports. No subject occupied as much attention in campus newspapers as did the fate of football, hockey, and basketball teams. Competition was carried on through regional leagues overseen by the Canadian Intercollegiate Athletic Union, founded in 1906. The three "controlling" members of the association (owing to their highly developed sports' programs) were Queen's, McGill, and the University of Toronto. Universities would be allowed full membership into this privileged circle only if they achieved "senior" proficiency in five sports, though associate membership was granted those able to mount teams in particular sports. The Western Canada Intercollegiate Athletic Association and the Maritime Intercollegiate Athletic Union also facilitated intra-regional competition, as did various city leagues, and throughout the country exhibition games were periodically arranged with visiting American rivals.[44] No matter what the quality of their teams, students enthusiastically cheered them on, convinced that their campus's image would thrive with success on the sports field. As major exhibitions these events elicited from students sentiment and institutional loyalty. They also provided an authorized release from the academic routine and a great excuse to party. Festivities at the Royal York Hotel following the annual football game between Western and Toronto at Varsity Stadium were considered by many the biggest social event of the year.[45]

The growth of organized inter-university sports reflected a variety of influences: industrial capitalism, Americanization, and the pronounced tension between professionalization and amateurism. The once informal conduct of athletic competition yielded in the late nineteenth century to the phenomenon of the organized spectacle, for which property had to be purchased and games had to be formally scheduled to coincide with the leisure time of urban audiences. Improved communications made intercity and inter-university competition possible, now enthusiatically promoted by the popular press. Coaching and the training of players demanded increasing expertise and were tasks American universities undertook with extreme seriousness. They actively recruited and subsidized athletes, constructed expensive stadiums, and commercialized in a pervasive manner American university athletics.[46] Among Canadian campuses, the University of Western Ontario was unmistakably impressed by this approach. In the 1930s Mustang football games were used to promote the university, particularly in southwestern Ontario, where the contests provided a substitute for professional spectator sports. Tickets were sold throughout the area; games were well attended, and championships were greeted with regional euphoria.[47]

As with fraternities, however, the American example was double-edged. Lacking large private endowments and wealthy alumni, Canadian universities offered no athletic scholarships, devoted relatively few of their funds to athletic resources, particularly in the Depression, and, reflecting their British past, applauded the noble and enduring tradition of amateurism in national sports. According to historian Allan Metcalfe, middle-class Canadians in the early twentieth century, including those in universities, associated the integrity and elitism of sports with the preservation of its amateur status. "Rough play, the use of ringers, fan conduct, and any other evils all coalesced into one ailment – professionalism," defined as the playing of sports for the purpose of making money and "obtaining a livelihood." Sports, it was believed, should reinforce the university's goal of cultivating character and should never become an end in themselves.[48] Thus, for Canadian university officials the route to excellence and status in the academic arena – professional training – led to cultural atrophy if allowed to dominate in the athletic arena. Total insulation from professional and American influences was impossible, but for administrators and students alike, Canadian modesty in the conduct of competitive university sports was a distinct asset. "We don't give athletic scholarships," noted Alberta's *Gateway*, "nor does the athlete necessarily become a campus god. Sports have their place, but it should not be foremost in a university. This is the Canadian attitude and we believe it to be the correct one."[49] McGill principal Arthur Currie agreed: "Competitive athletics have an educational value. They teach men how to win and how to lose. They should develop manliness and character. But I dissociate myself most strongly from any idea that we need athletics at McGill for advertising purposes ... McGill's well-earned reputation rests on a more permanent foundation – one of solid educational achievement." The absence of "million-dollar stadiums" in Canada made it sometimes necessary to "field losing teams," according to the Saskatchewan *Sheaf*, but "it also made it possible to field winning students."[50]

Intercollegiate athletics for women was not unknown but was de-emphasized in favour of intramural and recreational sports. The Women's Intercollegiate Athletic Union sponsored leagues in basketball, badminton, swimming, hockey, and tennis. But female university sports were affected by a "reform" movement in this period that attempted to reflect the "special" characteristics and perceived needs of women. As male athletics become more commercialized and competitive in the United States, concerted efforts were taken to protect women from these aggressive forms of athletic endeavour. While organized college sport for women had attained legitimacy by the 1920s and 1930s, North American teachers, coaches, and doctors promoted physical activity designed to protect both the gentility and the child-bearing function of females. In hockey and basketball women were subjected to special rules designed to prevent bodily contact. "Play Days," in which colleges would be brought together for a "friendly athletic competition" requiring "minimal levels of skill and intensity," emerged as an alternative to intercollegiate athletics for women in the 1930s.[51]

Whatever cultural and physiological needs they were intended to serve, female athletics were marginalized in Canadian universities, particularly in the Depression. While male athletes were far from over-indulged, women's sports faced chronic shortages in facilities, equipment, and travel funds, nor were they considered spectator events. Women were barred from using the elaborate athletic facilities of Hart House at the University of Toronto and faced similar forms of discrimination at McGill. At Western in 1936, while constituting one-third of the student enrolment, women were allotted only one-eighteenth of the funds assigned to university sports.[52]

When given the opportunity, however, most students, male and female alike, participated enthusiastically in intramural athletics. Three-quarters of University of New Brunswick students in 1931 engaged in some form of athletic activity.[53] Public health in general, particularly in the wake of the First World War, the disastrous flu epidemic of 1917, and the periodic spread of communicable diseases, gained prominence throughout the interwar period. A worrisome flu contagion broke out in 1937, and throughout the period tuberculosis was acknowledged as the leading cause of death among college-aged students. At Memorial College in St John's, poorer students were found to have a higher incidence of health problems than the more affluent.[54] In light of such knowledge, educators increasingly viewed the maintenance of adolescent health as part of the school's responsibility. Students were subjected to annual physical medical examinations, inoculated if necessary, and in most universities compelled to take physical education. While some students objected to this last regulation as an unwarranted restriction on their freedom of choice, most appeared to favour it, agreeing with administrators that compulsory physical training flowed logically from mandatory mental training.[55]

The priority given physical and health education led to a major conflict at Dalhousie University in 1938. Sven Korning, a Swede, had been hired the previous fall to manage the gymnasium and provide students with physical education instruction. According to the students' athletic association, however, he proved incapable of "promoting and developing" the North American games that Dalhousie students favoured, such as tennis, badminton, football, basketball, and softball. Korning's interest in such European games as handball found few enthusiasts in the Dalhousie gym. In an organized protest – rare at Dalhousie – more than two hundred students passed a resolution requesting that "a capable physical instructor be appointed to look after the Dahousie gymnasium and to instruct in games and physical training." Supported by the Council of Students and by the *Halifax Citizen* – which objected to "the appointment of a foreigner while our own fellows are overlooked" – Korning's critics succeeded, though not immediately, in pressuring the university to replace him.[56]

Sports thus extended the university's role of making men and cultivating the supposedly gentler tendencies of women. Respectable Canadian youth were expected to attend to their fitness while avoiding both physical and social excess. Students accepted this direction, and were even known to criticize university administrations for failing to fulfil their responsibilities in this area. The organization of university athletics bore the imprint of both British and American influences, though the synthesis appeared uniquely Canadian. Lacking large private resources, and restrained further by the Depression economy, Canadian universities offered basic but frequently ill-equipped athletic programs – to enthusiastic students. As spectators or participants, university youth made campus sports an important part of their associational culture.

IV

If participation in campus sports contributed to the segregation of university men and women, other social activities brought them together. While no president would proclaim the coupling and courting of students to be one of the university's purposes, in practice this was an important institutional function, an inevitable consequence of coeducation. There were, of course, no guarantees that one would find an ideal date – let alone marriage partner – but the search for one or the other (or both) occupied a significant place in the conduct of student life.

As a select group, students dreamed of meeting mates with the kinds of personal qualities that fit their expected social position. Unscientific surveys of what women looked for in men, and vice versa, found that students favoured a "collegiate style," less ostentatious than what had allegedly characterized the 1920s but still consistent with middle-class pretension. The ideal man would be educated but not pedantic; ambitious but not a "grind"; intelligent but not "conceited"; well dressed but not flashy. If he was also athletic, sincere, witty, and a good dancer, he would be considered socially successful.[57] Men seemed less inclined to respond seriously to such surveys; none the less, 74 per cent of a University of Western Ontario sample did express a preference for college-educated wives. Such women would ideally be attractive, charming, intelligent (but not intellectual), and adept at some sports, bridge, and dancing.[58] These "types," of course, could be easily parodied, and the average student would never have measured up. Still, they indicated that style and presentation mattered a great deal − more than strict academic success − in the world of one's peers.

The main forum in which students tested their mastery of social skills was the college dance. The school year featured dozens of such events, from casual sock hops to formal "proms," for which men rented tuxedos and women wore gowns. At major balls, live orchestras were hired, dance cards were filled out in advance, and men enhanced their reputations by fox-trotting or waltzing with the most popular women.[59] Poorer students were at a great disadvantage. Unable to afford the costs of dating, they missed the most elaborate balls. Still, there were other, less expensive opportunities. Dances took place on campus, in local hotels, or in private homes, sometimes so frequently that university officials feared they were reaching epidemic proportions. Between the second and twenty-seventh of February 1933, Dalhousie students held at least sixteen dances.[60] Efforts by faculty or student councils to limit, or worse, eliminate these socials met with vigorous opposition. This was one outlet that students jealously guarded, and its popularity extended even to those denominational campuses where dancing was officially scorned. Unable to prevent the staging of dances at Winnipeg's Fort Garry Hotel, the faculty of the Methodist Wesley College finally lifted its ban in 1931 and permitted its students one on-campus dance per week. McMaster students lost their appeal for an end to dance-bans in 1932, but they circumvented Baptist tradition by continuing to sponsor a full calendar of parties and proms elsewhere in Hamilton.[61]

American music always attracted Canadian youth, and the last part of the decade witnessed the spread of the latest fads. The "swing jazz" of Benny Goodman and Tommy Dorsey (replacing the "nice jazz" of

Guy Lombardo and Paul Whiteman) came to Canadian campuses with a flourish. Its upbeat and feisty tones blared alongside the compelling sounds of "coloured" musicians – Fletcher Henderson, Bessie Smith, and Count Basie.[62] Believing, prematurely, that the Depression was over, student writers explained the popularity of this music and the dances that accompanied it as the result of a surge of optimism about the future:

To many older people this mad dancing craze is bewildering. They are unable to fathom modern American youth's hysteria for 'swing' and 'jams' and 'truckin' and the rest of the whirl. But is it not comparable to the rise of jazz music after the Great War? Is not this virtual release from the gloom and scarcity of the depression period a natural analogy? ... Most of the dance music written during the 'slump' was of the slow, almost melancholy variety; life was restrained, pocket books were thin ... Let us have no more of the depresssion dance – couples close against each other shuffling their feet slowly in time to minor music. All hail the Big Apple, the prosperity peck, the triumphant truck, the shining shag. Welcome the dance designed especially for swing music. For the Big Apple is the young person's dance.[63]

Another symbol of renewed spirit and a loosening of restraints was the innovation in 1937 of the "Sadie Hawkins" dance, invented by American humourist Al Capp in his popular comic strip *L'il Abner*. Like the girls of Capp's Dogpatch, U.S.A., college women inverted social convention by inviting men to the annual Sadie Hawkins dance.[64] But the exceptionality of this temporary role reversal served mainly to reinforce the normal patterns in male-female relations on campus. Men continued to be the initiators in dating while women awaited invitations. They boosted each other's images by appearing in couples at the numerous public social events. A more difficult question, however, is what they did in private. "Officially," middle-class sexual morality was easy for students to decipher. Women should remain virgins until they married. Ideally, men would too, though if they chose to "sow their wild oats" before marriage, they should do so only with "non-respectable," non-university women with whom they should never become more deeply "involved." Thus, "pure" women with unsullied reputations were the ideal mates for well-behaved, though possibly more "worldly," men.

Aware of parental fears and public suspicions that universities were dens of iniquity for untamed youth, university authorities did their best to uphold the aura of respectability. Campus dances were always chaperoned; men's access to women's residences was strictly controlled, and the publication of sexually "explicit" material could elicit sharp rebuke. In a famous incident at the University of Toronto in 1929, the editor of the *Varsity* was fired for acknowledging that "petting" was a common practice among the university's youth. Student editors in other parts of Canada expressed amazement that the particularly conservative Toronto establishment could be so offended by this admittedly provocative but harmless editorial.[65]

In truth, campus sexual life was neither as loose as critics feared nor as pristine as officials pretended. In the absence of documentary evidence on this subject, a combination of anecdotal, impressionistic, and American research material permit some cautious conclusions. In 1938 Dorothy Dunbar Bromley and Florence Haxten Britten published a book on the sexual practices of American students based on 1300 interviews. They found that half of the men and one-quarter of the women claimed to have had pre-marital sexual intercourse. In addition, 4 per cent of women and 8 per cent of men admitted to being homosexual. Contrary to parental ideals, American college women evidently believed that sexual intercourse with one's fiancé was acceptable, though with anyone else it constituted promiscuous behaviour. The conduct of American students was only marginally influenced by religious values – in one survey only 6 per cent of men and 10 per cent of women admitted the importance of religion in their lives. In general, the American literature concluded, campus sexual activity in the 1930s was more discreet than in the 1920s, and even then had been wildly exaggerated by the popular press. During the Depression students were sexually curious but careful. According to one magazine, "sex is no longer news, and the fact that it is no longer news is news."[66]

Owing in part to the slower emergence of academic social psychology in Canada, statistical information on the sexual practices of students in the 1930s is not available. Interviews suggest, however, that some students were sexually experienced but, beyond necking and petting, which were socially acceptable, most, like their American counterparts, were not. The double standard was alive and well. Some men boasted about finding sexual partners off campus, but respectable women, if they had intercourse, risked ruining their reputations if they told anyone. They also risked pregnancy, for while the determined could obtain contraceptives, it was still technically illegal to sell or distribute them, nor were known birth-control methods terribly reliable.[67] The continuing importance of denominational colleges meant that religion, too, played a role in encouraging sexual restraint in Canada – more so, evidently, than in the United States "Moral values were stronger [in the 1930s] than today," recalled a Toronto woman, and a male's status could thus be forged without reference to his sexual experiences. "I feel certain that some students found the opportunity to engage in sex," noted one Ontario man, "but it was never a predominant diversionary urge." As a Nova Scotian concluded, there was little peer pressure "to go all the way."[68]

What students in both countries craved was more knowledge about sexual issues. Birth control was more openly discussed than in the past, in part the result of the eugenics movement, whose advocates sought to control the spread of poverty in the Depression by sterilizing the poor. For different reasons, feminists favoured greater public access both to contraceptives and to information about health and family planning.[69] These matters were discussed on university campuses, and across the continent students petitioned for courses and lectures on "marriage preparation." In December 1937 a major national student conference in Winnipeg endorsed a resolution demanding the inauguration of such education at all universities, though, reflecting Canadian sensibilities, an amendment was added that "called for respect to be paid to the religious conviction of students in all such discussions."[70]

While some universities refused to authorize them, the general trend was towards sponsorship of lectures by responsible authorities that students could attend on a voluntary basis. Frequently, what they were treated to under the guise of "frank discussion" were traditional homilies about the need for moral probity. Two hundred "enthusiastic" male students "jammed" Toronto's Hart House to hear the first of a series of talks on "youth and marriage" sponsored by the Student Christian Movement. The speaker was Reverend J.D. Parks of the High Park United Church. Similar talks were delivered elsewhere by equally respectable lecturers.[71]

As in other instances, university officials hoped both to temper student behaviour and to prevent public censure by responding flexibly – but within well-defined limits – to student initiatives. Of course some citizens would never be appeased. Following publication of an article in the University of Alberta *Gateway* entitled "Sex, Christianity and the Student," an outraged solicitor, appropriately named A. Gladstone Virtue, demanded that W.A. Kerr, the president, expel the students responsible for printing the piece. He claimed that it endorsed sexual education and that it did not condemn pre-marital sex. In a single-spaced, three-page letter, Kerr responded by explaining that students could only be expected to live responsible and disciplined lives if they were given the opportunity to think for themselves without rash interference from their elders. He found nothing morally offensive in the article and had no intention of punishing the students. Unswayed, Virtue wrote again demanding action by the equally unmoved president.[72]

The issue of male-female relations raises further questions about the distinct experience of women in campus associational life. While the value of coeducation was frequently debated, the vast majority of university women of the 1930s would not have considered themselves feminists. Women's-rights activists of previous generations were respected for having broken university admission barriers and having fought for female suffrage, but no such causes galvanized into a widespread women's movement in the 1930s. As historians have demonstrated, genuine equality with men was never really the goal of "maternal" feminists in the early twentieth century. Although she insisted that women had a major role to play in civilizing the world, even Nellie McClung believed marriage and child-rearing to be women's primary function. As we noted earlier, the occupational "sphere" of women had widened in the early twentieth century to include the possibility of professional work, particularly in teaching, nutrition, and social work. A handful of women also became lawyers and doctors in the 1920s and 1930s. But on and off campus, social, occupational, and economic discrimination – in no way eased by the Depression – endured. Highly educated women were expected, ultimately – perhaps after a temporary stint in the work-force – to make their "careers" in the middle-class household. While aware of and sometimes angered by their subservient role, women largely accepted it; moreover, in spite of continuing discrimination, they positively cherished their university experience. These attitudes merit further exploration.[73]

Always subject to greater paternalism than men with respect to residence living, athletic opportunities, and expected sexual deportment, women faced other inequities, both overt and subtle. Certain campus organizations, such as the Bridge and Political Economy clubs at McGill, simply excluded coeds.[74] Men virtually always ran student councils, edited student newspapers, and made women the butt of endless jokes and bad poetry. Modest advances by the 1930s, however, included the publication of annual women's issues of student papers, with guest female editors, and the introduction of all-female debating competitions. Normally, women's affairs were covered in regular "coed" columns, which focused on campus social activities, fashion, and etiquette. At the University of British Columbia women were not permitted to smoke on campus, a rule that women themselves voted to uphold on the grounds that their smoking would damage the public image of the university.[75] In other ways, though, coeds in western Canada were treated more liberally than students in the east. On a tour of western campuses the editor of Toronto's *Varsity* expressed surprise to see men and women lunching together in cafeterias, something that rarely happened at Toronto. There, men ate at Hart House and women at the Women's Union. Exchange students, too, found more genuine coeducation at the University of British Columbia than at the more conservative McGill.[76]

The separate and unequal treatment of women was justified on the basis of assumed physiological and emotional differences between the genders. Writing in respected journals, men still found it possible to conclude, on the basis of "scientific" evidence, that woman had less capacity for abstract thought than men, owing to the smaller size of their "frontal lobes." Another writer argued that "the maternal instinct ... makes [the woman's] view of life more personal, more bound up with the activities and sanctities of the home, likelier to be that of the family than of the tribe or the nation, more partial in judgment, less willing to be guided by the canons of abstract justice than the male." As late as 1939 a *McGill Daily* editorial contended that while men were suited to the economic function of production, "women's qualifications run in the sphere of consumption," supposedly reinforcing their natural connection to the household.[77]

While the presence of women on campus was an established fact, men contended – frequently in a jocular tone – that as husband-hunting "social butterflies," women were a constant source of distraction. "The Women – Ah, God bless all of 'em," declared one Dalhousie student, "but keep 'em away when we are trying to study."[78] In one of the crudest examples of such thinking, W.E. McNeill, the vice-principal of Queen's, claimed that the university – now a "dancing academy" – had become a "woman infested place."[79]

These demeaning stereotypes could provoke irate responses. A flood of letters to the student newspaper followed McNeill's speech at Queen's, one of which ominously reminded readers of the student strike of 1928, the result, in part, of faculty's similarly condescending treatment of students.[80] There were other occasions, too, when women denounced and fought such arrogance and prejudice. After years of exclusion, McGill women finally gained admission to the university student council in 1931. At the University of British Columbia in 1937 women protested the prohibition against their right to shoot .22 rifles on the campus range for fear that they might "hurt themselves." And at Western the limited facilities for female athletics aroused a campaign for a woman's union building.[81]

Such protest, however, was episodic, not sustained, and discrimination was addressed in more subtle ways, which made campus life for women – despite the inequities – endurable, worthwhile, and even enjoyable. In their struggles for coeducation, earlier generations of university women had left their descendants of the 1930s with an important legacy – the female-only student societies in which all women students were automatically members. Formed in 1911, the Wauneita Society at the University of Alberta sought to "uphold [women's] rights among an overwhelming number of males."[82] Levana at Queen's, Delta Gamma at Dalhousie, and the Women's Union at McGill were constituted and carried on with a similar mission. Through these associations women made contacts and friendships requiring neither male approval nor social qualifications for admission. Unlike the elite and selected sororities, these all-inclusive women's groups reached out unconditionally to female students, smoothing their initiation and integration into campus life.

Unquestionably, these organizations were preoccupied with social affairs. They sponsored orientations, teas, sing-songs, and dances, though they also engaged in fund-raising for charitable causes. Such activities confirmed the views of some male professors and students that women were trivializing the university experience – as though the social activities in which men engaged (fraternities, football, and residence parties) were somehow less frivolous. But such clichés missed the real significance of women's associational life.

Middle-class women in the 1930s were exposed to two apparently contradictory role-models. First, the accomplished professional or business woman – no longer such a novelty – received favourable treatment in the press, particularly in women's magazines like *Chatelaine*. Prominent individuals such as Agnes Macphail and Charlotte Whitton drew appreciative audiences when they spoke on university campuses. In Canada and the United States, Eleanor Roosevelt was one of the most admired public figures of her day. These revered examples of women forging successful careers outside the home appeared difficult to reconcile with the other – admittedly more pervasive – ideal type: the successful housewife and mother. *Chatelaine*, whose ads, features, and household tips were directed primarily to the housebound woman, illustrated this standard in an article entitled "When a Man Is Peevish," describing systematically how a "wise wife" could avoid creating an unhappy man. She should serve him supper only after he had rested for half an hour; if he complained about the meal, she should never argue for fear of aggravating his "mental upset." If she kept him out late at night, making him overtired, she would be "guilty of criminal negligence." In short, "it is a wife's job – a wife's privilege – to make home a happy place and to keep peevishness from spoiling it."[83] According to this model, the fulfilled woman was a knowledgable and caring domestic organizer.

But for university women, the successful homemaker and the admired professional were not necessarily irreconcilable ideals. Both required similar social skills. Younger women, aspiring to middle-class respectability, whether they worked in or outside the home should be meticulous in their presentation. They should be well-mannered, properly dressed, socially adept, poised, and confident. They should get involved in community and volunteer work, and even learn how to address a luncheon audience.[84] Educated women had both the opportunity and the obligation to master these talents. Women who did not would have an incomplete higher education and thus even fewer social and economic advantages. With their emphasis on the social world, then, female societies sought to enhance women's opportunities to succeed within their own domain. Women did not seek *en masse* to end male prerogatives or even to encroach in more than minor ways on traditional male territory. Yet they jealously guarded those institutions – the only ones on campus – over which they had exclusive autonomy. Both career women and future housewives had something to gain from what these associations promised.

Where women lacked these outlets, there was a felt need to create them. At the University of British Columbia a new women's club called Phrateres was organized in 1935 to assist the "unsocial and the socially inexperienced girls, and to bring them together under conditions which will break down the inhibitions caused by timidity, supersensitiveness, lack of money and other causes, and which, as a consequence will help to prepare them for the experiences which they will meet after leaving college."[85] The middle-class paragon that these and other young women were advised to emulate was embodied in the character of Mrs Brock, the late wife of the university dean. "She was utterly self effacing. Herself a university graduate, she revealed and exemplifed to all who knew her, and especially to numberless students, that harmony of disciplined culture and active goodness which has always been the University ideal."[86]

Most young women, of course, were neither totally timid nor perfectly poised. A realistic portrait of what middle-class parents expected and how typical university daughters might have responded can be found in a 1934 *Chatelaine* article by Garrett Elliott, called "What I Wish for My Daughter."[87] Like other parents, he faced the challenge of finding the legitimate reach of his authority. His daughter and her friends "conceded the weight of certain parental preogratives without at the same time conceding their essential justice." They respected their parents but kept a certain distance. What the writer hoped, in any event, was that his daughter would dress becomingly while maintaining her individuality; that she would spend money "to advantage" but live within her means; that she not smoke but that if she did she would avoid "ostentation and staining her fingers"; that she would eschew social snobbery but "recognize the essential qualities and obligation entailed by good breeding"; that she speak well and not in phony clichés; that she would be proficient in one or more sports; that she marry successfully "because she has more to lose by its failure ... [A wife's] interests, her activities, her friends, her social status focus entirely about her marriage. It behooves her to protect her investment, and so I would hope for her the wisdom to play her cards well." She should allow her husband "some place where she does not intrude ... he will find it anyway."

The author had expected his daughter's education would make her clever. The kind of intelligence she had in fact gained he found "more servicable in the workaday world than the cut-and-dried knowledge that I had hoped for her." This poignant account captures the essence of the prescription for the successfully cultivated middle-class woman of the day, and the Canadian university of the 1930s had a vital role to play in helping her to achieve or maintain this position. A college education would provide a young woman not with the social or economic status of men but with a legitimate degree of independence and sophistication considered valuable at home, at work, and in the community. For this reason her university years were both relished at the time and fondly recalled.[88]

V

Students spent most of their academic and social life on campus, but they were not bound there. In the evenings and on weekends they were drawn into the city by movies, theatres, eateries, and retail outlets. While unruly behaviour and youthful cockiness could arouse resentment and perpetuate town-gown conflict, public antipathy to students was offset by the considerable contribution they made to local economies, particularly during the Depression. Occasional surveys of student spending practices revealed the extent of their monetary worth. University of Saskatchewan students, far from the country's most affluent, spent $633,425 in 1937, of which $180,000 went to university fees. Local businesses thus took in $453,425 worth of student purchases. Between one-half and one-third of this total was spent on clothes, men averaging $78.00 annually and women $102.00. A total of $13,000 went to meals, over $11,000 on shows, about $9500 on dry-cleaning and laundry, some $7600 on carfare, and approximately $7500 on cosmetics and drugs. Men also spent $1.25 a month on dances, while women spent $0.09. Finally, men consumed an average of $3.64 worth of tobacco annually, and women $2.50.[89] A survey at the University of British Columbia revealed similar patterns, showing additional expenditures on rent, gas and auto repairs, doctors and dentists, books and magazines, and haircuts.[90] Those inclined to question the maturity and importance of students to the community were advised by the Saskatchewan *Sheaf* that "half a million dollars a year alone [of student spending] speaks with an adult voice."[91]

Though the Depression economy reduced the frequency of advertising, campus newspapers carried numerous displays from local merchants seeking student customers. Fall ads welcomed everyone back to university, and editors returned the favour by urging students to patronize those merchants who purchased advertising space.[92] Even the popular press advertised directly to students. Full-page Eaton ads in the Toronto

Globe congratulated the class of 1935 and urged its members to buy jewelry, luggage, golf clubs, and evening wear.[93] Whatever their aspirations and post-graduate fate, students were an immediate boon to local business, particularly in smaller communities. In Kingston they demanded – and received – discounts from theatre proprietors, one of whom happily estimated that 1600 students, taking advantage of reduced rates, saw at least one movie per week.[94]

In their passion for Hollywood movies, students were not alone. By 1939, according to the *Canada Year Book*, "the Motion Picture [had] become the most popular form of public entertainment and the business of satisfying the demand for such amusement [had] assumed a corresponding importance."[95] Despite Depression-induced shutdowns, there were still 950 motion-picture houses in Canada in 1936, 102 of which were in Toronto and 62 in Montreal.[96] Initially patronized mainly by the working class, following the First World War, movies successfully tapped a more affluent middle-class clientèle, fascinated by the innovation of sound and lured by sophisticated marketing techniques.[97] The five hundred productions churned out annually by Hollywood in the 1930s found regular and enthusiastic audiences north of the border.

Like other forms of popular entertainment, movies were a source of concern both to guardians of high culture and to proponents of moral reform. Particularly in the early 1930s, the steady cinematic diet of "free love," vice, crime, and drunkenness, combined with the legacy of scandal and financial impropriety in Hollywood itself, prompted censorship campaigns in both the United States and Canada. Advocates feared the corruption of youth and even wider social breakdown – especially worrisome in a Depression economy – if the "indecent" content of movies was not controlled. Hollywood did not await the strong arm of government. Worried also by a temporary decline in its audience, the industry opted for self-regulation. Following the creation in 1934 of the Production Code Administration, moral order was restored in moviemaking. Language and sexual relations were purifed, and attacks on social convention were replaced by comedic farce, romantic melodrama, and epic myth-making. The social commentary of Charlie Chaplin went unappreciated (until later), and the early satire of the Marx brothers dissolved into slapstick and buffoonery. "The movie moguls gave up their adversary stance because they suddenly found greater opportunities for profit and prestige in supporting traditional American culture, in themselves becoming its guardians."[98] Where impropriety still appeared on the screen, censorship was available to regulators in every Canadian province. The "glorification" of foreigners, the ridicule of clergymen and marriage, and the unrestrained use of revolvers particularly roused Canadian censors to action.[99]

In lamenting the insidious impact of Hollywood on Canadian culture, student editors periodically followed the lead of austere faculty critics. The *Varsity* noted in 1932: "As [part] of a British institution ... it is up to us to applaud and urge the British productions which are obviously of better tone and less artificial texture than those of Hollywood."[100] Students ignored such advice, however, and attended the theatre in droves, including those unintentionally hilarious American features that depicted Canada in the most clichéed, stereotyped form.[101] Like moral reformers of the day, however, one can err in making too much of the cultural significance of Hollywood films on the minds of Canadian university youth. Undoubtedly they contributed to the continuing Americanization of Canadian popular culture, counterbalancing the British North American influences to which English Canadian students were otherwise exposed. But primarily the movies provided an entertaining escape from campus routines and served as a relatively inexpensive vehicle for socializing and dating. As the Canadian Youth Commission later noted, they were a modern recreational outlet frequented by young people and their peers "independent" of their families.[102] In its glamour and sensationalism, the cinema indulged the fantasies and illusions of those whose future was open but terribly uncertain. Movies could still titillate youth, but parents and educators need not have worried: even as their popularity grew, Hollywood films were less than ever stimulators of cynicism, social criticism, or unconventional behaviour.[103]

A somewhat more cerebral – and nationalistic – outlet, radio, also attracted large audiences in the late 1920s and 1930s, on and off university campuses. American singers like Rudy Valee and Bing Crosby, and comedians Jack Benny, Amos 'n' Andy, George Burns and Gracie Allen were enormously popular among older and younger listeners alike. Through this medium, with the creation of the Canadian Broadcasting Corporation, a Canadian presence was preserved and promoted, though it hardly overwhelmed American programming. Musicians Guy Lombardo and Don Messer, playwrights Merrill Dennison and Fletcher Markle, and actor-announcers John Drainie and J. Frank Willis found outlets for their creative talents on the airwaves. None was as popular as Foster Hewitt, who mesmerized the country with his professional hockey broadcasts.[104] A number of well-known Canadian entertainers, such as Lorne Greene (Queen's), John Fisher (Dalhousie), and Johnny Wayne (Toronto), received their apprenticeship on the theatre stages of Canadian universities during the 1930s.[105] Radio provided two other dimensions that movies did not: immediacy – including the riveting reports from the site of the Moose River Mine Disaster in Nova Scotia in 1936; and elevated culture – including drama, opera, and classical music provided by symphonic orchestras in Vancouver, Toronto, and Quebec.[106]

University students, usually encouraged by faculty and administrators, used radio in a unique way by engaging in nationally or locally broadcast debating competitions, some of which were sponsored by the Canadian Radio Commission and its successor, the CBC. Extension courses arranged by the Canadian Association of Adult Education, and commentaries on public affairs by professors such as F.H. Soward (British Columbia), George Glazebrook (Toronto), and Herbert L. Stewart (Dalhousie) provided novel links between the educational and entertainment media. To the degree that these activities offset the mediocre productions of American commercial networks, even sceptics like Dalhousie president Carleton Stanley were convinced of radio's potential for cultural uplift.[107] When used for educational purposes, radio supplemented university teaching; more often, however, as pure recreation it provided students with a valued diversion from their studies.

There were other diversions, too. Because students were unable to take for granted a secure future, the Depression injected a note of sobriety into the campus mood. Still, the lives of those who *had* achieved wealth or notoriety inspired endless fascination. No one could escape – or wanted to – the prurient accounts of the Lindbergh kidnapping or the trials of the Dionne quintuplets. The astronomical salaries of movie stars, the tribulations of royalty, and the successes of brash entrepreneurs also piqued student interest. The death in 1936 of King George V, the abdication in the same year of Edward VIII, and the royal visit of George VI and Queen Elizabeth in 1939 were major news events in both the campus and popular presses.[108]

One might have expected struggling students to resent leisure-loving millionaires, but with respect to one Canadian capitalist, the opposite was the case. Numerous stories in the student press highlighted in 1938 the astonishing career of the country's youngest business tycoon, George McCullagh. At the age of thirty-two this "Boy Wonder" owned the Toronto *Globe* (Canada's "most powerful newspaper"), had made a fortune in mining, wielded enormous political influence in Ontario, and was being touted as a future prime minister.[109] Students were aware of McCullagh's extremely conservative views – one editorial worried about his fanning the flames of class conflict – but most commentators were in total awe of his position. As a publisher he attracted special interest among student journalists, who invited him to deliver the keynote address to the inaugural meeting of the Canadian University Press. Beyond that, his youth, outspokenness, and material success – achieved without a university degree – spoke to the values and ambitions of the ordinary student in the 1930s. McCullagh's career – exceptional as it was – seemed to prove that even in the Depression, youth still had reason to be hopeful. Evidently, one could succeed within the system and still retain one's verve and individuality. Socialist and communist sceptics aside, for most Canadian students the free-enterprise myth had survived the collapse of capitalism.

Whatever the fate of the larger economy and however lofty their dreams, students had to narrow their sights and ensure their personal fiscal viability each academic year. In order to be marketplace consumers, many were compelled to become part-time producers of goods and services. Students worked for two reasons: to earn spending money that would enable them to participate fully in the social life of the campus and the community, or, in the case of the poorest, to purchase bare necessities required merely to survive the term. Observers at the time contended that part-time work, both in the summer and throughout the year was anxiously sought and difficult to obtain during the Depression, particularly for women.[110] Queen's alumnus Rose Mary Gibson recalled her classmates doing volunteer work at the girl-guide and fresh-air camps in the absence of other opportunities.[111]

For those students who found work, successful entry into middle-class careers did not preclude temporary stints as unskilled labourers, and the opportunities for employment of even this sort varied with the strength of regional economies. Some women at Western were hired as demonstrators and library workers, but "the most usual form of occupation is domestic, whereby a student undertakes some household duties for the family with whom she is residing in return for room and board in part or in whole."[112] Men were hired in a wider variety of jobs, though they considered themselves lucky to find manual labour of any sort. H.S. Ferns, a student at the University of Manitoba, was relieved to have obtained work for a mere eight weeks between 1931 and 1935 – as a "chamber maid" for chickens. This "filthy" job involved watering the poultry, cleaning dung from their cages, and hosing the slaughterhouse after the animals were killed.[113] Some students, unable to find work at home, hitchiked across the continent or, like Marshall McLuhan and Tom Easterbrook, worked their way on cattle-boats to Europe.[114]

A rare statistical insight into part-time work patterns was provided by the University of Western Ontario for the year 1939, by which time jobs were somewhat more plentiful.[115] The survey found that 77 per cent of male arts students and 40 per cent of the women were employed in the summer. Almost one-quarter of the men worked at Christmas, compared to only 6 per cent of the women, and 23 per cent of men were employed during the university session, compared to 13 per cent of the women. Substantially more – 42 per cent of the males and 19 per cent of females – expressed interest in working part-time had this been possible.

In terms of job categories, 59 per cent of Western (arts) men employed during the summer of 1939 worked as manual labourers and 33 per cent in clerical or sales work. Only 35 per cent of employed women worked in the former category and 50 per cent in the latter. Wage disparities were pervasive. Whereas 73 per cent of employed men earned more than ten dollars per week in the summer, only 48 per cent of employed women did so. Having good family connections helped students to get summer jobs. Of those employed, 59 per cent of the men and 46 per cent of the women claimed that "personal influence," as opposed to "regular application," secured them their positions. Thus the networking methods, if not the privileged occupations, of the middle class helped many university students through the Depression. The good jobs, the quality incomes, and the comfortable lifestyles, if one were fortunate and adequately prepared, would come later.

Because it rounded out one's academic training, extracurricular life was considered by students and "modern" administrators alike both legitimate and necessary. The challenge for university officials was to contain and channel associational life, while students were inclined to stretch their autonomy to its limits. For the most part the authorities maintained the upper hand. Yet students were not empty vessels into which all the lessons of Western civilization could be easily poured. No simplistic theories of social control can explain campus life of the 1930s.[116] The student-faculty relationship was complex and dynamic. As in the past, students were always a potential source of disorder, and administrators had to learn when to bend and when to resist. They used a variety of means: discipline, paternalism, flexibility, and the institution of student government to enforce the rules and preserve the peace.

What helped keep order, irrespective of faculty actions, was first the sheer scope of extra-curricular outlets, and second the fact that students, of their own volition, shared the dominant values of their parents and teachers. They were preparing for middle-class lives, which they hoped would provide both immediate respite from the Depression and long-term security. Accomplishing this mission required learning applied social skills that went beyond mere academic success. "University spirit," explained one editorial, "is a loyalty to a definite and coherent body animated by a specific spirit, which evokes a sense of gratitude, of obligation and service. The student is given opportunity and means whereby he may develop his personality along chosen lines under the aegis of the university with which he has identified."[117] The campus culture rewarded intelligence more than pure intellect; it made leaders out of those with poise and polish; it admitted women but confined them to a particular social space; it allowed minimal access to religious and ethnic minorities, and proceeded to marginalize them. Students consumed the continental popular culture, which spoke more directly to their youthful tastes than anything offered by stodgy, aging educators. Still, despite deploring their lack of discernment, adults could take heart in the enduring patriotism and "common sense" of Canadian students.[118] Lured by American fads, students resisted American excesses, represented by the organization of fraternities and team sports. Students were told, and they believed, that Canadian campus life was more restrained and balanced than that south of the border.

The Depression did not transform the nature of student associational life, although its impact was not without significance. It heightened students' importance to local economies as consumers and cheap labourers. Hard times made them more serious on the one hand, but determined to enjoy campus life on the other. And in some, as we shall see in the next chapter, the Depression stirred social conscience and stimulated political activism.

CHAPTER SIX

Politics and Social Change: The Student Movement

Canadian students placed a high priority on campus social life, but like previous generations of youth they were not oblivious to politics and world affairs. Throughout history students have participated fervently in reformist and revolutionary movements. The 1930s provided conditions particularly conducive to student activism in Europe and North America. Collapsed capitalist economies, the rise of fascism, and the imminence of war threatened to deface or destroy the world that youth was preparing to enter. Even privileged, educated youth could not be insulated from these enormous pressures. How would they face the challenge? To what degree did their responses involve collective political action? While historians have examined the student movement of the 1930s in the United States and Europe, there are no such detailed treatments of the Canadian experience.[1] This chapter explores the extent to which Canadian students of that era participated in efforts to transform the political and social order of Canadian society.

I

Their denominational origins still in the recent past, Canadian universities in the more secular environment of the early twentieth century faced the challenge of preserving their cultural integrity while adapting to modern currents. As we have seen, they portrayed themselves as non-doctrinaire, God-fearing institutions, responsible for graduating middle-class professionals with sound moral values and the qualities of good citizenship. The social crises of the 1930s, in the eyes of university authorities, made such a mission even more important.[2]

While periodically menaced by the high jinks of unruly students, university campuses prior to the 1930s had largely been spared the potentially more serious challenge posed by politically militant youth.[3]

The political moderation of university students was reflected in the program of the National Federation of Canadian University Students (NFCUS), an organization founded at a Montreal conference of student council representatives from eleven universities in December 1926.[4] Inspired by the encouragement of Ralph Nunn May, a member of the Imperial Debating Team and a former president of the National Union of Students in England, NFCUS arose in part out of the post-war desire for international harmony and peace among students in Europe and North America. NFCUS resolved to "promote national unity" through campus co-operation and to facilitate the exchange of information on student concerns. It was soon evident that NFCUS perceived itself primarily as an apolitical service organization for students. It gained some respect for its promotion of inter-university debating competitions, of which it had sponsored some five hundred by 1935, and its university exchange program, in which students from one region of the country would spend a year of university in a different region. NFCUS also sought to obtain reduced transportation rates for students travelling within Canada and abroad.[5]

Only a handful of students actively participated in the affairs of NFCUS on a regular basis, though it generally elicited positive, if perfunctory, editorial comment from the student press. Throughout the Depression, when other student groups promoted peace and social reform, NFCUS stood on the sidelines, studiously avoiding taking controversial positions on issues of the day. As an editorial in the University of Manitoba student newspaper explained, NFCUS "may be compared to a mechanical robot. It carries out its obvious duties, but posseses none of the dynamic quality which can only be obtained with a solid body of student support for its activities and student thought on its problems."[6] University authorities and the Royal Canadian Mounted Police agreed. According to a 1939 RCMP surveillance report, NFCUS, unlike more radical groups, was a "reliable and approved institution."[7]

Somewhat less "reliable," and far more committed to raising the political consciousness of Canadian students, was the Student Christian Movement (SCM). Founded in January 1921, when the student departments of the YMCA and YWCA joined forces with a group of young Christian activists, SCM was an outgrowth of the social gospel, a Christian reform movement "seeking to realize the Kingdom of God in the very fabric of society."[8] The SCM was the most important and enduring element of the Canadian student movement of the 1930s. Inspired by the activities and writings of reformist theologians such as Reinhold Niebuhr and J. King Gordon, it convened chapters on most Canadian campuses, sponsored talks by controversial speakers, raised relief funds for war victims in China, and, most importantly, campaigned relentlessly for peace and social justice. While there were political differences within the organization, with some students promoting religion over politics and others promoting radical ideology and mass action, the scm (unlike other student groups) remained unified and reasonably well organized at both national and local campus levels.[9]

With its tradition of mission-oriented Methodism, Victoria College at the University of Toronto was a particularly important centre of scm activity; approximately 10 per cent of the college's one thousand students participated in the movement in the mid-thirties.[10] At the University of Alberta twelve scm study groups met throughout the 1930–31 year, drawing an average of 130 students (some 10 per cent of the student body), while the Universities of Manitoba, Dalhousie, McGill, and Mount Allison had equally active though smaller constituencies.[11] Although scm's left-wing politics roused periodic concern in more conservative quarters, its righteousness and moderation earned it the support of most university authorities. R.C. Wallace, president of the University of Alberta from 1928 to 1936 and principal of Queen's from 1936 to 1951, was an scm booster who served as its honorary national president in 1937, and Chancellor E.W. Beatty of McGill, no enthusiast of radical politics, believed that scm played an important role in helping to shape students' "moral development."[12] Thus, because of its protected niche on Canadian campuses, the scm provided a "haven of legitimacy" for some student radicals; more importantly, it served as an outlet for the minority of students interested in combining Christian living with social change.[13]

Another national student organization worthy of note was the Canadian Student Assembly (csa), founded in January 1938 following a national student conference in Winnipeg organized by the scm.[14] Under the leadership of its national secretary, Grante Lathe, a graduate medical doctor from McGill, the csa posed a serious challenge to the politically listless nfcus, and the rivalry continued until the csa broke up in a swirl of controversy over its policy on the war in 1940. Composed of local "student assemblies," which students could join as individuals or club members, the csa established a presence on most campuses by 1939. It opposed militarism and favoured greater educational opportunity, closer relations between French and English Canada, and the preservation of civil liberties.[15]

The csa's most important undertaking was a campaign to pressure the federal government to provide a thousand "national scholarships," worth five hundred dollars each, for university students. On 6 March 1939 a csa delegation of six students, bearing petitions and documentation of the low level of financial support available to Canadian students, met the minister of labour, Norman Rogers, to press their claims. Their efforts yielded mixed results. Bursaries totalling $225,000, to be distributed to students over three years, were incorporated into the Dominion-Provincial Youth Training Plan in 1939, but because the program required provincial co-operation at a time of considerable federal-provincial conflict, the provinces of Ontario, Quebec, New Brunswick, and Nova Scotia refused to participate in the scheme, thus depriving their students of financial assistance. Students in the west received more benefit.[16]

While the CSA never succeeded in its efforts to build a mass movement, attracting by its own (probably exaggerated) estimate the active involvement of 2 per cent of Canadian students, along with other groups it played some role in making the public more aware of the problems and needs of Canadian youth.[17] Canadian historians of the 1930s have ignored the emergence of a significant youth movement in Canada in the last half of the decade, which attracted wide and generally favourable public attention. At the centre of the movement was the Canadian Youth Congress (CYC), of which the CSA and the SCM, were member groups. At its peak in the late 1930s the CYC represented every major youth organization in Canada, with a total constituent membership of over four hundred thousand. Beginning in 1936 it held annual national conferences (with up to 730 participants), out of which it issued a Declaration of the Rights of Youth and a program favouring youth employment training, improved health, recreational, and educational facilities, and world peace. It also sent a number of delegates, representing the political spectrum from conservative to communist, to the 1936 World Youth Congress in Geneva. On the whole, middle- class university students were far less involved in the activities of the CYC than were volunteer agencies representing working-class youth, although a group of students from the University of Toronto played a major role in the events leading to the founding of the CYC, and one of its graduates, Kenneth Woodsworth, became the full-time national secretary of the organization.[18]

Communist youth played an important role in the CYC and took a less influential part in the university-based student movement of the 1930s. While most of the considerable energy of the Young Communist League (YCL, the youth branch of the Communist Party of Canada) was channelled to the organization of workers, the unemployed, and the campaign against fascism and war, some of this effort spilled on to university campuses through the CP's united-front and popular-front policies.[19] Where possible, co-operative work was engaged with groups like the SCM and the CSA, although YCL members rarely declared publicly their major affiliation. The fear of harassment and repression in part explains this tactic. Applying draconian municipal laws, the Toronto police force broke up numerous Communist meetings in the late twenties and early thirties, some of which included students.[20] Then, in 1931, under Section 98 of the Criminal Code, which made it illegal simply to "advocate" political change "by the use of force," the Communist Party was declared "an unlawful association" and eight of its leaders were tried, convicted, and jailed. The law lapsed in 1936, allowing Communists to operate more openly, but was reimposed in Quebec in 1937 in the form of the Padlock Law, which made it a criminal offence to circulate literature "tending to propagate communism."[21]

RCMP informers infiltrated student meetings where Communists were present and filed reports on others merely suspected of having Communist links. One account contained the names of three McGill professors who were scheduled to attend a scientific conference in Moscow, and others reported on speeches by a (non-Communist) socialist student named David Lewis and a political science lecturer, Eugene Forsey, both from McGill.[22] When right-wing spokesmen charged that university campuses were filled with communists, an accusation hurled frequently at McGill University, the claims were found to be without substance. In 1931 even RCMP Inspector J.W. Phillips declared "ridiculous" the view that McGill was a "hot bed of communism." Still, most such charges, no matter how suspect the source, were followed up with investigations in the illiberal political climate of the 1930s.[23] The UBC student newspaper perhaps adopted the most appropriate response to these groundless complaints – sarcasm. After a British Columbia cabinet member, R.H. Poole, claimed that some university faculty were teaching communism, the *Ubyssey* titled an editorial, "Are Our Faces Red?" and a columnist in the liberal *Vancouver Sun* dismissed Poole's "communistic hallucinations."[24]

A Communist club was permitted to function openly at the University of Toronto in 1936, an "experiment" that received national attention in student newspapers, though because the membership was small and the majority of students were viewed by the university's president as "level-headed," this was not considered a particularly dangerous initiative.[25] Communists were known to be leading forces in the League against War and Fascism, which, as part of its united-front national campaign, held meetings on various campuses throughout the decade. In Winnipeg, the *Manitoban* recalled that the league had had a "short and unimpressive existence" at that university.[26]

Inspired by events in the United States, where a Communist-led National Student League was formed in 1932, a Canadian Student League emerged later that year at the University of Toronto and established small groups in other Canadian cities. It held at least two conferences, where it attempted to unite university and high-school students in a common organization favouring scholarships for the poor, freedom of speech and assembly, the abolition of campus officers' training corps, opposition to fascism and fascist propaganda, and the creation of an economic system based on "use, not profit." Its most noteworthy activity was the role it played in a 1934 Montreal campaign against increased high-school tuition fees, which included a student walk-out from two schools. It also participated in a 1935 May Day "strike" by a reported three thousand Vancouver (mostly high-school) students, who marched in a demonstration with area relief-camp workers. Student League groups operated on several Canadian campuses, where they co-operated with other reform organizations but had a minimal impact on the student body as whole. At its peak the Young Communist League had seventeen hundred members across the country, and while it was most active in Montreal, Toronto, Vancouver, and Winnipeg, where it forged some effective alliances with non-Communist youth groups, only a small proportion of the YCL's members were university students.[27]

If Communist youth sometimes made their presence felt on Canadian campuses, so too did democratic socialists. The organization of the League for Social Reconstruction (LSR) and the Co-operative Commonwealth Federation (CCF) led to the formation of like-minded study groups and clubs on a number of campuses. Some of these were affiliated with the Co-operative Commonwealth Youth Movement (CCYM), formed in 1934, which, like the Young Communist League, focused most of its organizing efforts on working-class, not university, youth. In 1938 the CCYM was strongest in Alberta, where it drew upon links with the long-established United Farmers of Alberta. It was active as well in Ontario and Saskatchewan, where its members attracted the attention of some students by delivering speeches and selling newspapers on street corners.[28] Under the tutelage of professors such as W.H. Alexander at the University of Alberta, Leonard Marsh, Frank Scott, and Eugene Forsey at McGill, Eric Havelock, Frank Underhill, and Harry Cassidy at Toronto, A.W. Carrothers at the University of British Columbia, and J. King Gordon at the United Theological Institute in Montreal, sympathetic students sought to raise the political consciousness of their classmates along socialist lines. A University Society for Social Reconstruction (with the ironic abbreviation of the USSR) formed at United College in Winnipeg, as did similar groups at Mount Allison University in New Brunswick and Queen's University in Kingston. The most energetic and intellectual university socialist group was the McGill Labour Club, whose publication, the *Alarm Clock*, was banned from the campus in 1933 by Arthur Currie, the McGill principal, and whose activities were followed closely by the RCMP.[29]

Off campus, youth associated with the CCF continually battled those tied to the Communist movement (particularly in organizations such as the Canadian Youth Congress), but within universities left-wing students maintained a greater degree of unity in the SCM, the CSA, and various peace-movement activities. Their small numbers made open conflict futile.[30]

No event demonstrates the unity and promise of the student movement more than an unprecedented national student conference held in Winnipeg in December 1937. The idea of the conference originated in discussions between individual members of the SCM and the CYC who sought to create a "live, all embracing" assembly of students, comparable to the dynamic meetings of the CYC.[31] The SCM, considered the only national body capable of organizing such an event, agreed to do so, and in the fall of 1937 its associate general secretary, Margaret Kinney, toured campuses generating interest among student councils, the politically active student groups, and the press. Open meetings were held on many campuses, where agenda topics were discussed and delegates chosen.

The conference was deemed a considerable success. In the ebullient view of the *Manitoban*, the three hundred plus delegates from some twenty universities were treated to "the greatest student intellectual marathon" ever organized.[32] Speeches by the internationally known Reinhold Niebuhr and by T.Z. Koo (the secretary of the World Student Christian Federation) attracted considerable attention, but what made the conference particularly lively were the open debates among students themselves on issues ranging from educational reform to Canadian foreign policy. French Canadians participated actively, explaining to bemused but engrossed English Canadians their support for the repressive Padlock Law, their opposition to free speech for Communists, and the importance of Catholicism in their lives. The conservative views of Quebec students were offset by resolutions calling for labour's right to bargain collectively, political equality for Canadian-born Orientals in British Columbia, and an independent foreign policy for Canada (supported by French Canadians). The conference ended in idealistic high spirits, leading to its two major accomplishments, the founding of both the Canadian Student Assembly and the Canadian University Press. The conference's largely left-of-centre policies drew less public attention than the favourable contribution it was perceived to have made to national unity. Returning to their campuses, the politically active Christian, socialist, communist, and pacifist students re-encountered the reality that building and sustaining a reform movement was more easily said than done.[33]

II

Despite the abundance of concerns that might have inspired it, there was no mass political movement of university students during the 1930s.

At best perhaps 5 per cent of students joined or participated regularly in reform-oriented organizations, though the last half of the decade involved more students than the first.[34] Socialist students and others moved by the plight of workers and the unemployed joined marchers in the "On-to-Ottawa trek" in 1935 and supported coal-miners in a New Brunswick strike in 1937.[35] But they were a distinct minority. In 1937 an Indian student visiting Canada was "appalled by the lack of political movements amongst the Canadian youth. They are far behind the youths of other countries in this respect."[36] Student activists and non-activists alike agreed that the bleak economic climate did not rouse much protest among university students. If anything it had the reverse effect. According to University of Manitoba student Earl Beattie, "the students doing political things were just a minority. The bulk of students didn't give a damn." Gertrude Rutherford, an SCM organizer from the University of Alberta, observed in her tour of western campuses in 1931 that "nowhere had the social life of the universities been affected by economic conditions. There were the same number of dinners, dances, teas, and other events." While the outbreak of the Depression deepened the political commitments of those already inclined to activism, it made most students more cautious. Indeed, prior to the 1935 federal election the student newspaper at Western advised students to be wary of political movements and new ideas. "In times of crisis, we cannot afford to gamble on any new political system which is as yet largely theoretical and not proved by experience ... radicalism is a luxury of stability." An earlier editorial claimed that capitalism was "the only system for Anglo Saxons."[37]

Canadian students were not necessarily as conservative as the Western *Gazette* editorials implied, but they were far less politically conscious than activists thought appropriate for the times. Why? Students were privileged to be at university, but apart from an extremely well-heeled minority, they were not wealthy. The typical student was the child of a merchant or a teacher for whom university was first and foremost a stepping stone to a more secure professional career.[38] The Depression removed any guarantee of such employment, but as many observed, it made students work harder in the hope of enduring and surviving the difficult times.[39] Radical ideas were discussed and debated, but their advocates were perceived as well-intentioned dreamers out of step with reality. At best, recalled Kenneth Bradford, a University of Toronto student in the early 1930s, the typical student attitude towards politics was one of "pure inquiry without passion." "We were political observers," echoed Marjorie Bowker of the University of Alberta, "not participants."

Though they might challenge authority in other ways, students tended to support the political choices of their parents. When Prime Minister Bennett visited a number of Canadian universities in 1933, he was treated with near reverence by most student newspapers, one of which commented on the "inspirational qualities and sound common sense" of his platitudinous speech.[40] Two years later a student poll at the University of Saskatchewan gave 45 per cent support to the Liberals, 25 per cent to the CCF, 21 per cent to (Bennett's) Conservatives, and 8 per cent to the Communists, results consistent with those of the province of Saskatchewan in the imminent federal election. A similar survey of four thousand students at the University of Toronto gave the electoral edge to the Conservatives over the Liberals (35 per cent to 30 per cent), with the CCF receiving 13 per cent, the Reconstruction party 9.8 per cent, and the Communists 3.2 per cent of the vote. The polls signified, first, that student opinion followed the shift toward Liberalism in the country as a whole (though University of Toronto students proved *more* conservative than voters in Ontario generally, where the Liberals won handily), and second, that the Canadian university was, in the words of the *Sheaf*, "no hotbed of radicalism."[41]

This was not to suggest that students were reluctant to debate issues of social and political concern. Formal debating competitions were organized throughout the decade either by local university societies or by NFCUS, the latter featuring well-publicized encounters between representatives from Canadian and other British Commonwealth campuses. Topics ranged from the serious and seemingly subversive to the frivolous and irreverent: debaters resolved that "the British Empire must disintegrate," that "this House favours a dictatorship," that "this House would rather live in Moscow than Britain," that "Liberalism, though it speaketh, is dead", that "this House deplores the policies of the Bennett government," that "Hollywood should be razed," that "emotion has done more for the good of the human race than has reason," and that "it is better to walk than to run."[42]

Even if their supporters lost the arguments, Bennett, big business, and Hollywood had little to fear. Debating, like football, initiations, and student council elections, was judged more on style than substance. Students enjoyed the intellectual tussle; they were impressed by the articulate, intelligent, and witty debaters – all social skills prized by cultured and educated middle-class youth. A *McGill Daily* editorial favoured debates that featured "brilliant sallies ... , repartee, and a ready fund of little stories" and denounced those that were "drab" and pedantic.[43] Similarly, the Saskatchewan *Sheaf* condemned the "heavy, quasi-intellectual ... discussions of political and historical subjects," arguing that "social subjects" appealed more to the "listening public."[44] As mere entertainment spectacles, these intellectual skirmishes posed no real threat to campus political order.

Indeed, the *Queen's Journal* perceived debating as a valuable extra-curricular forum for professional and marketplace training. "From the beginning of the days of big business in the modern meaning of the phrase, the ability to express oneself clearly, concisely and forcefully has been a major factor leading up to that somewhat vague condition – success ... The act of public speaking is ... an essential source of education not only to enable one to consider current topics more intelligently, but also to train the individual in an asset so desirable in the highly competitive business and professional world of today."[45]

Debating was thus part of the vibrant associational life of the campus, which, as we have seen, included dances, sports, fraternities, and clubs. These activities, most of which politically active students joined, were cherished experiences through which social relationships were forged, youthful vitality expended, and Depression cruelties escaped. Students treasured the good times their universities offered, while radicals and other overly serious intellectuals unhappily reminded them of the misery and mundanity they sought to avoid.[46] As one campus editor noted, "A college newspaper should show students at play as well as at work. It has been my experience that features of a more intellectual sort will be ignored by the greater part of the student body on every occasion which they appear."[47]

The campus culture of conformity was reinforced by university officials, who periodically used repressive measures in order to discredit heretical ideas. Universities normally permitted students to express themselves freely, both in organized debates and in the student press, but there were many notable and remarkable exceptions to the liberal approach. University authorities did not consider students fully formed adults, and they did their best to shape the student environment in ways that fit the dominant cultural and political values of the community. When students badly overstepped the bounds of propriety and good taste and brought public criticism to bear on the university, this was considered unacceptable, even dangerous. Acknowledging publicly the existence of atheism at the University of Toronto cost a *Varsity* editor his job and forced the suspension of the paper's publication. Because of its irreverent, cynical, and off-colour quality, Arthur Currie, principal of McGill, banned a publication called the *Black Sheep*, and on another occasion warned the *McGill Daily* that if it did not "improve in tone and in character the articles it contains, it should be suppressed." In 1938 the university forced the McGill Social Problems Club to rescind an invitation to Tim Buck, the leader of the Communist Party, for fear of being charged under the Quebec Padlock Law. Notably, Adrien Arcand, the leader of the fascist movement in Canada, had spoken earlier at the university without interference. In 1931 the editor of the *Ubyssey* was suspended by the University of British Columbia board of governors after the paper denounced the educational spending policies of the provincial government. And at the University of Saskatchewan in 1938 a Remembrance Day article claiming that soldiers killed in the First World War "were fools and dupes" who fought to "make the rich richer" caused the resignation of the editor. More astonishing, perhaps, was the University of Toronto's cancelling of the library subscription to the *New Republic* because of its alleged slur on the king of England. It referred to his "dull and negative personality."[48]

A number of Canadian universities – particularly in western Canada, where, paradoxically, authorities were generally more liberal than in the east – did not permit students to form "partisan" political clubs on campus. While concerned students (and some professors) denounced these limitations on their freedom to assemble, the universities in question rationalized their actions by invoking liberal argument. They claimed that if students formed partisan clubs that antagonized the parties in office, then the university as a corporate entity might well be threatened, thereby jeopardizing everyone's ability to teach, learn, and pursue knowledge. From this perspective, keeping political parties at bay preserved the independence of the university. As Walter Murray, president of the University of Saskatchewan, explained, "when this University was projected in 1903, a dominating idea was to prevent it from becoming subservient to political parties." The policy also prevented professors from these institutions from running for political office.[49] Where such clubs could operate freely, Conservative and Liberal students formed groups alongside socialists and communists.

Such limits on the freedom of expression reduced further the outlets through which student political activism might be channelled and encouraged, and helped to reinforce a political culture that marginalized radical thought.[50] As the University of Alberta *Gateway* conceded, "it is unwise for us ... to tread on religious or ideological corns ... To antagonize the powers that be – those on whom the University must rely for its very existence – would be to harm our public, the students."[51] Yet censorship could, and sometimes did, have the reverse effect, by angering and, at least temporarily, mobilizing the normally apolitical. Student editors from one part of the country almost always came to the defence of their besieged colleagues elsewhere,[52] and students also rallied round professors victimized by university, government, or public censure.[53] For fear of aggravating campus tensions, University of Saskatchewan President Walter Murray found "friendly discussions" a more effective method than censorship in moderating student opinion.[54]

While students generally kept the campus peace, avoided joining political organizations, and provided university authorities with few headaches, there were other occasions when they behaved far less passively.

Incidents that roused their passion could turn them into a formidable force. Universities often incited student protests when dances were restricted or banned.[55] In 1931 students in residence at the University of Alberta organized a successful petition campaign demanding a reduction in the price of room and board.[56] Perhaps the most remarkable collective action based on local concerns was a massive student protest in Vancouver in 1932 against drastic provincial spending cuts and a proposal to close the University of British Columbia. An intensive organizing effort culminated in a petition campaign in which a reported two thousand students "tramped the streets of Greater Vancouver" and collected sixty-five signatures opposing the outrageous financial recommendations of the "Kidd" Report.[57] And in 1939 students from the University of Western Ontario conducted a similar campaign against a funding reduction of twenty-five thousand dollars imposed on the university by the Ontario government. Students marched to Labatt's Park, raised local support, and sent a petition with over twenty thousand signatures to the premier's office.[58]

Such impressive protests reflected less the politicization of the students than the spirited commitment they felt to their universities. The type of institutional loyalty that UBC and Western students expressed was common in the 1930s. Because their universities played such a significant role in their social lives and professional development, students happily sought to protect them from external challenges, a sentiment that was usually directed at rival football and debating teams and less frequently at threatening governments imposing punishing financial policies. As small, fairly intimate institutions offering a temporary haven from a gloomier world, universities successfully elicited the fidelity of their students. Yet while "school spirit" could spontaneously erupt, it contributed little to the sustenance of a politicized student movement committed to changing the social order. And unlike student radicals of the 1960s, who made the university itself a target of their antipathy, those of the 1930s focused almost all their critical attention on those governing the world, not the schools. Activists, too, were fond of their future alma maters.[59]

III

One external concern – the fear of world war – did touch the souls of otherwise politically quiescent students of the 1930s. While students quietly endured a Depression economy, hoping to use their education as an instrument of survival, the prospect of renewed war roused active concern because it brought the very ability to survive into question. Students were not obsessed with the issue on a daily basis, but it occupied a permanent place in the recesses of their minds, and even before 1939 it was periodically pushed to the forefront by activists in the student movement.

Several petition campaigns, usually initiated by international organizations such as the World Student Christian Federation or the International Student Service, were carried on to Canadian campuses by national groups such as the SCM, the League of Nations Society, or the Student Peace Movement. Almost ten thousand Canadian students signed a petition in late 1931 encouraging Prime Minister Bennett, in somewhat vague terms, to push for peace at the upcoming Geneva disarmament talks.[60]

The infamous Oxford Pledge of February 1933, in which students at the Oxford Union voted 275–153 in favour of the resolution that "this House will in no circumstances fight for King and Country," received wide international attention, helping to keep the campus peace movement alive in Canada and, particularly, in the United States. Nothing as sensational as the annual American "student strikes for peace" occurred in Canada, owing in part to a national culture that still stressed loyalty to Britain, but there were significant anti-war statements and events north of the border.[61]

In the fall of 1934 the *McGill Daily* circulated a questionnaire on war similar to those being distributed internationally, the results of which were to be collected in Geneva by the International Student Service. Most Canadian campuses participated in the exercise, though the response rate averaged only about 20 per cent and the opinions of students were difficult to define clearly. The results at the University of Alberta were representative. While students feared the prospect of war, 70 per cent would fight if Canada were invaded, and 55 per cent if Britain were attacked. If Britain declared war under other circumstances, only 10 per cent said they would fight. War was never justified in the opinion of 20 per cent of students, and an equivalent proportion would refuse war service of any kind.[62]

In the period after 1935, as international tensions increased, student activists held peace vigils, sponsored anti-war "counter" services on Remembrance Day, circulated new questionnaires and petitions, and protested military training in campus Canadian Officers' Training Corps. The fear of war was real and widespread, though it scarcely interrupted the normal campus routine. And, like other Canadians, students were uncertain of the best strategy to be followed to prevent war. Following a 1936 national survey, the *McGill Daily* was asked to produce a summary of campus opinion, based on reports from the campus press. It found a somewhat strained effort to reconcile a mood of isolationism with a belief in the value of collective security. "Campus papers showed a 50–50 stand on the question of increased defence," with students on the west coast and in the Maritimes somewhat less isolationist than those elsewhere. As the *Dalhousie Gazette* had observed earlier, students "want to punish Italy [for invading Ethiopia], but they don't want to have any part in the punishing." Canadian students do not, echoed the *McGill Daily*, "speak with one voice." Uncompromisingly clear, however, was the universal opposition of students to conscription for wartime service. The *Daily* concluded, "It is agreed, with scare a dissenting voice, that there is much less prospect of Canadian youth supporting the government to the extent that they did in 1914 if war came."[63]

Growing concern among students about the rise of European fascism was reflected in the student press and kept alive throughout the thirties by the periodic appearance on campus of spokesmen for such oganizations as the League against War and Fascism. Communists and others among the politically committed were especially active in the campaign on behalf of the besieged Loyalists in the Spanish Civil War. On a number of occasions student editors raised their voices on behalf of Jews persecuted by the Nazis, and an admirable effort by Mount Allison students in 1938 to sponsor the emigration of refugee Jewish students to Canada was spurned by the university president and federal immigration authorities.[64]

Yet until war actually erupted, student opinion, like that in the country as a whole, could be benign, even favourably disposed, towards the rulers of Italy and Germany. Periodic commentary in the campus papers described the sense of purpose, idealism, and nationalism that the Nazis and Italian Fascists seemed to be generating. According to an article in the *Dalhousie Gazette* in 1933, Hitler had succeeded in bringing the "German people out of their slough of despondency by a system of organization and national thought." An extremely sympathetic article in Laval's student newspaper, *L'Hebdo Laval*, claimed that Mussolini "est avant tout un patriote" (is above all a patriot).[65] Seeking to exploit and promote such sentiment, the Italian government sponsored a 1934 Canadian speaking tour that included lectures at several universities by apologists for the Italian regime. Denying the existence of a dictatorship and defending the country's economic and social reforms, the speakers elicited wide, uncritical coverage, both on and off campus. Notorious Canadian fascist Adrien Arcand also found an occasional platform at Canadian universities.[66]

Sympathy for fascism was notably stronger in French-speaking Quebec than in English Canada, and this led to an ugly political confrontation among Montreal students in 1936. During the last week of October three delegates from the anti-fascist, Loyalist government of Spain were invited to Montreal and, having been denied the right to speak at city hall, were asked by the McGill Social Problems Club to lecture at the university. A group of students from l'Université de Montréal gathered outside the McGill Union, where the event was to occur, and threw rocks at those on the steps of the building. Later a mob of some 250, consisting mostly of Université de Montréal students, marched through the city streets shouting anti-communist and anti-Jewish slogans. They proceeded to the Mount Royal Hotel, where the Spanish delegates were staying, and, apparently unprovoked, assaulted a McGill professor. The turbulent weekend ended with an anti-communist, pro-Catholic demonstration of an estimated one hundred thousand people at Champs de Mars.[67]

Termed a "riot" by the press, these confrontations seemed to symbolize deep political and cultural cleavages between students from the two universities. Certainly, student political attitudes at the French Canadian universities (Montreal and Laval) were shaped by an official ideology stressing Catholicism, conservatism, and militant anti-communism. The 1928 Annuaire Général of l'Université de Montréal promised to protect its students from the forces of "materialism, liberalism and modernism."[68] Anti-Semitism, too, while deeply rooted in English Canada and well reflected in the admission policies of its universities, was expressed more openly and with greater vitriol in French Canada.[69] The small Université de Montréal–based Les Jeune-Canada (founded in 1932) promoted the rights of youth in a populist, reformist, and nationalist program, but combined this with a powerful expression of anti-Semitism.[70] Left-wing students in Quebec could be found, but in minuscule numbers. The opposition of socialists and communists to the church and to the pervasive nationalism of the province contributed to their ostracization from university campuses.[71] Université Ouvrière, a French Canadian adult-education facility serving workers, where "anti-clerical and radical economic views" were taught, offered critical political education but remained well outside the mainstream of French Canadian education and was subject to considerable harassment, including an assault on its premises by a "band of students" from l'Université de Montréal in 1930.[72] A somewhat more respectable outlet for reform thinking was the school of social science founded by Father Georges-Henri Lévesque at Laval University in 1938.[73]

Despite the obvious contrasts, it is possible to exaggerate both the depth of conservative activism among Quebec students and the differences between student life in the "two solitudes." In their interests, extracurricular activities, and professional aspirations, English and French Canadian students shared a great deal.[74] Politically, too, rapprochement appeared possible. The good feelings generated at the 1937 national student conference in Winnipeg were one indication of this spirit. And in the wake of the 1936 October "riot," which the Montreal *Gazette* attributed to "schoolboys and adults looking for excitement," the student councils of McGill and Montreal "agreed to patch up their differences" by publicly shaking hands and symbolically "burying the beret." To encourage better communication, the editors of the *McGill Daily* and the *Quartier Latin* agreed to write columns in each other's papers.[75]

What inferences can be drawn from such events? An energetic minority of English Canadian student activists leaned left politically, while a minority of French Canadian students campaigned with enthusiasm on the (far) right. The ideological and educational environment of English Canadian universities was less conservative than that of French Canada, where the church still wielded enormous authority. But the majority of students in both cultural groups were not preoccupied with politics and did not join political movements of the left or right. Thus, the political differences between students in the two cultures should neither be overlooked nor overstated.

IV

The coming of the Second World War mobilized the student movement into one climactic assault on conventional values, only to leave it enfeebled and in disarray. The Canadian Student Assembly called its third national conference over Christmas in 1939 in the hope, once again, of stirring student activism on a wide range of issues, from curriculum reform to national unity. But as it had throughout the decade, the question of war dominated the students' political discussions, only now under very different conditions. In September war had actually been declared. The War Measures Act now made it a crime to issue statements that could be seen to undermine the war effort of Canada and Britain. Openly opposing Canada's participation in the war itself was therefore out of the question. For students promoting the cause of peace, the discussions were no longer academic.[76]

Situated at Ste Anne de Bellevue, Quebec, the conference elicited strong participation from francophone students, whose views on the meeting's most controversial issue – conscription – were unmistakable. Against a background of militant nationalism in a province with deep, bitter memories, French-Canadian students from Quebec gave powerful and unanimous support to a resolution opposing compulsory wartime service. Their position reflected the policies of Le Bloc Universitaire, a movement of students from the Universities of Ottawa, Laval, and Montreal created earlier in 1939 and devoted to a nationalist "plan" that opposed both massive immigration of European exiles to Canada "totalement" and "très énergiquement à tout développement des mesures de guerre actuellement adoptées, développement qui rendrait plus onéreuse notre participation à la guerre" (completely and vigorously all war measures presently adopted, and any developments that would render more onerous our participation in the war).[77] On the latter issue francophone students were not alone. With the additional backing of a block of English Canadian delegates, the CSA passed a resolution that "opposed conscription for the duration of the war, and ... military commitments such as a large expeditionary force which would prepare the way for conscription."[78]

This resolution would be the death-knell of the Canadian Student Assembly. The statement was opposed strongly by a significant section of the anglophone delegates, which was acknowleged in the conference report from the CSA executive: "It appeared that in the West large numbers of students are opposed to conscription; in Ontario fewer numbers are opposed but their opposition is more active; in the Maritimes there is no opposition, while French Canada is solidly opposed to conscription."[79] Debate climaxed with a widely publicized walk-out led by the Mount Allison delegation, whose spokesman, Dean of Men C.A. Krug, claimed that the conference was being manipulated by those who were "anti-British, anti-war, and anti all those principles which form the basis of our ties with the British Empire."[80] In light of the tension, the conference undertook to distribute a questionnaire at university campuses following the meeting "to ascertain the opinion of youth in this matter" and to publish the results.[81] Co-sponsored by the Canadian Youth Congress and Bloc Universitaire, the questionnaire surveyed youth opinion on conscription, civil liberties, war profiteering, and youth employment.[82]

The enemies of the CSA used the anti-conscription resolution and controversy generated by the questionnaire to mobilize withdrawals from the organization. By the end of January member groups from seven universities had seceded from the CSA, and more desertions followed. A particularly tense confrontation erupted at McGill University, where five hundred students reportedly "smashed a CSA rally in a riotous session."[83] According to the president of the student council, the CSA was suspended at the University of British Columbia "on the grounds that the national conference had brought adverse publicity to the university by its reported anti-war atmosphere."[84] Many English Canadian campuses voted not to distribute the CSA questionnaire, though at Laval and Montreal students were polled and almost unanimously favoured the CSA position on conscription.[85] Pockets of support for the CSA could still be found in English Canada, but the organization's influence and effectiveness, far from massive at the best of times, were quickly slipping away.[86]

The problems and demise of the CSA came as a great relief to the

RCMP, which followed closely the activities of the organization and particularly those individuals who remained sympathetic to it. Convinced in January that the CSA was "permeated thoroughly by the YCL and CPC," the superintendent commanding "O" Division included among his list of those "regarded in University life as being men of extreme thought, if not definitely Communist," five faculty resource leaders who participated in the CSA conference: Frank Underhill (Toronto), Father St Denis (Montreal), F.R. Scott (McGill), Professor Roy (Laval), and Arthur Lower (United College).[87] By March, however, Kemp concluded: "It is impossible to establish any tie-in between the Communist Party and the Canadian Student Assembly at the present time."[88] One RCMP report found it worth noting that the "amount of Jews in the CSA, mostly from the West and McGill, was remarkable."[89] The RCMP was equally concerned about the potential dangers flowing from the conscription survey of youth opinion: "It is considered that some form of education to combat this subversive activity and to instill into the minds of young Canadians the patriotic aspect of War Service in the present struggle is essential."[90] It is not clear what additional role the RCMP played in educating the student body "to think along patriotic lines" apart from monitoring CSA activities and the fate of the conscription questionnaire on every campus, but by April it could report that the CSA in Ontario and elsewhere was a "dead issue." Despite attempts by the CSA to confront its opposition and save its reputation, "a small number of radical thinkers," wrote one RCMP informant, "are becoming somewhat discouraged at their lack of progress."[91]

The extreme concern in the RCMP raised by the CSA position on conscription was ironic in the Canadian political climate of early 1940. Public opposition to conscription had been expressed by none other than Mackenzie King, prime minister of Canada, yet students who promoted the same position were considered potentially subversive, suspected of being communist, and subject to intensive surveillance. In any event, serious opposition to the war effort, with an active peace movement to lead it, all but disappeared from campuses in English Canada and was muted in Quebec. Across the country voluntary recruitments in campus Canadian Officers' Training Corps rose dramatically in the fall of 1939, doubling at Mount Allison, more than doubling to 600 at the University of Alberta, quadrupling to 700 at the University of Manitoba, and rising sixfold to 500 at the University of British Columbia.[92]

Once compulsory military training was imposed upon male students over eighteen in 1940, the number of conscientious objectors refusing COTC training appeared quite small. At the University of Saskatchewan fifteen students, most of whom were Mennonites or Doukhobors, declared themselves, as did "fewer than half a dozen" at McMaster.[93]

A detailed report concerning the University of Alberta's 1700 students revealed that COTC exemptions were granted to 47 students for medical reasons, 20 to married men over age twenty-four, 23 to final-year medical students, 3 to clergymen, and only 1 to a (Mennonite) conscientious objector. One other student refused training but was not exempted.[94] A 1941 "Discipline" report at the University of Manitoba noted that the expulsion of two students refusing military duty was "being considered."[95]

Across Canada students joined "parade," curtailed much of their frivolous activity, and supported the war effort in other ways. A campus mood that so recently had combined elements of cynicism, isolationism, and even pacifism, had by 1940 yielded to one of vigorous, public-spirited patriotism. As the *McGill Daily* observed, students appeared to be "against war until war arrives."[96]

Was there a student movement in Canada during the 1930s? Like campus activists elsewhere, small groups of Canadians undertook a vigorous campaign to raise students' awareness of social and political problems.[97] They successfully provoked discussion and debate but largely failed to elicit the active involvement of the vast majority of students in reform, let alone revolutionary causes. How can this be explained? The social-class background of university youth is one factor. Students were privileged, but they were not, for the most part, bathed in opulence. University provided these middle-class youth with the potential of surviving the Depression and achieving long-term security. Hard times made them more individualistic on the one hand and determined to participate fully in campus social life on the other. In this apolitical atmosphere, grim, erudite radicals promoting untried, collectivist ideologies could get a hearing, but not a large following.

The role of religion in shaping the direction and fate of the student movement cannot be overlooked. In Quebec, Catholic students had no time for atheistic communists and Protestant social democrats. While English Canada had become increasingly secular by the 1930s, the association of Christianity with higher education still lingered, particularly at universities like McMaster and Acadia, which maintained direct denominational links. This helped to preserve a campus environment of stability, piety, and paternalism. At the same time, reformers such as those in the Student Christian Movement derived their political inspiration from religious conviction, thereby gaining a secure place on university campuses and usually carrying out their activities in an unthreatening manner that university authorities could tolerate and oversee. Thus, in a subtle way religion both fuelled and restrained an important element of the student movement.

Of course, campus authorities sometimes used more direct means, including censorship, to temper opinion considered not only radical but inappropriate and distasteful. From their parents and teachers students had learned to be deferential, respectable, and patriotic. Universities did their best to reinforce these values, which students as a whole were disinclined to defy on an ongoing basis. Being occasionally drunk or rowdy was condemned but expected; being a student activist could involve more risks, particularly for those linked, by accusation or fact, to communist or other "subversive" activities.

However, students were not mere putty in the hands of university authorities. We have seen how they could sometimes be moved to protest arbitrary or punitive actions by those in control. Because the university was the centre of their existence at a critical time in their development, students resented actions that unfairly restricted their freedom of expression (such as bans on dancing) or threatened the survival of the institutions (including excessive funding cut-backs). But these were single-issue events, in which student activists participated but which they could not sustain and direct to other causes. Students wanted to benefit from being at university and did not want to devote much energy to changing the world. Activists could not convince them, even during the Depression, that these causes were linked. As the straw polls indicated, students followed the political mood in the country as a whole, which was far from radical.

The apparent exception to the rule of campus apathy was the alarm generated by the prospect of world war. The peace movement, with its mix of isolationists, pacifists, anti-fascists, and proponents of collective security, found its way on to Canadian campuses. Widespread involvement in the movement was intermittent and usually confined to the signing of petitions, but the anxiety was genuine. Haunted by the memory of war, students feared its renewal and the threat that it posed to everything they cherished. For most, however, this was not an overly controversial position. It was hard to find anyone in Canada who favoured war, and university presidents sometimes talked admiringly of the students who were part of the peace movement. At the same time, it was equally hard to find many students who believed, along with the highly political League against War and Fascism, that war and fascism were the products of capitalism, which should be abolished. Their concern about war, though heartfelt and instrumental in keeping the campus student movement alive, was not ideologically based.

If the fear of war inspired the student movement, the reality of war ended it. The Canadian Student Assembly, the Canadian Youth Congress, and even the National Federation of Canadian University Students were all its victims. The Student Christian Movement survived but was riven by division over its policy on Canada's participation in the war. When the Communist Party reversed its position in 1941 to one of support for the war effort, the politics of opposition it had previously brought to the student and youth movements also dissipated.[98] In the face of increased Nazi aggression, the clamouring for peace in vague and often contradictory terms seemed to university students and Canadians as a whole an inadequate national response.

Despite their small numbers and however limited their achievements, the student activists of the 1930s made campus life more vital, engaged, and interesting than it otherwise would have been. Like other "radicals," they were ahead of their time in the fight for civil liberties, minority rights, student assistance, and youth-employment policies. They left an important but largely unknown legacy.

Sardonic view of the curriculum
Pharos 1931
Dalhousie University Archives

The university of the future
Pharos 1934
Dalhousie University Archives

"Infant" freshettes, Dalhousie
University, 1931
Dalhousie University Archives

WILL VENTURE OUT INTO BIG WORLD SOON

Examination time is at hand at McMaster university, and the co-eds seen above are trying their finals this spring, after which they hope to venture out into the big world. The little group above posed for the Spectator photographer and include, first row: Patricia Doyle, Janet Ward, Doris Raycroft, Mary Westaway, Dorothy Matheson. Second row: Kay Sturt, Marion Day, Ruth McGowan and Thelma Mitcham.

Examination time, McMaster University
Hamilton Spectator, 3 April 1936

Residence life, Assiniboia Hall, University of Alberta, October 1939
University of Alberta Archives

We, the undersigned students in residence at the University of
Alberta, do hereby petition the Board of Governors to seriously
consider a reduction in the price of board and room in the
University residences, to take effect as from the beginning of the
spring term. We feel justified in making such a request since
the price of food-stuffs has fallen, since help is abundant, since
there is bound to be a large profit on such a large scale method
of preparing meals, since the University operated below its grant
last year, since the price of board and room is much lower in
private residences than it is at the University, and since the
price of board and room has been recently decreased at some other
residence colleges in the west.

SIGNED:

[signatures]

Alberta students campaign for residence rate reductions, March 1931
University of Alberta Archives

University of Toronto students pushing a TTC coach
Globe and Mail Collection, 8 October 1932
City of Toronto Archives

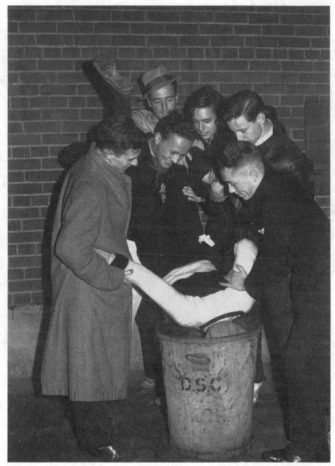

University of Toronto students ducking classmate in garbage can
Globe and Mail Collection, 28 October 1938
City of Toronto Archives

Junior Prom, University of Alberta, 1937
University of Alberta Archives

WOMEN'S FRATERNITIES

VOTE STRAIGHT
ANTI-FRATERNITY

VOTE FOR THESE

BERT WINNETT	NORAH McGINNIS	DON JAMES	JIM DAVIS	DUNC McINTOSH
FOR	FOR	FOR	FOR	FOR
PRESIDENT	VICE-PRESIDENT	TREASURER	SECRETARY	ALTHLETIC STICK

A VOTE CAST FOR THE ARTS-LEVANA-THEOLOGY PARTY IS A VOTE USED TO CRUSH FRATERNI-
TIES AT THIS UNIVERSITY. THERE IS NO ROOM FOR FRATERNITIES AT QUEEN'S. THEIR
INFLUENCE IS ALL TOWARDS CLOSED-DOOR ADMINISTRATION, POLITICAL BOSSING, INEF-
FICIENCY AND CORRUPTION. THE GROWTH OF FRATERNITIES HERE THREATENS TO DESTROY
THE SOCIAL LIFE OF THE UNIVERSITY AND TO UNDERMINE THE EXISTENCE OF A STRONG
QUEEN'S SPIRIT. THE ARTS-LEVANA-THEOLOGY PARTY STANDS FIRM UPON THIS VITAL DEC-
LARATION OF POLICY: ITS CANDIDATES, IF ELECTED TO THE A.M.S. EXECUTIVE, ARE PLEDGED
TO USE THEIR AUTHORITY TO MAKE STUDENT GOVERNMENT A REALITY BY RESTORING AND
ENFORCING THE BAN ON FRATERNITIES AT QUEEN'S.

Save Queen's and the A.M.S. from
The Fraternity Menace!

Intercollegiate track meet, University of Alberta, October 1938
University of Alberta Archives

Rugby practice, University of Toronto
Globe and Mail Collection, 9 September 1935
City of Toronto Archives

Student Christian Movement National Conference, Elgin House, Muskoka, Ontario, 1931
University of Toronto Archives

STUDENT ASSEMBLY LEADERS HOWLED DOW

RICHARD MURRAY, leader of the McGill students who yesterday broke up a meeting of the Ca dian Student Assembly at Strathcona Hall, is seen here attempting to obtain silence in order to reac resolution calling for the dissolution of the C.S.A. and the seizure of its funds. Behind him and to immediate right may be seen a member of the Montreal police force who was called in an atten to restore order and to order the students from the building Immediately behind Murray is

Above
Difficult days for the Canadian Student Assembly
Montreal Gazette, 7 February 1940

Right
Business careers in agriculture
Managra, March 1931
University of Manitoba Archives

A
Permanent
Business
. . . for College Trained Men

AGRICULTURE is just now entering a new era. Tractor farming has already reached a point where it affects the methods, habits and profits of every farmer—whether he owns a tractor or not. This is apparent in the greater prosperity of those farmers, everywhere, who have adopted power farming methods.

This condition offers to men of your training an opportunity you will find hard to equal. With your technical knowledge, a flair for salesmanship and ambition for financial independence, you can enter this business with reasonable assurance of success.

At the same time, you have the satisfaction of knowing that you are greatly benefiting every customer to whom you sell a new machine. You are helping him to cut down his power and labor costs; you are conserving his time and effort; you are adding to his profits and making life better for him.

As a permanent occupation, worthy of your best efforts and offering substantial rewards, investigate carefully the retailing of modern farm equipment. Possibly you can make arrangements to go into business in your home town or a neighborhood town where you are familiar with local conditions and know the people.

J. I. CASE COMPANY

Worthy of the name McGILL

McGILL—the name recalls a memory of grey walls, ivy-covered—of clipped lawns and stately trees. Recalls, too, traditions of a century of service— a century in which the name McGill has been associated with every phase of the development of the young Dominion.

And now the name is given to a new product—new, but with a solid background of experience and integrity behind it, a tradition of selection to exacting standards, of unvarying care in manufacture that makes the McGill Cigarette worthy of its name.

There is pleasure and satisfaction in smoking good tobacco and you will obtain full measure of both from this new cigarette.

There will be extra satisfaction to the friends of Old McGill in the knowledge that every package of McGill Cigarettes sold adds to the "Sir Arthur Currie Memorial Gymnasium-Armoury" Building Fund.

For the next three years fifty cents per thousand on all sales of McGill Cigarettes will be paid into the Building Fund and twenty-five cents per thousand will be contributed to the general maintenance fund thereafter.

In 1935 more than five billion cigarettes were sold in Canada. McGill students and graduates smoked some six million of these. At fifty cents per thousand that would mean $3,000.00.

At no cost to yourself you can help to build the new Gymnasium by asking for—

McGILL

. . . . *and it's a corking good cigarette*

McGill: Selling cigarettes to raise money for new gymnasium
McGill News 17, no. 4, 1936
McGill University Archives

YOUR YEARS AT COLLEGE HAVE
FITTED YOU FOR YOUR LIFE WORK.
YOU ARE NOW READY TO ENTER
THE ARENA OF BUSINESS. MANY
THINGS ARE NECESSARY FOR THE
ATTAINMENT OF SUCCESS. NOT THE
LEAST OF THESE IS THE ABILITY TO
SAVE. A MAN OF WIDE EXPERIENCE,
BROAD VISION AND HIMSELF AN
OUTSTANDING SUCCESS—JAS. J. HILL
—HAD THIS TEST:

" . . . . Are you able to save money? If not,
drop out. You will fail. You may think not
but you will fail as sure as fate. The seed of
success is not in you."

WE ARE SPECIALISTS IN SAVING

*For the location of the nearest branch
consult your 'phone book.*

PROVINCE OF ONTARIO SAVINGS OFFICE
EVERY DEPOSIT GUARANTEED BY ONTARIO GOVERNMENT
HEAD OFFICE   PARLIAMENT
                               BUILDINGS

Investing in Ontario
Torontonensis 1931
University of Toronto Archives

Overleaf
Eaton's: Promoting friendship
Torontonensis 1931
University of Toronto Archives

Enduring Friendships - - -

are to be considered one of the most valuable assets of your association with Toronto University. To know that they will last regardless of time, place or position is one of the greatest pleasures of your graduation. Your friendly dealings with The T. Eaton Co. can continue too . . . for wherever your profession may take you from Calgary to Halifax, you will find EATON'S ready to serve your needs . . . eager to solve your purchasing problems; and always in a way that should assure economy and satisfaction.

CHAPTER SEVEN

Making a Middle Class

During the Great Depression one could have done worse than be a university student. Unemployed workers, impoverished single mothers, and desperate prairie farmers endured far greater material deprivation than that experienced by typical college youth. And however bleak their immediate prospects, university graduates were armed with credentials that were expected, at some point, to pay rewarding dividends. But as this study has suggested, most students took nothing for granted. Unquestionably determined to enjoy the rich campus social life, they knew that occasional bouts of adolescent frivolity would soon give way to the more serious business of earning a living and bearing adult responsibilities. Their mostly modest social backgrounds had helped to prepare them for the challenges that lay ahead, rendered even more daunting by the continuing economic crisis. University students both inherited the insecurities and were sustained by the promise of middle-class life. Theirs was a culture of anticipation and "aspiration," not ostentation or presumption.[1] How, in fact, did they fare, and what part had higher education played in moulding their futures?

"We are leaving no stone unturned to hunt out such employment as may exist anywhere in the country, permanent or temporary, for graduating students," reported Gordon J. Smith, manager of the Queen's University employment service, in 1933, but in recent months "the results have been extremely disappointing."[2] This bleak experience was reflected elsewhere in the country as job-hunting students felt the full impact of the collapsed economy. Many graduates are "afraid of the unemployment bogey," echoed the Toronto *Globe*. "The hazards of unemployment [had] extended far through the ranks of the modern middle class," acknowledged sociologist Leonard Marsh, "particularly among the younger generation." It was thus "not hard to understand the desire for security, one of the fundamental 'drives' of the middle classes.[3] A sardonic – and exaggerated – view of the plight of the middle-class student was published in the irreverent McGill magazine the *Alarm Clock* during the depths of the Depression.

> The middle class was made to be
> The prop of our society;
> So clap your hands and jump for joy
> That you were born a bourgeois boy.
> And here's the game for you to play:
> Just close your cunning eyes and say:
> "Coloured collars can't be white,
>   And whatever is, is right."
> And so you'll keep the bourgeois flag unfurled
> And do your starving in a bourgeois world.[4]

Their expectations diminished, students graduating during the 1930s scoured the market for better news. The situation appeared to be more promising in the latter half of the decade as employment prospects showed signs of improvement, owing in part to a modest recovery in the non-ferrous-metal, hydroelectric-power, and forest-product industries.[5] The University of Alberta reported that 90 per cent of the 1935 engineering class, and all the graduates in law in the following year, had found positions.[6] For professional students, particularly in applied science, 1937 was an even better year, but degree-holders in the general arts were not yet out of the woods. University employment officers admitted that the latter proved "difficult to place even in the best of times" because their courses were considered "cultural rather than vocational."[7] Large surpluses of school teachers reduced opportunities within this field, particularly for women. According to the Dominion Bureau of Statistics, reporting in 1939, "Fewer girls have left teaching for other positions, or to be married, and former teachers have come back to the profession after spending some time at other work ... In the last four years men teachers have increased by about 3500 while the number of women teachers has been reduced by 800."[8] Indeed, the proportion of female teachers in Canada fell from 78 per cent in 1931 to 75 per cent in 1941.[9] Though they had good reason to worry, students were advised – even by their peers – not to despair. They had been conditioned to expect from higher education "something better in life than manual labour," but as the *Queen's Journal* declared, patience, endurance, and a positive attitude would help university youth through hard times. "When the fangs of depression lose their grip, the world will have a place for you."[10]

The individual experiences of students suggest that instead of slipping into bitterness or despair, they pounded the pavement, surviving the grim years while awaiting better times. For many the Second World War provided the first opportunity for steady employment. Arthur Hackett, who obtained an arts degree from the University of Toronto in 1930, was promised a job with an advertising agency, only to be told upon graduation that "it's all off buster." He trekked to Flint Michigan intending to train as an engineer while working for General Motors, did a variety of other odd jobs, and finally landed a government position in war-related work. Later he went into the insurance business, where he spent his remaining working years.[11]

Gordon Henry graduated from the Ontario Agricultural College in 1934 to a job as a labourer in the cheese department of Canada Packers. Eventually he became a successful local businessman and mayor of the town of Ingersoll, Ontario. Like so many others who may have had reason to feel otherwise, he had only positive memories of the value of his university years. "Without the leadership qualities developed while at OAC I feel I could not have been successful."[12] Similarly, Lew E. Oakley, a graduate engineer, worked as a labourer for eighty hours a week, later landing a permanent managerial position with a woollen company. He had no regrets about his time in university. It provided him with the "ability to search for information, assess the facts, and visualize results."[13]

Wilbur Bowker received a law degree from the University of Alberta in 1932, a time "when you couldn't buy your way into a law office in Edmonton." Eventually, however, seven of the eleven students in his class became successful lawyers, while one became a journalist and one died in the war. Of the two female graduates, one was stricken by ill health, and the other also practised law only occasionally.[14] Later in his career Bowker joined the faculty and served as dean of the University of Alberta law school.

Evelyn Eaton graduated from Western in 1939 and found work as a secretary at the "huge sum" of $65 a month. Following an even better-paying job working for a lawyer, she joined the war effort as an employee of Alcan in Kingston, making aluminium sheet and castings for planes. Later, she married.[15] Her classmate Jean Courney also did secretarial work for a lawyer. "Marriage came after the war and although I have never held a position since then, I have been able over the years to help in our own retail business. The training received at Western [was] most beneficial."[16]

Like most of her female classmates, Jean Begg, a Dalhousie alumnus, had no specific occupational ambitions, but upon graduation she obtained a job that required only minimal education – running a ledger-posting machine. She was eventually hired by a bank, where she

Table 8
Annual Graduates from Canadian Universities and Colleges, 1927–41

Degree or Program	Total	Women No.	%	Degree or Program	Total	Women No.	%
Bachelor of Arts				Library Degree			
1927–31	11,541	4,524	39.2	1927–31	146	144	98.6
1932–36	14,800	5,650	30.2	1932–36	282	272	96.5
1937–41	16,734	5,760	34.4	1937–41	310	296	95.5
Bachelor of Commerce				Teachers' Diploma Men & Women			
1927–31	643	70	10.9	1927–31	2,493		
1932–36	1,086	131	12	1931–36	3,594		
1937–41	1,199	134	11.2	1936–41	2,699		
Bachelor of Science				Degree in Education			
1927–31	994	134	13.5	1927–31	235	65	27.7
1932–36	1,537	205	13.3	1931–36	363	96	26.4
1937–41	1,620	220	13.5	1936–41	603	116	19.2
Engineering Degree, Diploma				Social Service Diploma			
1927–31	1,951	3	0.2	1927–31	110	109	99
1932–36	3,003	7	0.2	1931–36	282	212	95.2
1937–41	3,222	1	0	1936–41	343	295	86
Bachelor of Agricultural Science				Nursing Degree, Diploma			
1927–31	576	8	1.4	1927–31	539	539	100
1932–36	1,044	22	2.1	1931–36	799	799	100
1937–41	1,189	26	2.2	1936–41	1,120	1,120	100
Forestry				Occupational, Physical Therapy			
1927–31	145	0		1927–31	81	81	100
1932–36	149	0		1931–36	83	83	100
1937–41	147	0		1936–41	208	208	100
Bachelor of Architecture				Physical Training Degree Diploma			
1927–31	108	1	0.9	1927–31	210	210	100
1932–36	159	3	1.9	1931–36	141	139	98.6
1937–41	127	12	9.4	1936–41	179	175	97.8
Bachelor of Veterinary Science				Medical Doctors			
1927–31	111	1	0.9	1927–31	2,702	139	5.1
1932–36	212	0	0	1931–36	2,451	108	4.4
1937–41	319	3	0.9	1936–41	2,798	119	4.3
Bachelor of Household Science				Dentists			
1927–31	399	399	100	1927–31	549	3	0.5
1932–36	713	713	100	1931–36	417	4	1
1937–41	941	941	100	1936–41	534	5	0.9

Table 8 (continued)

Degree or Program	Total	Women No.	Women %	Degree or Program	Total	Women No.	Women %
Pharmacists				**Master of Arts**			
1927–31	981	51	5.2	1927–31	1,215	394	32.4
1931–36	865	54	6.2	1931–36	1,262	432	34.2
1936–41	884	81	9.2	1936–41	1,378	348	25.3
Law School				**Master of Science**			
1927–31	1,143	50	4.4	1927–31	262	17	6.5
1931–36	1,172	41	3.5	1931–36	391	23	5.9
1936–41	1,302	34	2.6	1936–41	564	24	4.3
Roman Catholic Colleges				**Bachelor of Divinity**			
1927–31	1,301			1927–31	160	0	
1931–36	1,410			1931–36	180	0	
1936–41	1,694			1936–41	207	0	
Protestant Theological Colleges				**Licentiate**			
1927–31	853	87	10.2	1927–31	403	8	2
1931–36	913	85	9.3	1931–36	560	30	5.4
1936–41	843	81	9.6	1936–41	949	36	3.8
Doctorate in Course				**Honorary Doctorate**			
1927–31	239	24	10	1927–31	524	7	1.3
1931–36	401	40	10	1931–36	452	7	1.5
1936–41	427	33	7.7	1936–41	500	28	5.6
				Other Post-graduate Degrees			
				1927–31	389	7	1.7
				1931–36	460	10	2.2
				1936–41	281	24	8.5

Source: Dominion Bureau of Statistics, *Supply and Demand in the Professions in Canada* (Ottawa 1945), 24–5.

remained, and in 1962 she became the first female branch manager in Nova Scotia. For the discipline and enduring friendships it offered, Begg cherished her university experience.[17]

Other women – a distinct minority – also defied convention by forging full-time careers in male-dominated professions, although they made little headway in increasing their proportionate presence in most such fields during the 1930s (see Table 8).[18] They constituted 4 per cent of chemists in 1931 and 3 per cent in 1941; and 8 per cent of professors and college principals in the former year, compared to 7 per cent in the latter. The proportion of female lawyers and notaries increased from 1 to only 2 per cent over the decade, and of physicians and surgeons from 2 to 3 per cent. By contrast, women continued to dominate nursing (100 per cent in 1931 and 99 per cent in 1941) and librarianship (80 per cent in 1931 and 85 per cent in 1941).[19]

These personal histories and statistical patterns reflect the fate of graduates of the 1930s. Typically, men unable to enter their chosen fields immediately after graduation worked at low-paying jobs temporarily, then enlisted in the armed forces, and finally were able to find more prestigious and secure positions in the professions or business. A far higher proportion of women never entered the labour-force. Those who did worked for a short period in offices or in the "helping professions," which they abandoned, sometimes voluntarily, frequently by compulsion, once they married.[20] Single female graduates also found jobs in diverse fields when the war broke out, which they were usually forced to give up when peace returned.[21] A small minority, including some who had entered male-dominated employment areas, continued their trades in the post-war period.

Some institutional case studies provide further insight into the life-courses followed by students attending university during the decade. Alumni records from Acadia, a university whose curriculum concentrated on undergraduate liberal arts as opposed to professional training, revealed that of 234 known graduates from 1931, 1936, and 1940, 28.6 per cent became teachers, 11.5 per cent clergymen, 9.9 per cent businessmen, 8.1 per cent professors, 8.1 per cent dieticians, 5.6 per cent doctors, 4.7 per cent scientists, 3.4 per cent engineers, 3 per cent librarians, and 2.1 per cent secretaries or stenographers. While 99.2 per cent of all known men engaged in full-time "careers," only 47.9 per cent of the women who worked did so on on a long-term basis.[22]

A survey that drew responses from 7 per cent of all graduates from the University of Saskatchewan between 1930 and 1935 found that 71 per cent of the 107 men became professionals primarily in teaching, engineering, science, and medicine, 13 per cent became business executives or manager-supervisors, 6.5 per cent farmers, 3.7 per cent civil servants, and 1.8 per cent manual workers. Of the 63 women who responded to the questionnaire, fully 97 per cent were employed at least temporarily. A total of 54 per cent taught school, and 9.5 per cent worked as secretaries, 9.5 per cent as dieticians, and 6.3 per cent as librarians. Among the remaining women were two professors (3.1 per cent), two social workers, two laboratory technologists, a psychologist, a doctor, and a nurse.[23]

The careers of the 1936 graduating class of McMaster University (reporting in 1950) revealed that of 53 male graduates, 17 per cent went

Table 9
Occupations of Male Graduates, Dalhousie University, 1921–40

Occupation	1921 No.	1921 %	1926 No.	1926 %	1931 No.	1931 %	1936 No.	1936 %	1940 No.	1940 %
Lawyer	23	27.4	25	24	33	23.9	30	20	26	17.8
Doctor	20	23.8	37	35.6	31	22.5	27	18	42	28.8
Dentist	6	7.1			9	6.5	16	10.7	12	8.2
Professor	8	9.5	4	3.8	5	3.6	7	4.7	3	2
Clergyman	11	13	4	3.8	8	5.8	11	7.3	7	4.8
Engineer	2	2.4	11	10.6	6	4.3	1	.4	3	2
Teacher[1]	3	3.6	6	5.8	3	2.2	6	4	1	0.7
Pharmacist	1	1.2	1	1	3	2.2	1	0.4	4	2.7
Scientist	2	2.4	2	1.9	2	1.4	3	2	4	2.7
Businessman[2]	2	2.4	3	2.9	5	3.6	4	2.7		
Accountant					1	0.7	3	2	1	0.7
Supervisor					3	2.2	1	0.4	2	1.4
Journalist	1	1.2					1	0.4		
Officer in armed services					1	0.7				
Musician			1	1						
Total known	79	94	94	90.4	110	79.7	111	74	105	72
Total unknown	5	6	10	9.6	28	20.3	39	26	41	28
Total	84		104		138		150		146	

1 Includes principals.
2 A number of lawyers, engineers, and accountants also were businessmen. They are counted only in their professional categories. Note also that others with double occupations (e.g., "lawyer-army officer"), are counted in only one category.
Source: Directory of Graduates and Former Students of the University, Corrected to 1937, Dalhousie University Archives (DUA); University Lists of Degrees Conferred 1921–40, DUA; *Dalhousie Alumni News*, 1920–27 (various issues), DUA; *Alumni News*, 1930–80 (various issues), DUA.

into various business endeavours, 15 per cent became scientists (mostly working in private corporations), 15 per cent teachers, 13.2 per cent ministers, 11.3 per cent lawyers, 7.5 per cent civil servants, and 7.5 per cent doctors and dentists. At least half of the men served in the Armed Forces. Among the 25 female alumni, 40 per cent either did not work or reported no work following graduation. The overwhelming majority of those who did became teachers or secretaries. Only two women appeared to be still employed in 1950.[24]

The results of a systematic investigation of Dalhousie students who

Table 10
Occupations of Female Graduates, Dalhousie University, 1921–40

Occupation	1921		1926		1931		1936		1940	
	No.	%	No.	%	No.	%	No.	%	No.	%
Teacher	8	22.2	8[1]	16.3	3	6.5	1	1.7	4	10
Clergy	4	11.1	3	6.1	3	6.5	5	8.5	3	7.3
Librarian	1	2.8	2	4	1	2.2	2	3.4	2	4.8
Nurse	10	27.8	1	2			1	1.7		
Social Worker			2	4	1	2.2	1	1.7		
Lawyer			4[2]	8.2					1	2.4
Doctor	1	2.8					1	1.7		
Professor							2	3.4		
Secretary	1	2.8					1	1.7		
Journalist					2	4.3				
Administrator					1	2.2			1	2.4
Scientist					1	2.2	1	1.7		
Technician					2	4.3				
Civil servant							1	1.7		
Researcher							1	1.7		
Musician	1	2.8			1	2.2				
Total known[3]	26	72.2	20	40.8	15	32.6	17	28.8	11	26.8
Total unknown[4]	10	27.8	29	59.2	31	67.4	42	71.2	30	73.2
Total	36		49		46		59		41	

1 Includes one woman who was a teacher-nurse-nun. She was counted only as a teacher.
2 Includes two women with law degrees whose work record is unknown.
3 Includes women known to have worked on both short-term and long-term bases.
4 Includes unknown, no occupation, and married women not reporting occupations.
Sources: Directory of Graduates and Former Students of the University, Corrected to 1937, DUA;
University Lists of Degrees Conferred, 1921–40, DUA; Dalhousie Alumni News, 1920–27 (various
issues), DUA; Alumni News, 1930–80 (various issues), DUA.

graduated in 1921, 1926, 1931, 1936, and 1940 are reported on Tables
9 and 10. They reveal that of the graduates who could be traced, men
were concentrated in law, medicine, dentistry, teaching, and the clergy.
Graduating women who were employed found work primarily in teaching, libraries, and the clergy. That a far higher percentage of men than
women reported to alumni magazines on their working histories indicates that females, particularly those graduating in the Depression, were
the most likely to remain out of the labour-force. As we have already
noted, and as others have demonstrated, the depressed economy had a

more damaging impact on employment opportunities for women – in both professional and non-professional areas – than for men.[25]

There can be no question, then, that university graduates eventually found it possible to live secure and relatively comfortable lives within the middle class, with men overwhelmingly situated within the workforce and women sharing their lives as marriage partners. The Acadia experience, for example, reveals that 76 per cent of men and 74 per cent of women who graduated between the wars married. Based on the reporting of their husbands' occupations, women, like those at Acadia, were found to marry predominantly within the middle class or higher, an observation confirmed by informal surveys of other university alumni magazines.[26]

Did university graduates rise beyond the middle class, and was it possible to do so without a university education? The answer to these questions, of course, depends on a working definition of the middle and upper classes – an exercise that draws the historian into an exploration of a complex and much debated literature. For reasons explained in Appendix A, the middle class is defined to include families whose major income-earners were non-manual workers enjoying social status but exercising limited economic power and whose standards of living ranged from the very modest to the very comfortable. The upper class, by virtue of its ownership of extraordinary amounts of property and wealth, exerted immense influence on the economic and often the political life of the nation.[27]

In his examination of the 985 members of the Canadian corporate elite in the early 1950s, a significant proportion of which would have been of college age between the wars, John Porter found that 58.3 per cent had university education and a further 5.4 per cent had some professional schooling beyond high school.[28] A notable minority, therefore (36.3 per cent), ascended to the top of the corporate ladder without university education, but Porter noted that this was truer of the older rather than the younger members of the elite. Increasingly, higher education had become one important qualification for access to the upper class, but it was not normally a sufficient criteria. A significant proportion of the Canadian-born corporate elite (22 per cent of 611 individuals) inherited their positions directly from their fathers or uncles. In addition, 34.2 per cent of the Canadian-born attended elite private schools, where they forged social connections and were exposed to appropriate forms of socialization.[29]

Some additional evidence for these patterns can be found in Peter Newman's study of *The Canadian Establishment*, published in 1975. Like Porter's elite, Newman's consisted of fewer than 1000 individuals, 173 of whom were listed "selectively" in an appendix.[30] The basis for this selection is unclear; however, in light of their leading executive positions with Canada's largest corporations there is no question of the paramount importance of these individuals in the business community. Of the 173, 101 were found to have been of university age between the late 1920s and early 1940s. A total of 78 per cent of this group had university education, most with degrees. Of the 22 individuals who lacked university credentials, 11 (50 per cent) were leading executives in banks, investment, or securities companies, and 2 (9 per cent) were presidents of publishing companies, having begun their careers in journalism. The remaining 9 (41 per cent) were executives in a variety of industries, including forest products, tobacco, construction, and military production.[31] Half of those without university education had attended private schools (such as Upper Canada College in Toronto, Ridley College in St Catharines, Lower Canada College in Montreal, or Shawinigan Lake School in British Columbia), as had at least 41 (or 52 per cent) of the university educated.

For both Porter's and Newman's university-trained elites, the University of Toronto and McGill were popular choices, reflecting their special status within the Canadian establishment.[32] Law, which had traditionally been considered a useful form of training for the upper class, was the chosen profession of one in four of Newman's and one in seven of Porter's economic elites. Scientific and engineering degrees were also held by a significant proportion of this group, though relatively few graduates of the 1930s who entered top corporate echelons had obtained business degrees.[33] For those corporate executives attending university in the post-Second World War era, however, a degree from the Harvard Business School brought with it considerable prestige.[34]

Most university graduates of the 1930s, of course, settled for less lofty social positions, sharing neither the upper-class backgounds nor the immensely affluent lifestyles of wealthier classmates and alumni. As Porter noted, the economic elite tended to be self-perpetuating, normally being "recruited from the upper levels of the social class sytem."[35] The ability of those from relatively humble origins to work their way up to the top of the corporate ladder was not unknown, though it was far from common. Porter estimated that 54.5 per cent of the Canadian-born economic elite had "started out at or fairly near the top," and an additional 12.5 per cent had the benefit of private-school educations.[36] Only about 15 per cent originated from below the middle-class rank. The remaining 18 per cent came from "professional or middle-class families." There is always a degree of social mobility from one class to another within market economies, but financial barriers, religious discrimination, cultural and ethnic bias, continuing cycles of generational poverty, and uneven access to advanced education tend to solidify class lines and limit equality of opportunity in capitalist societies. Despite some individual success stories, these patterns have prevailed in Canada throughout the twentieth century.[37]

Taking into account the material presented in chapter 2 on students' social origins and in this chapter on the careers of graduates, the social and economic significance of higher education in the 1930s can be summarized in this way. Except in rare cases, university training did not provide a means through which the the poor and working class could rise to the ranks of the rich. At the other end of the class structure, a university degree supplemented the social and economic advantages already held by the economic elite. Higher education proved to be of most critical importance to those seeking occupational mobility *within* the middle class. The rich – including the minimally educated – could negotiate their futures on the basis of abundant material assets and influential family connections, but among degree-holders, the more modestly endowed were normally confined to trading professional credentials for social standing and material well-being. University graduates who became middle-level businesmen or managers instead of practising, licensed professionals, as we have seen, also extolled the important (albeit more indirect) role that higher education played in smoothing their paths to the future.

The Depression did produce its share of graduates whose eventual influence in a variety of fields earned them national, or at least regional prominence. Noteworthy politicians who attended university in the 1930s included ex-Ontario premier John P. Robarts (Western), former premier of Nova Scotia and leader of the national Progressive Conservative party Robert Stanfield (Dalhousie), and another Nova Scotia premier, Henry Hicks (Mount Allison and Dalhousie). The three most prominent New Democratic Party politicians of their generation – Tommy Douglas (Manitoba and McMaster), Stanley Knowles (Brandon and Manitoba), and David Lewis (McGill) – all graduated during the decade. Former Supreme Court Chief Justice Bora Laskin (Toronto and Osgoode) and his successor, Brian Dickson (Manitoba), studied in the 1930s, as did a number of individuals active in scholarship, education, and the arts: poets Dorothy Livesay (Toronto) and Irving Layton (who received a bachelor of science in agriculture from Macdonald College), critic Northrop Frye (Toronto), novelist Robertson Davies (Toronto and Queen's), philosopher Marshall McLuhan (Manitoba), historians W.L. Morton (Manitoba) and J.M.S. Careless (Toronto), political scientist C.B. Macpherson (Toronto), composers Violet B. Archer (McGill) and Louis Applebaum (Toronto), folklorist Edith Fowke (Saskatchewan), editor Francess Halpenny (Toronto), and university presidents Claude Bissell (Toronto) and Murray G. Ross (Acadia and Toronto). Jean Sutherland

Boggs, former director of the National Gallery of Canada, and Pauline McGibbon, patron of the arts and first female lieutenant governor of Ontario, both attended the University of Toronto in the 1930s. Publishers John W.H. Bassett (Bishop's) and George M. Bell (McGill) headed Baton Broadcasting and FP Publications respectively. Other leading business-men included H.J. Clawson (Saskatchewan), an executive with the Steel Company of Canada, Ian Sinclair (Manitoba), chairman of Canadian Pacific, Ray Wolfe (Toronto), chairman of Oshawa Group Ltd, Thomas Bell (Toronto), chairman of Abitibi Paper Co., William J. Bennett (Toronto), president of Iron Ore Co. of Canada, Alan Burton (Toronto), president of Simpson's Ltd, Arthur J. Little (Western), partner with Clarkson-Gordon Co., and A.G. Archibald (Dalhousie), chairman of the Board of Maritime Telegram and Telegraph Co. Ltd.[38]

Increasingly utilitarian in their orientation, Canadian universities in the early twentieth century found themselves responding to the occupational requirements of an evolving capitalist economy – which entered an unprecedented trough in the 1930s. The short-term career prospects of graduates were thus highly uncertain, but the long-term need for pro-fessionals and managers remained, and students (predominantly males) eventually found their way to these positions. While capital was mobi-lized by the upper classes outside universities, occupational qualifications required in the administration and servicing of the economy were now being mobilized within the halls of higher learning, and middle-class youth were the chief participants in this process.

In the course of their academic training students were exposed, in both formal and informal ways, to a set of values that were intended to sustain professional and middle-class culture. In the first instance, as we have seen, higher education provided its recipients with theoretical and specialized knowledge considered appropriate for those engaged in mental as opposed to manual or menial labour. Licensed, certified prac-titioners were particularly well placed because they were best able to cultivate a mystique around the distinctiveness, the rationality, and the supposed indispensability of professional work. In a world in which knowledge, social class, and corporate (including professional) organi-zation were hierarchically ordered, mere laymen with limited education were considered incapable of grasping the technical language used and complex tasks carried out by those with select credentials. At the same time the public was compelled to turn to these professionals exclusively for the services they provided. Where they were obtained from govern-ment, legal charters secured professional monopolies and the privileges that accompanied them. Where access to the profession was less rigidly guarded, as in engineering, social work, or teaching, practitioners used their powers of persuasion and propaganda to warn consumers of the dangers they faced in employing the services of undertrained amateurs. The image of excellence was extended by professional codes of ethics that made up in high-minded sentiment what they lacked in rigorous application. In the words of historian Burton Bledstein, "By portraying heroes whose professional code of behavior transcended a concern with payment for their services, middle-class culture prevented people from believing that they were working for mere money."[39]

The service component of middle-class work was underlined by the applied orientation of higher education. While outsiders remained sceptical of traditional academics who stressed the critical importance of classical education, they had far greater sympathy for those who upheld the problem-solving potential of university education. As R.C. Wallace argued, "The utilitarian flair which has possessed us and has given its own atmosphere to educational thought has produced results which have justified themselves." The greater their perceived contribution to the modernization of Canadian society, the more respected were the skills earned by university graduates.[40]

But most university officials would not have been satisfied with a "doctrine of utility" that overlooked the importance of appropriate character development among Canadian students.[41] Conceding that strict religious training could no longer provide the educational foundation for the effective preparation of community leaders, educators hoped to preserve the integrity of their institutions by cultivating in students personal attributes that would encourage civility and order within a secular society. "Pure" arts courses emphasizing literacy, English literature, philosophy, and colonial history were combined with "applied" subjects in politics, economics, psychology, and sociology to promote the concept of "social citizenship." To former Prime Minister Robert Borden this meant that graduates should "be mindful of the things of the spirit holding high the torch of idealism so that men may sometimes turn aside from the din of the factory and the clamor of the marketplace to behold and to realize." Or, as another politician, Ernest Lapointe put it, "We need energies, men of worth, conscious of their responsiblities; we need thoroughly competent men in all places and for all tasks ... The most urgent work is to prepare that leading class which must derive its name by its services, its initiatives and its power of action." In short, "the university man must be a social man."[42]

Though they had far fewer career options, university women seeking middle-class respectability were expected to be no less socially minded. To university officials this had less to do with women's participation in campus life as dating and dancing partners – which the prudish often deplored – than it did with their "natural" role as nurturers both in the community and in the home. As teachers, social workers, housewives, or volunteers, female graduates were considered more genteel, cultivated, and refined than their less educated counterparts, and the university was credited with providing this finish.

Social norms and prejudices might be periodically scrutinized in the classrooms and common-rooms of the nation, but there is little question that universities perpetuated cultural and ideological conventions. Like gender roles, racial and ethnic biases were sustained through campus life. Overwhelmingly white, Anglo-Celtic and Protestant, the English Canadian campus successfully preserved its cultural homogeneity. Where the growing number of Jewish students was perceived as a challenge to this uniform image, extraordinary steps were taken to limit their presence. Had other minority groups sought to enrol in the same proportion as Jews, undoubtedly they would have experienced a similar fate.

It is not that students passively bowed to the whims of their educational masters. Like university youth before and since, they had the power, if they had chosen to use it, to challenge and undermine authority. Bourgeois communities had always spawned oppositional movements through which small groups of militant youthful heretics assailed both political conventions and the values of materialistic cultures.[43] In the 1930s, too, a minority of politically conscious activists called into question the ideas and practices of capitalist society, rendered even more suspect by the onset of the Depression. Their views were debated, but contrary to the claims of their severest critics, their influence among the student body was limited.[44]

Although there were exceptions, students absorbed the dominant liberal-conservative ideology of the era. The economic system, however strained, still offered middle-class students some promising employment prospects, if not immediately, then at least down the road, and they were not inclined in the meantime to follow unproven routes. As the Queen's Journal noted, "there is a wide general supposition that university students as a class are in revolt against convention, religion and such things. That is hardly so, but true enough that the outside world is disturbed by its glimpses of student radicalism. Radicals and free thinkers do not predominate, however."[45]

When political activists turned their attention to the dangers of renewed world war, they struck a more responsive chord on campus. Memories of the recent conflagration still lingered, and students feared the threat that future wars posed to their very existence. Craving peace, most students still eschewed political radicalism. Thus petition campaigns and silent vigils posed no serious challenge to campus order — even as the leaders of the student peace movement attracted the regular attention of zealous RCMP informants. The actual outbreak of the Second

World War further dampened campus activism, confirming the faith of those who viewed the university as "a school of patriotism."[46]

A vigorous associational life, far more than politics and world affairs, absorbed the abundant energies of students in the 1930s. The extra-curriculum provided both an outlet for youth to assert its presence and an effective medium for the dissemination of middle-class values. Once they realized that they could not prevent students from forming clubs, publishing newspapers, or embracing popular fads, university officials sought to contain campus social life within the realm of respectability. Occasionally, student behaviour transcended the bounds of good taste, and culprits involved in the most shocking episodes were punished for supposedly damaging their institutions' reputations. But such disruptive incidents were relatively rare. More commonly, students wrote freely and critically about such matters as rigid teaching methods, bothersome restrictions on campus dancing, and the failure of many adults to respect sufficiently the intelligence and independence of youth. Students sought, with some success, to increase their autonomy in the social sphere, and with equal success university officials loosened the bonds without losing control. The most effective presidents were those who governed with a combination of paternalism and flexibility, and who used student governments – always prepared to demonstrate their maturity and responsibility – to regulate clubs and impose discipline.

Like the culture of professionalism, student life was hierarchically organized, replete with mystical rites of passage, racially and ethnically exclusivist, not deeply intellectual, and male dominated. Despite some generational conflicts, students in the end emulated the middle-class values and ideals preached by their parents and teachers. In flowery prose reminiscent of scores of presidential addresses, a Dalhousie vale-dictorian answered his own question: "What has been the fruit of the four year sojourn at Dalhousie? If nothing else, one might say we have developed a certain cultural attitude, the breadth of view, the spirit of toleration which is the distinguishing mark of men and women with a university background."[47] A *McGill Daily* editorial similarly summa-rized the purpose of university training by inventing an acronym from the word "success":

S – stability in character
U – understanding of people
C – consecration of purpose
C – consecration to one purpose in life
E – energy
S – sociability
S – sobriety in our daily actions[48]

While English-Canadian universities fostered a common student culture, shaped by professionalism, middle-class beliefs, and the aspirations of upwardly mobile youth, the tone of student life resonated with regional particularities. Exchange students participating in the program sponsored by the National Federation of Canadian University Students were struck by certain institutional differences. Campus life on the west coast, for example, was considered more informal, less elitist, and more influenced by American trends than was the case in central and eastern Canada. The University of British Columbia's "breezy liberalism" appealed to an easterner more accustomed to Toronto's "conservatism entrenched in Gothic."[49] In addition, the relative prosperity of central Canada appeared to produce a class of students with more disposable income than was common among their counterparts in the Maritimes and the prairies. Smaller residential universities were perceived to generate a greater degree of unity and spirit among the student body than was true of larger, multifaceted commuter institutions.

There were regional differences, too, with respect to the future destinations of university graduates. Where economic circumstances allowed, alumni chose to live and work relatively close to home. Of nearly five thousand graduates of the University of British Columbia (up to 1940) whose addresses were known, more than 83 per cent resided in the province and 7 per cent elsewhere in Canada.[50] On the prairies and in eastern Canada, however, the tradition of out-migration persisted – even among the ranks of the highly educated. While more than 80 per cent of Acadia graduates between the wars had been born in the Maritimes, only 49 per cent (as of 1953) remained in the region. Almost one-quarter resided in Ontario and Quebec, 4 per cent in other provinces, and more than one-fifth in the United States.[51] The graduate exodus from Saskatchewan was even more dramatic. Only 27 per cent of students who obtained degrees from the University of Saskatchewan from 1932 to 1942 remained in the province.[52]

Whatever their differences, Canadian universities were considered by students and faculty alike to be collectively more civil, temperate, and respectful of academic tradition than American institutions (with the possible exceptions of Harvard and Yale). Like other Canadians, students emulated and consumed aspects of American popular culture while retaining their nationalist and (particularly in central and eastern Canada), imperialist sensibilities, which were reasserted with renewed vigour during the Second World War.[53]

In subsequent years, changing social and educational conditions would subtly transform the cultural lives of highly educated middle-class youth. As "mass" higher education emerged in the post-war period, universities became somewhat less exclusive, attracting more women and ethnic minorities. Furthermore, the process of secularization continued apace, with religious values leaving only trace elements in the life of post-secondary education. Reflecting a greater intellectual pluralism, the curriculum became far more diverse. And in the wake of the turbulent youth movement of the 1960s, students gained more autonomy and administrators governed universities with less paternalism.[54] In a less intimate more impersonal university environment, presidents were now more likely to be selected for their managerial skills than for their perceived effectiveness as campus father-figures.[55]

But in basic ways the middle-class values that pervaded Canadian campuses in the early twentieth century persisted in the years that followed. Genuine equality of educational opportunity eluded women, minority groups, and the working class as white, middle-class males continued to be the chief beneficiaries of higher education.[56] The culture of credentialism became more influential than ever as universities extended professional and business administration training with great enthusiasm, encouraged, at least until the 1970s, by the popular "human-capital" theory of educational investment.[57] Public fascination with science and technology reached new heights, and universities fuelled this interest by undertaking nuclear, space, and computer-systems research. The humanities survived, though as always their proponents perceived themselves to be under siege by the forces of anti-intellectualism and utilitarianism.[58] Students continued to use the university as a stepping-stone to higher status, though the general rise of educational levels reduced the negotiating value of the BA. As in the depressed economy of the 1930s, students of the 1970s and 1980s wondered if they would successfully maintain, let alone improve, their social positions. This insecurity – always lurking in middle-class culture – once again infused campus life, contributing to the spread of a more conservative political aura.[59] Finally, frustrated, aging professors could still be found lamenting in hyperbolic prose the supposed collapse of academic standards and the deteriorating quality of students.[60] As we have seen, they were not the first academics to attempt to save the middle class from itself. They would not likely be the last.

A Note on Methodology and Sources

Historians, particularly those in Canada, do not pay much explicit attention to theory – some seem utterly allergic to discussing, let alone applying it. The reasons for this are not entirely invalid. Imposing theoretical preconceptions on a body of evidence can lead to selective reading and rigid, formulaic conclusions. There are too many examples – in Canada and elsewhere – of non-historians (or alleged historians) abusing evidence and distorting the past in the interests of arriving at theoretically "valid" conclusions.

Historians who claim that theory has no bearing whatsoever on their work are equally myopic, however. What topics they choose to study and how they interpret the massive, complex body of documents on any given subject arise from scholarly or cultural influences, ideological orientations, or "theories" – acknowledged or not – that they have assimilated and incorporated into their academic work. Though they should always avoid mechanistic thinking, and while evidence must be allowed to take the researcher in unanticipated directions, historians should at least be aware of – and even applauded for openly recognizing – the conceptual proclivities that underlie their scholarship. Being a reputable historian does not require, or even arise from, theoretical or ideological neuterdom – assuming that such a bland condition could be achieved, which is unlikely.[1]

In striving for conceptual clarity but avoiding an interruption of the text with an elaborate methodological discussion, I have chosen to outline in this appendix the basis for my application of the well-used but loosely defined term "middle class." Historians looking for guidance from previous writers on the meaning and values of this social category face a number of challenges. Some authors, adopting a consensus approach to the study of history and contemporary life, either never mention class in their examination of social dynamics or assume that most people are in the same social class.[2] Others devote considerable energy to describing the characteristics and culture of the middle class without adequately defining the term itself.[3] There are also writers who fail to distinguish between the middle and upper classes, or who "resolve" the problem by collapsing the two into the same category, sometimes referred to generally as the "ruling classes," which are contrasted, in a "two-class model," with the "working classes."[4]

Further conceptual differences arise between those using Marxist (or neo-Marxist) models and those employing more traditional sociological notions based on "social stratification." The former approach defines class position with respect to the ownership of the "means of production." For the latter, one's location in the class structure depends on a variety of criteria such as income, education, standard of living, or prestige.[5] Within each of these traditions there are more subtle and sophisticated treatments of the issue. Critics (including neo-Marxist critics) contend that Marx's identification of two basic classes – the bourgeoisie and the proletariat – does not account carefully enough for emerging and enduring class formations that lie between the two main class antagonists. Others contend that Marx acknowledged the existence of the middle classes but either marginalized or read them out of history prematurely. In addition, neo-Marxist scholars, following the example of English historian E.P. Thompson, have wisely stressed the importance of studying class not merely as a static, statistical entity but as a phenomenon shaped by living collectivities of workers or businessmen who, in the course of pursuing their respective interests, have forged shared interests and a common "consciousness."[6] Critics of stratification theory object to its proponents' use of too many "subjective" variables (such as prestige or status) at the expense of "objective," scientific criteria that focus more directly on the exercise of economic and political power. Furthermore, stratification theorists are sometimes accused of being purveyors of mythology and apologists for the status quo because their work implies that individuals, whatever their social origins, can attain upward social mobility by dint of proper attitudes and diligent work.[7]

This study proceeds from the conjecture that distinctions between the experiences and cultures of working-class, middle-class, and upper-class Canadians are real and worthy of further investigation. My exploration of the backgrounds, beliefs, activities, aspirations, and destinies of university students in the 1930s confirms my belief in the promise and rationality of this sort of inquiry, which I hope is borne out in the text. I am also convinced that the type of class analysis that speaks most eloquently to the reality of student life in the 1930s is that which takes into account the three issues mentioned above: economic position, collective class consciousness, and perceived social status.[8]

As this book argues, one's relative social status mattered enormously to university youth and their families, and to dismiss this preoccupation as merely "subjective" is to disregard a critical motivation underlying middle-class behaviour. Instead, I have attempted to demonstrate how middle-class students incorporated these perceptions into a system of values that shaped their collective consciousness. (Chapters 3 to 7 discuss how these beliefs were transmitted through both the academic and social life of the university.) But I also accept the argument that individuals are not always the best judges of their true class position, which is why it is important to frame social-class categories on the basis of more concrete criteria than those employed by some sociologists (a process engaged in chapters 2 and 7). The deepest literature suggests that wealth and property ownership are the most convincing bases for this ordering. Once one's "objective" class position has been determined, however, one's values and self-image deserve careful attention if the complex dynamics within the social class are to be understood. Thus Marxists who focus on economic power and class consciousness, and non-Marxists who concentrate on the question of social status, all have valuable insights to offer students – at least this student – of social class. The theoretical, sociological, and historical studies I have found most helpful (drawn from various "schools") are those that grapple directly with the "problem" of the middle class – particularly the rise of the "new" middle class – and are particularly sensitive to the process of historical change. This work is also based on an approach to political economy that seeks to explore the relationship between internal institutional life and the broader social and economic forces surrounding the institution.[9]

To ignore the middle class in favour of a simple two-class model misses the essence of both the typical university student's self-perception and his or her actual experience. To overlook or excessively minimize the differences between the middle and upper classes is to suggest, in defiance of logic, that the child of a clergyman and the child of a fabulously wealthy businessman share a common material and cultural reality. Furthermore, to conclude that there are no important distinctions to be made between the student who becomes a teacher, earning an extremely modest income, and the student who eventually rises to the top of a major corporation also runs in the face of reason. Not only do the elite corporate executives wield more influence in the community, but they also enjoy a standard of living vastly superior to that of the middle class. At the same time, it would be fair to conclude – particularly with respect to the 1930s – that the cultures of the upper and middle classes have more in common than either does with the culture of the working class, whose material conditions, expectations, degree of working autonomy, and access to economic power and political influence are, by comparison, severely limited.[10]

A three-class model – upper, middle, and working – thus offers the best context within which to study the experience and significance of student life, and probably other social phenomena.[11] While I make no attempt to define the exact level of propertied assets or the degree of social status and power that distinguish the middle from the upper classes (although some useful approximations are offered in chapter 2), and while debatable gradations will exist no matter where such lines are drawn, the application of this approach, particularly with respect to the social composition and culture of students in the 1930s, still bears fruit. I am defining middle-class families as those whose major income-earners were non-manual workers who enjoyed social status but exercised limited economic power, and whose standard of living ranged from the very modest to the very comfortable.

In employing this definition, I am aware of certain qualifications, limitations, and anomalies. Collective consciousness among students and other Canadians was shaped by values arising from the forces of religion, ethnicity, gender, regionalism, nationalism, and generational tension, and the book demonstrates how these influences also touched university life. It would be fair to conclude that they affected the culture of all social classes in Canada, so that any discussion of "class consciousness" must take them into account. For example, the values and social conditions that confined women to inferior positions in Canadian society transcended class divisions, though the actual lives led by middle-class and working-class women differed considerably. Furthermore, the class identity of certain individuals and groups sometimes proves elusive. The middle-class teacher or small businessman, for instance, who attained considerable authority by becoming a mayor or a cabinet minister might straddle the dividing line between the middle and upper classes.

The most problematic category is that of "white-collar workers," whose status – working class or middle class – remains a widely debated subject. Most historians agree that the social position of white-collar workers, while relatively high at the end of the nineteenth century, diminished as capitalism went through its consolidation phase at the beginning of the twentieth century. The 1930s can be seen as part of the transitional period in which a portion of white-collar workers – including clerks in private industry and civil servants – could be located within the middle class. Mostly male, they retained prestige, a degree of autonomy on the job, the prospect of advancement, and thus their middle-class identities. Others, mostly women, found themselves confined to low-level, routinized, and dead-end office work, earning minimal salaries and few promotional opportunities. Though technically white-collar employees, they should be perceived as part of the working class.[12] Students whose fathers worked in white-collar jobs were most likely to emerge from families with middle-class values or aspirations, which were reinforced by the university environment.

This study finds that a minority of students came from extraordinarily wealthy families whose fathers held considerable economic authority. But the upper class constituted too small a proportion of the Canadian population to account for the size of the university population of the 1930s. A minority of students came from the working class, which constituted the largest proportion of the Canadian labour-force. Thus the university could be considered neither an upper-class nor a working-class institution. The largest portion of students originated from middle-class business and professional families whose material existence ranged from the relatively humble to the relatively affluent. Some were in fact poor, particularly in the wake of the Depression, but by virtue of the values they held, the expectations they had for their children (particularly the importance assigned to higher education), and the life-courses their children actually followed, such families retained their middle-class identities. University education was perceived by middle-class parents as a means by which their offspring could retain, or preferably improve, their social positions.

A large proportion of the fathers of Canadian students were professionals, and an even greater proportion of students subsequently became professionals. Was there a distinction between middle-class and professional culture? Some historians have used the terms interchangeably, and while this is understandable given certain similarities between the two, simply equating them can lead to confusion.[13] In the quest for greater clarity, this study portrays professionals as a branch, albeit a critically important branch, of the middle-class "family" tree. The particular educational credentials required by professionals and the unique organizational culture within which elite professionals worked, and to which other professionals aspired, provided them with a generally higher status, though not necessarily a higher standard of living, than that of businessmen without professional qualifications (see chapter 4). The prestige that professional credentials brought the individual explains why many students who aspired to business success also sought university degrees.

It should be noted, however, that a university education was not the only road to middle-class security. In all likelihood, high-school graduates of the 1920s and 1930s (as compared to the 1960s and later) could also achieve comfort and relative prestige without more advanced education, largely by rising through corporate ranks to managerial or executive positions.[14] As chapter 3 points out, some employers, in fact, remained suspicious of the university educated; nevertheless, by the 1930s, business leaders, more so than in earlier generations, were assigning value to the commercial importance of college education.

The perception of the university as a middle-class institution with a large, though not exclusive, investment in professional training is reinforced by an understanding of the context within which higher education emerged in the early twentieth century (see chapter 1). The burgeoning capitalist economy of Canada increasingly required professionals, middle-range corporate employees, and civil servants with more sophisticated and specialized schooling, and the middle class itself sought to preserve and, if possible, enhance its status by accumulating exceptional qualifications unavailable to the majority of the population. In addition, the university was a forum in which students' social relations could be forged and extended and the culture of middle-class youth could be articulated, sometimes in the form of opposition to authority (see chapters 5 and 6). As the book argues, such opposition did not imply a rejection of middle-class values. Universities were agencies of social control, but they were not prisons, and students found ways of shaping their own culture while participating – not merely as passive objects – in the socialization process.

There are a number of theoretical complexities that arise from this study, and while I share with others the inability to resolve them fully, I am convinced that the integrity and utility of the approach described above survives the imprecisions. At the very least it provides a useful way of conceptualizing the experiences of university students in the 1930s. Theory, after all, is always subject to debate and revision, but my presentation of the empirical evidence that sustains it, I trust, is less open to question.

A final note on sources. Primary research was conducted not at every English Canadian university but at universities in every region (Dalhousie, McGill, Queen's, Toronto, Western, Manitoba, Saskatchewan, Alberta, and British Columbia). Additional archival material on student careers came from Acadia University, and the Robarts Research Library at the University of Toronto houses a complete collection of academic calendars from universities across the country. The archives at Laval University and the University of Montreal contained material on student activism in Quebec, while the McMaster University Archives holds the records of the National Federation of Canadian University Students. Additional material on student political activity was obtained from the Canadian Security Intelligence Service following application through the Access to Information Act. Archive sources were more extensive at some institutions than others, though they generally included student newspapers, annual and presidential reports, presidential papers and correspondence, senate and board of governor minutes, student registration and club records, and alumni magazines. The evidence gathered on the history of religious colleges affiliated with non-denominational institutions was supplemented by excellent secondary sources on the history of other denominational colleges, particularly by John Reid on Mount Allison, by Charles Johnston and John Weaver on McMaster, and by Kevin Quinn and George Rawlyk on Queen's Theological College. Other institutional studies, including Michael Hayden on Saskatchewan, Frederick Gibson on Queen's, and Stanley Frost on McGill, as well as a variety of older, though less analytical histories, provided some useful data.

I have gained insights as well from the growing literature on the history of women in Canada, identified throughout the text in the notes. National statistics on occupation and education were gathered from publications by the Dominion Bureau of Statistics, Statistics Canada, and the Department of Labour. In what was perhaps the most challenging aspect of this study, the exploration of academic and professional culture, I attempted to synthesize, where secondary sources (including theses) permitted, the disparate literature in intellectual and cultural history. University calendars, annual presidential reports, private collections, and professional association journals also contained important source material on this subject. Much research remains to be done in this field – in every era. I only wish more had been done before I undertook this study.

Quantitative data on the social backgrounds and destinies of students (see chapters 2 and 7) were tabulated by computer. In addition, biographical information was derived from interviews, previously conducted oral histories available in university archives, and correspondence with ex-students. Approximately one hundred in total, these stories provide anecdotal and impressionistic material that help to personalize the account and sustain literary and quantititative evidence. Rarely were generalizations drawn exclusively from these sources. More individual testimony could have been collected, and additional oral documentation will undoubtedly emerge as further research is undertaken. I became convinced, however, that patterns repeated themselves in the oral testimony with sufficient frequency to justify their incorporation into this study. While sociologists might bristle at my failure to select interviewees on a more "scientific" basis, historians will understand the great value of using these sources as individual biographies. Finally, published research from the United States and Europe provided some basis for national comparisons.

Classification of Occupations

This list, though not comprehensive, is representative of fathers' occupations most commonly identified by students at four universities on their registration forms. It was compiled from the original forms for Dalhousie, Queen's, and Toronto, and from aggregated data, assembled by the university and published in annual reports, for Alberta. (See Table 4 for bibliographical information.)

As always, the categorization of certain occupations demanded choices that some might dispute. For example, should a self-employed "photographer" be categorized as a skilled worker-artisan or as a businessman? (I chose the former.) Is a "foreman" a supervisor or a skilled worker? (I chose the latter.) I was guided, in part, by Donald Treiman's *Occupational Prestige in Comparative Perspective* (New York: Academic Press 1977), which argues, on the basis of occupational scales used in more than sixty societies, that with few exceptions the ranking and "prestige" of occupations has been remarkably consistent over time. However the handful of difficult placements are ranked, the overall percentages presented in Table 4 would be only marginally affected.

PROFESSIONAL

Accountant
Architect
Barrister/solicitor
Clergyman
Doctor/physician/surgeon
Dentist
Deputy minister
Dietician
Engineer

Geologist
Journalist
Judge
Lawyer
Librarian
Mayor
Missionary
Musician (with higher education)
Nurse
Optometrist
Politician/member of Parliament/senator
Professor
Public notary
Scientist
Teacher
Veterinarian

BUSINESS

Businessman
Broker
Contractor
Corporation president/vice-president
Dealer
Druggist
Gentleman
Grocer
Importer/exporter
Insurance agent
Landlord
Manufacturer
Merchant
Proprietor
Publisher
Retailer
Speculator
Trader

SUPERVISORY

Army-navy officer
Captain
Chief of police

Civil service manager/director/supervisor
Commissioner
Deputy provincial secretary
Fire Chief
Inspector
Manager
Probation officer
Registrar
School board member
Secretary-treasurer
Superintendent
Town clerk

WHITE COLLAR

Bookkeeper
Cashier
Clerk
Civil servant
Commercial traveller
Customs' official
Guide
Salesman
Secretary
Social-service worker
Tax collector

ARTISAN-SKILLED

Baker
Blacksmith
Boat builder
Bookbinder
Cabinet maker
Carpenter
Chemist
Chef
Designer
Draughtsman
Electrician
Foreman
Glazier
Goldsmith
Machinist

Mason
Master mariner
Mechanic
Musician
Photographer
Plumber
Pressman
Printer
Tinsmith
Surveyor
Tailor
Technician
Wireless operator
Writer

SEMI-SKILLED, UNSKILLED

Barker
Barber
Bus driver
Caretaker
Fireman
Gardener
Labourer
Lightkeeper
Messenger
Packer
Policeman
Sailor
Soldier
Steel worker
Waiter
Watchman
Weighman

FARMING-FISHING

Dairyman
Farmer
Fisherman
Grower
Planter
Rancher
Shepherd

Notes

INTRODUCTION

1 Konrad Jarausch, ed., *The Transformation of Higher Learning 1860–1930* (Chicago: University of Chicago Press 1983), 11.
2 For example, see John G. Reid, *Mount Allison University, 1843–1963*, 2 vols. (Toronto; University of Toronto Press 1984); Michael Hayden, *Seeking a Balance: The University of Saskatchewan, 1907–1982*; Frederick G. Gibson, *"To Serve and Yet Be Free": Queen's University, 1917–1961* (Montreal: McGill-Queen's University Press 1983); C.M. Johnston and John Weaver, et al., *Student Days; An Illustrated History of Student Life at McMaster University from the 1890s to the 1980s* (Hamilton: McMaster University Alumni Association 1986); Margaret Gillett, *We Walked Very Warily: A History of Women at McGill* (Montreal: Eden Press Women's Publications 1981); Keith Walden, "Respectable Hooligans; Male Toronto College Students Celebrate Hallowe'en, 1884–1910," *Canadian Historical Review* 68, no. 1 (Mar. 1987): 1–34. These and other such sources are cited in the text. For an extended discussion of the historiography, a comprehensive list of Canadian and non-Canadian sources, and a new collection of articles in the field, see Paul Axelrod and John G. Reid, eds., *Youth, University, and Canadian Society: Essays in the Social History of Higher Education* (Montreal: McGill-Queen's University Press 1989).
3 American and European books on this topic include Helen Lefkowitz Horowitz, *Campus Life: Undergraduate Cultures from the End of the Eighteenth Century to the Present* (New York: Knopf 1987); Paula Fass, *The Damned and the Beautiful: American Youth in the 1920s* (New York: Oxford University Press 1977); David O. Levine, *The American College and the Culture of Aspiration, 1915–1940* (Ithaca: Cornell University Press 1986); David Allmendinger, *Paupers and Scholars: The Transformation of Student Life in Nineteenth Century New England* (New York: St. Martin's Press 1975); Colin Burke, *American Collegiate Populations: A Test of the Traditional View* (New York: New York University Press 1982); Konrad Jarausch, *Students, Society and Politics in Imperial Germany: The Rise of Academic Illiberalism* (Princeton: Princeton University Press 1982); Geoffrey Giles, *Students and National Socialism in Germany* (Princeton: Princeton University Press 1985).

CHAPTER ONE

1 Abraham Flexner, *Universities: American, English, German* (London: Oxford 1968), 6.
2 Robin Harris, *A History of Higher Education in Canada, 1663–1960* (Toronto: University of Toronto Press 1976), 28.

3 See Harris, *A History of Higher Education*; J. Donald Wilson, Robert
  M. Stamp, and Louis-Phillipe Audet, eds., *Canadian Education: A
  History* (Scarborough, Ont.: Prentice-Hall 1970); Laurence K.
  Shook, *Catholic Post-Secondary Education in English-Speaking Canada*
  (Toronto: University of Toronto Press 1971); D.C. Masters, *Protestant
  Church Colleges in Canada* (Toronto: University of Toronto Press 1966);
  John G. Reid, *Mount Allison University, vol. 1, 1843–1914* (Toronto:
  University of Toronto Press 1984); Hilda Neatby, *"And Not to Yield":
  Queen's University, vol. 1, 1841–1917* (Montreal: McGill-Queen's Press
  1978); Stanley B. Frost, *McGill University: For the Advancement of
  Learning, vol. 1, 1801–1895* (Montreal: McGill-Queen's University
  Press 1980); W.S. Wallace, *A History of the University of Toronto,
  1827–1927* (Toronto: University of Toronto Press 1927); George
  Rawlyk ed., *Canadian Baptists and Christian Higher Education*
  (Montreal: McGill-Queen's University Press 1988).

4 On the backgrounds of university professors in the nineteenth century,
  see Janet Scarfe, "Letters and Affection: The Recruitment and
  Responsibilities of Academics in English-speaking Universities in the
  mid-Nineteenth Century," doctoral Diss., University of Toronto 1981,
  vii, chaps. 1, 3.

5 Wilson, Stamp, Audet, *Canadian Education: A History*, pt II; Susan
  Houston and Alison Prentice, *Schooling and Scholars in Ninteenth-
  Century Ontario* (Toronto: University of Toronto Press 1988); Alison
  Prentice, *The School Promoters* (Toronto: McClelland and Stewart
  1974); Bruce Curtis, *Building the Educational State: Canada West,
  1836–1871* (London, Ont.: Falmer Press and Althouse Press 1988); Ian
  Ross Robertson, "The Bible Question in Prince Edward Island from
  1856–1860," *Acadiensis* 5, no. 2 (Spring 1976): 3–25.

6 Some readers will be aware of the historiographical debate about
  the existence of the "middle class" in the nineteenth century, though
  there is a greater degree of consensus about its entrenched position in
  twentieth-century capitalist countries. A "two-class" model is presented
  by Michael Katz, Michael Doucet, and Mark Stern in *The Social
  Organization of Early Industrial Capitalism* (Cambridge: Harvard
  University Press 1982), chap. 1. My use of the term is explained in
  Appendix A, to which readers are referred. Historians of the mid- to late
  nineteenth century who argue, in my view convincingly, for the presence
  of the middle class include Mary Ryan, *Cradle of the Middle Class:
  The Family in Oenida County, New York, 1790–1865* (Cambridge:
  Cambridge University Press 1981); Stuart Blumin, "The Hypothesis of
  Middle-Class Formation in Nineteenth Century America: A Critique
  and Some Proposals," *American Historical Review* 90, no. 2 (Dec.
  1985): 299–338; John Gilkeson. *Middle-Class Providence, 1820–1940*

(Princeton: Princeton University Press 1986). On the emergence of the "new middle class" in the early twentieth century, see, among a variety of sources, Burton Bledstein, *The Culture of Professionalism: The Middle Class and the Development of Higher Education in America* (New York: W.W. Norton and Company Inc. 1976); Barbara and John Ehrenreich, "The Professional-Managerial Class," *Radical America* 11, no. 2 (Mar.–Apr. 1977): 7–31; C. Wright Mills, *White Collar: The American Middle Classes* (London: Oxford University Press 1951); Eric Olin Wright, *Class, Crisis and the State* (London: Verso 1979), chap. 2.

7 Graham Lowe, "The Rise of Modern Management in Canada," in Graham S. Lowe and Harvey J. Krahn, eds., *Working Canadians: Readings in the Sociology of Work and Industry* (Agincourt: Metheun 1984), 164; Graham S. Lowe, "Mechanization, Feminization, and Managerial Control in the Early Twentieth Century Canadian Office," in Craig Heron and Robert Storey, eds., *On the Job: Confronting the Labour Process in Canada* (Montreal: McGill-Queen's University Press 1986), 177–209. On scientific management, see also Paul Craven, *"An Impartial Umpire": Industrial Relations and the Canadian State, 1900–1911* (Toronto: University of Toronto Press 1980), chap. 2; M.S. Larson, *The Rise of Professionalism: A Sociological Analysis*, (Berkeley: University of California Press 1977), 140–1.

8 R.D. Gidney and W.P. Millar, "The Origins of Organized Medicine in Ontario, 1850–1869," in Charles Roland, ed., *Health, Disease and Medicine: Essays in Canadian History* (Hamilton: Hannah Institute 1984), 65–95; Colin Howell, "Reform and the Monopolistic Impulse: the Professionalization of Medicine in the Maritimes," *Acadiensis* 11, no. 1 (Autumn 1981): 3–22; Colin Howell, "Elite Doctors and the Development of Scientific Medicine: The Halifax Medical Establishment and 19th Century Medical Professionalism," in Roland, ed., *Health, Disease and Medicine*, 105–22; James Struthers, "'Lord Give Us Women': Women and Social Work in English Canada, 1918–1953," Canadian Historical Association, *Historical Papers* 1983, 96–112; James Pitsula, "The Emergence of Social Work in Toronto," *Journal of Canadian Studies* 4, no. 1 (Spring 1979): 35–42. On urban reform activities, see J.M.S. Careless, *Toronto to 1918: An Illustrated History* (Toronto: James Lorimer 1984), 161–93; John C. Weaver, *Hamilton: An Illustrated History* (Toronto: James Lorimer 1982), 96–127; Paul Rutherford, "Tomorrow's Metropolis: The Urban Reform Movement in Canada, 1880–1920," in Gilbert Stelter and Alan F.J. Artibise, eds., *The Canadian City: Essays in Urban History* (Toronto: McClelland and Stewart 1977); John C. Weaver, "Tomorrow's Metropolis Revisited: A Critical Assessment of Urban Reform in Canada, 1890–1920," in Stelter and Artibise, eds., *The Canadian City*, 393–418.

9 Michael Katz, in *The People of Hamilton, Canada West* (Cambridge: Harvard University Press 1975), notes that members of the upper and middle classes in the 1850s and 1860s constantly worried about the prospect of downward social mobility (chap. 4, and 309–10). Mary Ryan, in *Cradle of the Middle Class*, writes that the story of the Utica middle class is "not a dramatic case of upward mobility but rather a sustained battle to maintain middle-range occupations for themselves and their children" (184). One way of later securing position was through higher education. Chad Gaffield, Susan Laskin, and Lynne Marks, "Student Population and Graduate Careers: Queen's University, Kingston, Ontario 1895–1900," in Paul Axelrod and John Reid, eds., *Youth, University and Canadian Society: Essays in the Social History of Higher Education* (Montreal: McGill-Queen's University Press 1989), 3–25, show that the fathers of full-time students at Queen's University from 1895 to 1900 included 31 per cent farmers, 24 per cent professionals, 16 per cent manufacturers, managers, and civil servants, and 16 per cent skilled, semi-, and unskilled workers (12). See also Stuart Blumin, "The Hypothesis of Middle-Class Formation in Nineteenth Century America," and John S. Gilkeson, *Middle-Class Providence, 1820–1940*, chap. 1.

10 There are some inconsistencies in the numbers cited in the two reports used as sources for this table in the categories of engineers, dentists, and clergymen, owing in all probability to slightly different occupational definitions used in succeeding censuses. For figures cited in these occupations I have used the more recent (1963) report. On the admission of women to university, see John G. Reid, "The Education of Women at Mount Allison, 1854–1914," *Acadiensis* 12, no. 2 (Spring 1983): 3–33, and Margaret Gillet, *We Walked Very Warily: A History of Women at McGill* (Montreal: Eden Press 1981).

11 This was true for the 1930s as well. See chap. 3, 59–61, and chap. 7, 157–60, for a discussion of this issue.

12 Randall Collins, *The Credential Society: An Historical Sociology of Education and Stratification* (New York: Academic Press 1979), 41; Colin Howell, "Reform and the Monopolistic Impulse," 4.

13 On efforts by businessmen to eliminate competition, see Michael Bliss, *The Living Profit: Studies in the Social History of Canadian Business, 1883–1911* (Toronto: McClelland and Stewart 1974), 33–54.

14 M.S. Larson, *The Rise of Professionalism: A Sociological Analysis*, 38; Randall Collins, *The Credential Society*, 132–5.

15 Colin Howell, "Elite Doctors and the Development of Scientific Medicine," 106.

16 Howell, "Elite Doctors," 115–19, and Gidney and Millar, "The Origins of Organized Medicine in Ontario, 1850–1869," 65–95. See also Paul

Axelrod, *Scholars and Dollars: Politics, Economics, and the Universities of Ontario, 1945–1980* (Toronto: University of Toronto Press 1982), 131–3, for a summary of this process in Ontario. On Europe and the United States, see Konrad Jarausch, ed., *The Transformation of Higher Learning: 1860–1930* (Chicago: University of Chicago Press 1983).

17 Howell, "Reform and the Monopolistic Impulse," 14. Other sources on the history of professionalism and professional education in Canada include Abraham Flexner, *Medical Education in the United States and Canada: A Report to the Carnegie Foundation for the Advancement of Teaching*, Carnegie Foundation for the Advancement of Teaching, bulletin no. 4 (New York 1910); D.W. Gullet, *A History of Dentistry in Canada* (Toronto: University of Toronto Press 1971), esp. chap. 5. According to Gullet, "Indentureship training was subject to many abuses ... The better practitioners took great care both in selecting a student and in training him, but other dentists, greater in number, simply used indentured students to their own advantage [in the 1870s]" (57). See also B.D. Bucknall et al., "Pedants, Practitioners and Prophets: Legal Eduation at Osgoode Hall to 1957," *Osgoode Hall Law Journal* 6 (1968): 142–229; Curtis Cole, "'A Hand to Shake the Tree of Knowledge': Legal Education in Ontario, 1871–1889," *Interchange* 17, no. 3 (1986): 15–27. In the case of law, Osgoode Hall was run by the Law Society of Upper Canada independently of universities until 1957. For a general account of the expansion and timing of the development of professional education in Canadian universities, see Robin Harris, *A History of Higher Education in Canada*, chaps. 10, 16.

18 Arthur Engel, "The English Universities and Professional Education," in Konrad Jarausch, ed., *The Transformation of Higher Learning*, 302. According to Ellen Condliffe Lagemann, in *A History of The Carnegie Foundation for the Advancement of Teaching* (Middletown, Conn.: Wesleyan University Press 1983), following the publication of the Flexner Report in 1910, "most of the leaders of the medical profession, a number of the leaders of the legal profession, and some members of the engineering and teaching professions, among others, also looked to the university to develop, transmit, and certify the special knowledge that would augment and sustain the authority and autonomy they wished to claim" (59).

19 W. Peterson, *Canadian Essays and Addresses* (London: Longman's Green and Co. 1915), 318, cited in Marni De Pencier, "Ideas of the English-Speaking Universities in Canada to 1920," doctoral diss., University of Toronto 1978, 623. See also Yves Gingras, "Financial Support for Postgraduate Students and the Development of Scientific Research in Canada," in Axelrod and Reid, eds., *Youth, University, and Canadian Society*, 301–19. The importance placed on the university's service to

agriculture was evident in western Canada. See Michael Hayden, *Seeking a Balance: A History of the University of Saskatchewan, 1907–1982* (Vancouver: University of British Columbia Press 1983), 37–8.

20 As University of Toronto President Robert Falconer wrote, "The modern Canadian university could not have been brought into being, unless during the period of its rapid growth this country had added greatly to its wealth. This material enrichment was itself due to the application of science to industry, which filled the harbours of the world with a tide on which rode abundant commerce": in "From College to University," *University of Toronto Quarterly* 5, no. 1 (Oct. 1935): 15. On the United States, see Laurence Veysey, *The Emergence of the American University* (Chicago: University of Chicago Press 1965), 3.

21 Condliffe-Hagemman, *Private Power for the Public Good: A History of the Carnegie Foundation for the Advancement of Teaching*; Donald Fisher, "The Role of Philanthropic Foundations in the Reproduction and Production of Hegemony: Rockefeller Foundations and the Social Sciences," *Sociology* 17, no. 2 (1983): 206–33. On Canada, see John G. Reid, "Health, Education, Economy: Philanthropic Foundations in the Atlantic Region in the 1920s and 1930s," *Acadiensis* 14 no. 1 (Autumn 1984): 64–83; and Lawrence J. Burpee, "Canada's Debt to the Carnegie Corporation," *Queen's Quarterly* 45, no. 2 (1938): 232–7.

22 While no one has done an analysis of this phenomenon in Canada in the early twentieth century, useful information on the demand and supply of professional labour can be found in Dominion Bureau of Statistics, *Supply and Demand in the Professions in Canada* (Ottawa 1937). My own work on the post–Second World War period demonstrated the obstacles to linking educational training with labour-markets. Even the use of manpower planning, largely unknown earlier in the century, proved unreliable and capricious in the market economy: see Axelrod, *Scholars and Dollars*, chaps. 5–6. See also Nicholas Abercrombie and John Urry, *Capital, Labour and the Middle Classes* (London: George Allen & Unwin 1983), chap. 6.

23 See Table 1, chap. 2.

24 Statistics Canada, *Historical Compendium of Educational Statistics: Confederation to 1975* (Ottawa 1978), Table 23, 216. In 1930, 54.6 per cent of the 31.5 thousand full-time undergraduates in Canadian universities were enrolled in arts and science courses and the remainder in "professional programs."

25 Gaffield, Laskin, and Marks, "Student Populations and Graduate Careers," 15–21.

26 Cited, 1904, in Stanley B. Frost, *McGill University*, 2: 54.

27 Cited in Janet Scarfe, "Letters and Affection," 417.

28 Brian McKillop, "Science, Humanism, and the Ontario University," in

McKillop, *Contours of Canadian Thought* (Toronto: University of Toronto Press 1987), 36.

29   Brian McKillop, *A Disciplined Intelligence: Critical Inquiry and Canadian Thought in Victorian Canada* (Montreal: McGill-Queen's University Press 1979); S.E.D. Shortt, *The Search for an Ideal: Six Canadian Intellectuals and Their Convictions in an Age of Transition* (Toronto: University of Toronto Press 1976); Patricia Jasen, "The English Canadian Liberal Arts Curriculum, 1800–1950: An Intellectual History," doctoral diss., University of Manitoba 1987, chaps. 1–2.

30   Executive Minutes, 30 May 1925, Wesley College Board of Directors, WC-5–6, University of Winnipeg Archives, cited in Gerald Friesen, "Principal J.H. Riddell: The Sane and Safe Leader of Wesley College," in Dennis L. Butcher et al., eds., *Prairie Spirit: Perspectives on the Heritage of the United Church of Canada in the West* (Winnipeg: University of Manitoba Press 1965), 256. For a discussion of how McMaster University, a Baptist institution, attempted to maintain its religious idealism in the face of creeping modernism, see Charles M. Johnston, *McMaster University, vol. 2, The Toronto Years, 1930–1957* (Toronto: University of Toronto Press 1976), chaps. 7–10.

31   Cited in Marni De Pencier, "Ideas of the English-Speaking Universities to 1920," doctoral diss., University of Toronto 1974, 533. See also James. G. Greenlee, *Sir Robert Falconer: A Biography* (Toronto: University of Toronto Press 1988), 144.

32   See chap. 3, p. 40, for examples.

33   Daniel Gordon, "The Functions of the Modern University," 1903, cited in De Pencier, "Ideas of the English-Speaking Universities," 502.

34   DePencier, "Ideas," 436.

35   Michael Hayden, *Seeking a Balance*, chap. 1; Walter H. Johns, *A History of the University of Alberta, 1908–1969* (Edmonton: University of Alberta Press 1981), chap. 1.

36   University of British Columbia Minutes of Convocation, 1912, 4, cited in De Pencier, "Ideas," 577. F.F. Wesbrook, offered the position in 1912, appeared to meet the requirements.

37   Cyrus MacMillan, "The University and the Freshman," *The University Magazine* 10, no. 2 (Apr. 1911): 210. See also Henry Newbolt, "Literature and Science", *The University Magazine* 17, no. 3 (Oct. 1918): "Education is not another word for information, it stands for the development and enrichment of the intellectual powers, including the practical powers which we include under the name of character, and which are fostered by mental spiritual experience. Both literature and science may be the means of education but only if they supply this mental or spiritual enrichment over and above the merely informing facts with which they deal" (354–5).

38 Brian McKillop, "Marching as to War: Elements of Ontario Under-
    graduate Culture, 1880–1914", in Axelrod and Reid, eds., *Youth,
    University, and Canadian Society*, 78, 82.
39 McKillop, "Marching as to War," 77–8. See also John D. Thomas,
    "Servants of the Church: Canadian Methodist Deaconess Work, 1890–
    1926," *Canadian Historical Review* 65, no. 3 (Sept. 1984): 385; and
    Diana Pedersen, "'The Call to Service': The YWCA and the Canadian
    College Woman," in Axelrod and Reid, *Youth, University, and Canadian
    Society*, 187–215.
40 Stanley B. Frost, *McGill University* 2: 98; *Charles M. Johnston and
    John Weaver, Student Days: An Illustrated History of Student Life at
    McMaster University from the 1890s to the 1980s* (Hamilton:
    McMaster University Alumni Association 1986), 18–19; Paul Axelrod,
    "Moulding the Middle Class: Student Life at Dalhousie University in the
    1930s," *Acadiensis* 15, no. 1 (Autumn 1985): 121; McKillop,
    "Marching as to War," 84–5. On emerging conceptions of middle-class
    masculinity, see Peter N. Stearns, *Be a Man: Males in Modern Society*
    (New York: Holmes and Meier Publishers Inc. 1979), chap. 5.
41 Hilda Neatby, *"And Not To Yield': Queen's University*, vol. 1., *1841–
    1917* (Montreal: McGill-Queen's University Press 1978), 295–9; John G.
    Reid, *Mount Allison University: A History, vol. 2, 1914–1963* (Toronto:
    University of Toronto Press 1984), 1–19; Frost, *McGill University* 2:
    95–112; Hayden, *Seeking a Balance*, 83; Barry Moody, "Acadia Fights
    the Great War," in Axelrod and Reid, eds., *Youth, University, and
    Canadian Society*, 143–60.
42 Yves Gingras, "Financial Support for Postgraduate Students and the
    Develoment of Scientific Research in Canada," in Axelrod and Reid,
    eds., *Youth, University, and Canadian Society*, 301–19; B. Sinclair, N.R.
    Ball, and J.O. Peterson, eds., *Let Us Be Honest and Modest: Technology
    and Society in Canadian History* (Toronto: Oxford University Press
    1974), 271–80.
43 See Brian McKillop, "Science, Authority and the American Empire," in
    Contours of Canadian Thought: "By the 1920s, this sense of [inherited
    cultural] tradition had been significantly shaken, and the decade
    witnessed as a consequence the attempts of some Canadian leaders to
    shore up the old cultural institutions, while others searched just as
    earnestly for ideals with which to build the country along new lines"
    (128). On the attempt to reconcile faith and reason, see also Ramsay
    Cook, *The Regenerators: Social Criticism in Late Victorian English-
    Canada* (Toronto: University of Toronto Press 1985). See also Marlene
    Shore, *The Science of Social Redemption: McGill, the Chicago School,
    and the Origins of Social Research in Canada* (Toronto: University of
    Toronto Press 1987), chap. 1.; and Patricia Jasen, "The English-

Canadian Liberal Arts Curriculum," 154–6.

44 Walter Murray, president of the University of Saskatchewan, cited in De Pencier, "Ideas," 567. On professional values, see also Burton Bledstein, *The Culture of Professionalism*, 5–7.

45 Cited in an editorial, "The Educated Man," Toronto *Globe*, 24 Oct. 1932, 4.

46 On the extension of education and the demographic changes affecting the family, see Canadian Youth Commission, *Youth, Marriage and the Family* (Toronto: Ryerson Press 1948), 1–13, 22. On the decline in the birth rate at the turn of the century, see Warren E. Kalbach and Wayne M. McVey, *The Demographic Bases of Canadian Society* (Toronto: McGraw Hill 1979), 94–5. On the decline of child labour, the Dominion Bureau of Statistics noted that the the the number of male workers 10–15 years of age fell from 58,074 in 1921 to 43,995 in 1931. The number of female workers fell from 15,134 to 8,635 over the same period. The working population as a whole increased 22.3 per cent during the decade: DBS, *Trends in Occupation, 1891–1931* (Ottawa 1939), Table 4, p. 5. On child-saving, see Neil Sutherland, *Children in English-Canadian Society: Framing the Twentieth Century Consensus* (Toronto: University of Toronto Press 1976), passim. For a view that raises questions about the impact of the child-saving movement on the decrease of child labour, see Lorna Hurl, "Restricting Child Factory Labour in Late Nineteenth Century Ontario," *Labour/Le Travail* 21 (Spring 1988): 87–121.

47 Stanley Hall, *Adolescence: Its Psychology, and Its Relations to Physiology, Anthropology, Sociology, Sex, Crime, Religion, and Education* (New York: D. Appleton and Co. 1904). Hall's theory of adolescence as a period of "storm and stress," and his concept of "recapitulation," which contended that each individual lived out the stages of human evolution, from primitive to modern, were well known. Hall considered adolescence to be a period during which the individual regressed to the "primitive" state, where natural physical and emotional needs are instinctively expressed, sometimes in a socially disruptive way. Evidence that Hall's theories were known and influential in Canada is provided in Leila Mitchell McKee, "Voluntary Youth Organizations in Toronto, 1880–1930," doctoral diss., York University 1982, chap. 2. Hall spoke in Toronto in 1891 at the meeting of the National Education Association. See also John Demos and Virginia Demos, "Adolescence in Historical Perspective," *Journal of Marriage and the Family* (Nov. 1969): 636–8; and John Demos, "The Rise and Fall of Adolescence," in Demos, *Past, Present and Personal: The Family and the Life Course in American History* (New York: Oxford 1986), 92–113. For a demonstration of the gender bias in Hall's theories, see Carol Dyhouse, *Girls Growing Up in Late Victorian and Edwardian England* (London:

Routledge and Kegan Paul 1981), chap. 5. On child-rearing, see
Norah. L. Lewis, "Creating the Little Machine: Child Rearing in
British Columbia, 1919–1939," *B.C. Studies* 56 (Winter 1982–83):
44–60; Veronica Strong-Boag, "Intruders in the Nursery: Childcare
Professionals Reshape the Years One to Five, 1920–1940," in Joy Parr,
ed., *Childhood and Family in Canadian History* (Toronto: McClelland
and Stewart 1982), 160–78. On sex education, see Michael Bliss, "Pure
Books on Avoided Subjects: Pre-Freudian Sexual Ideas in Canada," in
Michiel Horn and Ronald Sabourin, eds., *Studies in Canadian Social
History* (Toronto: McClelland and Stewart 1974), 326–46. See also
Robert Stamp, "Canadian High Schools in the 1920s and 1930s: The
Social Challenge to the Academic Tradition," Canadian Historical
Association, *Historical Papers* 1978, 76–93. For general accounts of the
American experience, see Joseph Kett, *Rites of Passage: Adolescence in
America, 1770 to the Present* (New York: Basic Books 1977); and Paula
Fass, *The Damned and the Beautiful: Amerian Youth in the 1920s* (New
York: Oxford 1977).

48 Robert Stamp, "Canadian High Schools," 76.

49 Paula Fass, *The Damned and the Beautiful*; James Pitsula, "Student Life
at Regina College in the 1920s," in Axelrod and Reid, eds., *Youth,
University, and Canadian Society*, 122–42; and Charles M. Johnston
and John C. Weaver, *Student Days: An Illustrated History of Student
Life at McMaster University*, chap. 3.

50 Natalie Zemon Davis, "The Reasons of Misrule," in Davis, *Society and
Culture in Early Modern France* (Stanford: Stanford University Press
1975), 97–123; Joseph Kett, *Rites of Passage*, esp. chap. 2; John Gillis,
Youth and History (New York: Academic Press 1981), chap. 1. There is
a large literature on the student movement of the 1960s; see Cyril
Levitt, *Children of Privilege: Student Revolt in the 1960s* (Toronto:
University of Toronto Press 1984).

51 Observers of the youth movement of the 1960s were particularly
inclined to the apocalyptic view. For an insightful analysis of public
portrayals of youth activism in the United States, see Todd Gitlin, *The
Whole World is Watching: Mass Media in the Making and the
Unmaking of the New Left* (Berkeley: University of California Press
1980). Examples of inflamed perceptions of students and youth in the
nineteenth and twentieth centuries can be found in Paul Axelrod,
"Romancing the Past: Nostalgic Conservatism, The Great Brain
Robbery, and the History of Education," paper presented to the
Canadian History of Education Association conference, Halifax,
October 1986. See also Patricia Meyer Spacks, *The Adolescent Idea:
Myths of Youth and the Adult Imagination* (New York: Basic Books
1981), 3–4.

52 Janet Scarfe, "Letters and Affection," 79. For accounts of unrest and violence at American universities in the nineteenth century, see David Allmendinger, *Paupers and Scholars: The Transformation of Student Life in the Nineteenth Century* (New York: St Martin's Press 1975), chap. 7; Helen Lefkowitz Horowitz, *Campus Life: Undergraduate Cultures from the End of the Eighteenth Century to the Present* (New York: Alfred Knopf 1987), chap. 2; Joseph Kett, *Rites of Passage*, chap. 2. However, even these accounts may overstate the degree of unrest by highlighting the episodic and tumultuous.

53 Scarfe, "Letters and Affection," 424. One of the leaders of the strike at the University of Toronto was Mackenzie King, future prime minister of Canada. See Harry Ferns and Bernard Ostry, *The Age of Mackenzie King* (Toronto: James Lorimer 1976), 21–9; Paul Craven, *"An Impartial Umpire,"* 50–1; W. Stewart Wallace, *A History of the University of Toronto*, 154–6.

54 Keith Walden, "Hazes, Hustles, Scraps, and Stunts: Initiations at the University of Toronto, 1880–1915," in Axelrod and Reid, eds., *Youth, University, and Canadian Society*, 94–121; Keith Walden, "Respectable Hooligans: Male College Students in Toronto Celebrate Hallowe'en, 1884–1910," *Canadian Historical Review* 68, no. 1 (Mar. 1987): 1–34.

55 Walden, "Hazes, Hustles," 110.

56 Natalie Zemon Davis, "The Reasons of Misrule."

57 Gibson, *Queen's University* 2: 66–81.

58 Reid, *Mount Allison* 2, 30, citing classics professor J.W. Cohoon in 1922. See also Donald Kirkey, "Building the City of God: The Founding of the Student Christian Movement," MA thesis, McMaster University 1983; Richard Allen, *The Social Passion: Religion and Social Reform in Canada, 1914–1928* (Toronto: University of Toronto Press 1971), 219–23. On the YWCA, see Diana Pederson, "The Call to Service."

59 McKillop, "Marching as to War"; Bledstein, *The Culture of Professionalism*, 223–47; Lefkowitz-Horowitz, *Campus Life*, chap. 2, 41–55.

60 Neatby, *Queen's University* 1: 205–10; Margaret Gillett, *We Walked Very Warily: A History of Women at McGill*, chap. 3.

61 Judith Fingard, "College, Career and Community: Dalhousie Coeds 1881–1921," in Axelrod and Reid, eds., *Youth, University, and Canadian Society*, 38–9. See also chap. 5 of this book.

62 Fingard, "College, Career and Community"; Gaffield, Laskin, Marks, "Student Populations and Graduate Careers."

63 McKillop, "Marching as to War," 76.

64 W.H. Alexander, classics professor at the University of Alberta, noted that "discipline sagged after the war ... There was a veritable craze for social affairs. Youth felt it had been cheated out of a good deal, and was

in haste to make up arrears": Alexander, *The University of Alberta: A Retrospective, 1908–1929* (Edmonton 1929), 34. For a description of a conflict over free expression between the publishers of a new literary magazine called *Fortnightly* and Principal Arthur Currie of McGill, see Leon Edel, "The Young Warrior in the Twenties," in Sandara Djwa and R.St.J. Macdonald, eds., *On F.R. Scott: Essays on His Contributions to Law, Literature, and Politics* (Montreal: McGill-Queen's University Press 1983), 25–6. Currie was worried that the magazine would "dishonour" the university. An interesting case of students taking the initiative on behalf of their university occurred at the University of British Columbia, where in 1922 students collected fifty thousand signatures on a petition calling for the relocation and expansion of the university. The campaign received public support and the move was accomplished in 1925: see John Rodenhizer, "The Student Campaign of 1922 to 'Build the University of British Columbia,'" *B.C. Studies*, no. 4 (Spring 1970): 21–37.

65 D.L. Thomson, "McGill Between the Wars," cited in Harris, *A History of Higher Education*, 351.

CHAPTER TWO

1 Statistics Canada, *Historical Compendium of Educational Statistics: Confederation to 1975* (Ottawa 1978), 208, 250–1. Quebec's total income went from 7.4 million in 1930 to 3.9 million in 1935; that of the western region from 4.7 to 2.9 million; of Ontario from 8.5 to 6.6 million; and of the Atlantic region from 1.3 to 2 million, owing largely to grants from the Rockefeller and Carnegie foundations. See John G. Reid, "Health, Education, Economy: Philanthropic Foundations in the Atlantic Region in the 1920s and 1930s," *Acadiensis* 14, no. 1 (Autumn 1984): 64–83.

2 At the University of British Columbia five faculty in Arts and Science and six of the fifteen professors in the Faculty of Agriculture were laid off in 1931–32: see Report of the President of the University of British Columbia for the Academic Year Ending *1932*. At Acadia there were staff reductions and "drastic" reductions in salary until by 1938 full professors were paid $2200, associates $1900, assistants $1780, and lecturers $1600: see Ronald Stewart Longley, *Acadia University, 1838–1938* (Wolfville, NS: Kentville Publishing Co. 1939), 8; Watson Kirkconnell, *The Fifth Quarter Century: Acadia University 1938–1963* (Wolfville: Governors of Acadia University 1968). See also A.G. Bedford, *The University of Winnipeg: A History of the Founding Colleges* (Toronto: University of Toronto Press 1976), 232. Salary cuts were imposed at the University of Western Ontario in 1932: see James J. and

Ruth Davis Talman, *Western 1878–1953* (London: University of Western Ontario 1953), 111; and John R.W. Gwynne Timothy, *Western's First Century* (London: University of Western Ontario 1978), 251–9. At McMaster in 1933 salary cuts were implemented of 5 per cent for those earning under $4000 and 6 per cent for those earning over that: see Charles M. Johnston, *McMaster University: The Early Years in Hamilton*, vol. 2, (Toronto: University of Toronto Press 1981), 40. Mount Allison reduced salaries by 5 per cent in 1932, 10 per cent in 1933, and 5 per cent in 1934: see Reid, *Mount Allison*, 2: 120–2. Salary reductions were imposed at the University of Saskatchewan in 1931, 1933, and 1935 at Saskatchewan. While no permanent employees were dismissed, some part-time faculty and assistants were: see Hayden, *Seeking a Balance*, 161–3. At Queen's the deficits grew and fees increased, but there were no salary cuts, and no full-time faculty were dismissed, as the university imposed a "rigid economy": see Gibson, *Queen's University*, 2: 92–102. At the University of Manitoba, the board chairman, John Machray, was tried and jailed for embezzlement: W.L. Morton, *One University: A History of the University of Manitoba, 1877–1952* (Toronto: University of Toronto Press 1957), 147–52.

3 The 1376 faculty constituted approximately 40 per cent of all full-time university teachers in Canada. See "Salaries of Teachers at 17 Universities by Rank and Region, 1937–8 to 1959–60," in Dominion Bureau of Statistics, *University Teachers' Salaries 1937–1960* (Ottawa 1961), 19. The average working wage is drawn from *The Economic Welfare of Canadian Employees: A Study of Occupations, Earnings, Hours, and Other Working Conditions, 1913–1937*, Queen's University, Industrial Relations Section, School of Commerce and Administration, bulletin no. 4 (Kingston 1940).

4 See sources cited in Tables 1 and 2.

5 *Vancouver Sun*, 6 Apr. 1936.

6 *Queen's Journal*, 8 Mar. 1935.

7 Garry John Burke, "An Historical Study of Intercollegiate Athletics at the University of Western Ontario, 1908–1945," MA thesis, University of Western Ontario 1979, notes the amount of money spent by students on sporting events, 249; see also University of Western Ontario *Gazette*, 29 Nov. 1939. See chap. 5, 121, on student spending practices.

8 National Conference of Canadian Universities (NCCU), *Proceedings* 1934, 75–82.

9 W.E. McNeill, in NCCU, *Proceedings* 1939, 16.

10 *Managra* 24, no. l (Nov. 1930): 10–11, UMA. The problem persisted. See also Report of the President, in University of Manitoba Annual Report *1935–36*, 3, UMA. John G. Reid, *Mount Allison University, vol. 2* (Toronto: University of Toronto Press 1984), 143, shows that between

1930 and 1939 the percentage of students from small communities decreased significantly, while the reverse was true of those from larger cities.

11 In French Canada the patterns were similar. At Laval University between 1930 and 1940, among 1508 first-year students, 28.3 per cent of students' fathers were professionals, 30 per cent were in business, 6 per cent were supervisors, 8.3 per cent were white-collar workers, 12.2 per cent were skilled workers, 4.1 per cent were semi- or unskilled workers, and 10.9 per cent were farmers. This material was collected from registration forms at the Bureau de diplome, Laval University. At Acadia University, 28.3 per cent of students' fathers were professional, 26.4 per cent businessmen, 6.3 per cent supervisors, 9.9 per cent white collar, 5.5 per cent skilled workers, 6.9 per cent semi- or unskilled workers, and 16.7 per cent farmers and fishermen. See Don Dowden, "Acadia University in the 1930s: Social Trends in Depression Era Higher Education," graduate research paper, Acadia University 1988, 17.

12 Report of the President of the University of British Columbia for the Year Ending *1933*, 25, UBCA. See also Robert Falconer, president of the University of Toronto, cited in *Saturday Night*, 17 June 1939, "Higher Education: Whither?" Quoting a recent Dominion Bureau of Statistics study, he noted, "There can be no doubt that the lowering of family income since the 1920s, unaccompanied by a corresponding drop in the cost of a university education, has made it more difficult for talented young people to find their way to the university." These impressions were confirmed in various interviews – e.g., Arthur Hackett, 10 Jan. 1987 (University of Toronto BA 1930).

13 *Ubyssey*, 2 Feb. 1932. See also *The Totem* 1938 (yearbook), n.p., UBCA.

14 President's Report, University of Western Ontario 1934–35, 9, UWOA. His views were echoed by W.H. McNeill, the vice-principal of Queen's, who contended that "the majority of [Canadian] students come from homes of very limited means": "The Increasing Costs of Education," NCCU, *Proceedings* 1939, 15.

15 *Queen's Journal*, 8 Mar. 1935.

16 John Porter, *The Vertical Mosaic* (Toronto: University of Toronto Press 1965), 274, 282–3.

17 Leonard Marsh, *Canadians In and Out of Work* (London: Oxford 1940), 390–1.

18 DBS, *Supply and Demand in the Professions in Canada* (Ottawa 1945), 35–6. In 1930 teachers and clergymen represented 7.7 per cent of students' fathers at the University of Western Ontario; in 1935, 5.8 per cent of the students at Alberta, and 5.1 per cent at the University of British Columbia. Doctors represented 4 per cent of students' fathers at UBC and 2.4 per cent in Alberta in 1935, and engineers represented

3.5 per cent of Alberta students' fathers in 1935, and 6.2 per cent of those at UBC. For sources see Table 3, and Report of the President of the University of British Columbia 1935–36.

19 Queen's University, *The Economic Welfare of Canadian Employees*, 44.

20 Gordon Stead, in *Vancouver News-Herald*, 9 Mar. 1934, clipping in university scrapbook, UBCA.

21 R.G. Dun and Co., *The Mercantile Agency Reference Book for the Dominion of Canada*, various issues, 1920–32, and R.G. Dun and Bradstreet, *The Mercantile Agency Reference Book for the Dominion of Canada*, various issues, 1933, 1934; Dalhousie University calendar 1921–39. Years selected for analysis were 1930–31, 1935–36, 1939–40.

22 Marsh, *Canadians In and Out of Work*, 39.

23 Interview, Marjorie (Montgomery) Bowker, 7 July 1984.

24 Jean Barman studied the destinations of graduates from three exclusive private schools in British Columbia. At one, Brentwood, it was reported in 1931 that of the school's 295 graduates, "151 had gone to thirteen different universities in Canada, England and the United States": see *Growing Up British in British Columbia: Boys in Private Schools* (Vancouver: University of British Columbia Press 1984), 154.

25 Interview with P.S. (UBC BA Science 1934), 20 Dec. 1985. Marion Cummer, who attended the University of Toronto from 1929 to 1933, was the daughter of the owner of a cattle buyer whose business "collapsed" in the early 1930s. Future Nova Scotia premier Henry Hicks, a student at Mount Allison and Dalhousie, recalled that his father mortgaged his home following financial losses (interview, 8 Aug. 1983). The same was true of the parents of Gladys Murray (Queen's BA 1933), which enabled her to go to university: interview 14, Aug. 1978, in *Hidden Voices*, Queen's University Oral History Project, QUA. Also interview with Earl Beattie (United College 1938–42), 19 Dec. 1985. His father was an unemployed accountant. He described himself as "lower middle class but poor."

26 DBS, *Higher Education in Canada, 1936–1938* (Ottawa 1939), 18–23. See also Jack Chernick, "National Scholarships," *Manitoba Arts Review* 1, no. 2 (Fall 1938): 30–2.

27 C.W. Hendel, "Scholarships and Student Aid at McGill," *McGill News* 19, no. 2 (1938), 16; Senate Minutes, 13 May 1933, Dalhousie University, DUA; C.H. Mitchell, treasurer of Student Loan Fund, to Board of Governors, 7 Apr. 1932, Board of Governor Minutes, 7 Apr., 1932, DUA; Report of the President of the University of British Columbia, Year Ending 31 Aug. 1934, 22, UBCA; *Queen's Journal*, 20 Feb. 1934; President's Report, University of Western Ontario 1930–31, 24, UWOA.

28 Reported in the *Sheaf*, 2 Oct. 1936. There was a run on Province of

Alberta Savings Certificates in the summer of 1935 as consumers feared they were becoming worthless. The provincial government stopped issuing them but the university continued to accept outstanding certificates in payment of fees.

29 W.P. Thompson, *The University of Saskatchewan: A Personal History* (Toronto: University of Toronto Press 1970), 124–5. See also Michael Hayden, *Seeking a Balance: The University of Saskatchwan, 1907–1982* (Vancouver: University of British Colubmia Press 1983), 157–8, 181. See also Presidential Papers, ser. 1, B66, USA.

30 Interview, 11 July 1984. Cherry later became an English professor at Saskatchewan.

31 She graduated in geology in 1934 and eventually became the director of McGill University Museums. She tells her story in "As The Twig is Bent," in Margaret Gillet and Kay Sibbald, eds., *A Fair Shake: Autobiographical Essays by McGill Women* (Montreal: Eden Press 1984), 113–14.

32 UBC Senate Minutes, 8 May 1935, UBCA. The dean of women at UBC cited a case of a first-year student who had won a scholarship at matriculation. She missed classes in November 1933 because she was "lacking car fare ... She now receives $5.00 a month for this purpose," as was the case with other students in a similar position: Report of the Dean of Women, in Report of the President of the University of British Columbia, Year Ending 31 Aug. 1934, 22, UBCA. See also interview with Lola Henry (assistant to Dalhousie President Carleton Stanley in the 1930s), 16 Aug. 1983; Student Correspondence Files, President's Office Papers, DUA, which contain letters to and from Stanley on the financial problems of students; and "Funds To Help Students Are Near Exhaustion," *Globe*, 12 Jan. 1935, 23 Sept. 1932.

33 Interview, Rose Mary Gibson, 24 July 1978, *Hidden Voices*, QUA; see also letters from organizations and individuals offering to sponsor poor or disadvantaged students at Alberta: President's Papers, 1928–36, Student and Alumni Affairs, Admission: Correspondence, 3281.1, UAA. According to U of T's *Varsity* (29 Sept. 1932), struggling students interviewed "held up the financial end by devious means and diverse manner – but with considerable success." In the same year the price of meals at the University of Toronto's Great Hall were reduced "because of the great financial strain" (*Varsity*, 28 Nov. 1932). See chap. 6 on the partially successful campaign initiated by Canadian students to increase the number and value of scholarships.

34 Fees rose by a low of 11 per cent at Dalhousie and a high of 300 per cent at Saskatchewan. McGill's fees rose by 79 per cent, Toronto's by 67 per cent, British Columbia's by 50 per cent, and Alberta's by 37.5 per cent: DBS, *Higher Education in Canada, 1936–38* (Ottawa 1939),

14, and various interviews on the costs of education, which were consistent with the DBS study.

35 Interview with Carney Morris, 20 Sept. 1985, and the Toronto *Globe* (12 Jan. 1935), which predicted that the casualty rate would be significant again in 1935. The president of the student council at UBC reported that as a result of a fee increase in in the fall of 1938, "200 to 300 students have been prevented from attending university" (*Ubyssey*, 8 Nov. 1938), but it is not clear whether this referred to the number of students who dropped out or those who would have entered for the first time had they been able to afford it.

36 Report of the Board of Governors of the University of Alberta 1930–31, 32, UAA.

37 C.W. Hendel, "Scholarships and Student Aid at McGill," *McGill News* 19, no. 2 (1938): 15, MUA.

38 DBS, *Canada Year Book 1934–35* (Ottawa 1935), 1054; Robin Harris, *A History of Higher Education in Canada, 1663–1960*, 393–4.

39 Anonymous letter to Robert Stamp, 29 Nov. 1980. See also University of Alberta, Report of the Board of Governors 1938–39, 17, UAA; Michael Hayden, *Seeking a Balance: The University of Saskatchewan, 1907– 1982*, 158–60; Toronto *Globe*, 11 Oct. 1932, 9, 10, on extension lectures at the University of Toronto. There is a variety of literature on the Antigonish Movement. See, for example, Laurence K. Shook, *Catholic Post-secondary Education in English-speaking Canada: A History* (Toronto: University of Toronto Press 1971) 84–5; and Alexander Fraser Laidlaw, "The Campus and the Community: A Study of the Adult Education Program of St. Francis Xavier University, Antigonish, Nova Scotia," D. Ed thesis, University of Toronto 1958.

40 Interview, Doug Cherry, 11 July 1984. Marjorie Montgomery Bowker (7 July 1984) recalled the university as a social "equalizer." According to Eric Mercer (Dalhousie 1933–37), "we were all in the same boat. We had no great expectations": interview, 11 Aug. 1983.

41 *McGill Daily*, 27 Nov. 1930, editorial entitled "Class Distinctions." See also David M. Solomon – "My Life as a Student and Teacher 1935– 1974," unpublished memoir, Aug. 1974, MUA – who had strong memories of class distinctions at McGill.

42 Interview with Walter Harris (University of Alberta 1933–37), 6 July 1984. Similar conditions and attitudes prevailed at McMaster University. According to Charles Johnston and John Weaver, "McMaster attracted very few sons and daughters of the extremely wealthy. Access to family cars and ownership of evening wear were evident, as hallmarks of a raffish crowd, but were exceptional enough to have seemed extraordinary": C.M. Johnston and John Weaver, *Student Days: An Illustrated History of Student Life at McMaster University from the 1890s to the*

1980s (Hamilton: McMaster University Alumni Association 1986), 59.

43 Interview with P.S. (UBC), 20 Dec. 1985. Carney Morris, cited above, recalled being treated no differently from his wealthy roommate, whom he never resented: interview, 20 September 1985. Gladys Munnings (Queen's BA 1933), interviewed in *Hidden Voices*, 14 Aug. 1978, noted that everyone was in the same predicament: that all students wore academic gowns to class at Queen's cut down on distinctions made on the basis of dress.

44 Interview with Arthur Hackett, 10 Jan. 1987.

45 Various interviews and student newspapers.

46 While oral testimony from Dalhousie supports this conclusion, the statistics are less clear than those from Toronto. At Dalhousie, 60 per cent of women (for the years 1930, 1935, and 1939) came from professional and business families, compared to 59 per cent of men, and 12 per cent of women had fathers who were manual labourers, compared to 14 per cent of men. Percentages from sources cited in Table 3.

47 At U of T for the year 1935, 55 per cent of first-year female students came from the city of Toronto, compared to 51 per cent of males. Oral testimony of women at Queen's in the 1920s suggests similar patterns. See also Nicole Neatby, "Preparing for the Working World: Women at Queen's during the 1920s," *Historical Studies in Education* 1, no. 1 (Spring 1989): 56–7, which found that the 1925 class of women came from more prestigious occupational backgrounds than did the men. Comparable statistics for Manitoba, Saskatchewan, Alberta, and UBC were not available, though oral testimony would suggest the patterns were the same. Sources on limited part-time work for women can be found in chap. 5, 125–6. Rose Mary Gibson, in *Hidden Voices*, 24 July 1978, recalled that women did volunteer work in summer in the absence of paid employment. Marion Cummer (Toronto 1933) recalled that there was no part-time work for girls from out of town: correspondence, 12 May 1986.

48 Mary J. Wright to Robert Stamp, 1 Apr. 1981. An interesting reflection of this attitude is found in R.C. Wallace, "The Function of the Universities in Western Canada," in Report of the Board of Governors of the University of Alberta 1931–32, 52–3. He wrote that universities in western Canada "have been at the centre of [the region's] life and thinking." This perspective is corroborated by an ex-student (and future scholar) from the University of Manitoba, H.S. Ferns, in *Reading from Left to Right*, 30. He noted that the creation of the University of Manitoba was considered "an essential part of [the province's] political economy." See also University of Alberta *Gateway*, 22 Feb. 1935.

49 Statistics on students' place of residence come from DBS, *Annual Survey*

of Education, 1935 (Ottawa 1937), 122–3, Table 46. The information
on national origins is taken from registration records, published in
aggregate form by the University of Alberta and collected from individual forms at Toronto and Dalhousie. The Toronto data include first-
year students only, while the other institutions include students in
all years. Unknowns are excluded from the calculations. While the
Alberta material is published under the heading "Registration of
Students According to National Origin," the Toronto and Dalhousie
information is in the category of "Father's Nationality." There is
additional information for other universities from which individual cases
can be cited, but, because of slight variations in the collection of data,
the categories are difficult to compare on an aggregate basis. Because
the student populations of the University of Manitoba and McGill
University were larger than average, the actual percentage of those in
the category of "Other" was likely somewhat higher than that cited in
this table.

50 *Gateway*, 5 Oct. 1934.

51 DBS, *Annual Survey of Education, 1935* (Ottawa 1937), 122–3,
Table 46.

52 In Manitoba in 1941, 47 per cent of the population was of non-English
European origin, compared to 32.4 per cent of the student population
in 1938–39: "Proportion of Various Stocks in the Student Enrolment for
the Session 1938–39," UA13, box 5, Registrar's Records, UMA.

53 At 24, 23.4, and 29.4 per cent respectively, Catholics, Jews, and Baptists
constituted a higher percentage of working-class students than did
Presbyterians, Anglicans, and United Churchmen, at 14.6, 10.3, and
7.3 per cent respectively.

54 Charles M. Johnston, *McMaster University: The Early Years in
Hamilton, vol. 2, 1930–1957* (Toronto: University of Toronto Press
1981), 55. See also Johnston and Weaver, *Student Days*, 55. At Acadia
the proportion of freshmen students who were Baptist fell from 63.2
per cent in 1929 to 52.6 per cent in 1938: Don Dowden, "Acadia University in the 1930s: Social Trends in Depression-Era Higher Education,"
graduate paper, Acadia University 1988, 7.

55 Report of the President, University of British Columbia 1934–35, shows
that 2 per cent were American, as were 7 per cent of the student body
at Alberta in 1930–31.

56 Laurence Shook, *Catholic Post-secondary Education in English-speaking
Canada*, 171–2.

57 See Marcia G. Synnott, "The Admission and Assimilation of Minority
Students at Harvard, Yale and Princeton, 1900–1970," *History of
Education Quarterly* 19, no. 3 (Fall 1979): 285–304; and George
Rosen, *The Structure of American Medical Practice, 1875–1941*

(Philadelphia: University of Pennsylvania 1983), 69. In his memoirs, John Kenneth Galbraith describes the workings of the quota system at Princeton: *A Life in Our Times: Memoirs* (Boston: Houghton-Mifflin 1981), 19–20.

58 UAI3, box 5, Registrar's Records, University of Manitoba, UMA.

59 Michael Hayden, *Seeking a Balance*, chap. 3.

60 MacKay to Currie, 23 Apr. 1926: Jewish Students at McGill, RG2 C48, Principal's Papers; and MacKay to Currie, 21 July 1933: Jews – Protestants, RG2 C48, Principal's Papers, MUA.

61 Stanley Frost and Sheila Rosenberg, "The McGill Student Body: Past and Future Enrolment," *McGill Journal of Education* 15, no. 1 (Winter 1980): 41–3, and Frost, *McGill University* 2: 128. Frost uses different figures on Jewish proportions in 1939 in the article and the book. I have cited the more recent percentages. Jewish students were restricted to a quota of eight to ten positions a year in the medical faculty: J.C. Simpson, associate dean of Faculty of Medicine to L.W. Douglas, 14 Jan. 1938, Jews: Matriculation, RG2 C48, Office of the Principal, MUA.

62 Percy Barsky, "How 'Numerus Clausus' Was Ended in the Manitoba Medical School," *Canadian Jewish Historical Society Journal* (Oct. 1977): 75–81; see also *Winnipeg Free Press*, 16 Mar., 14 Sept. 1944; 20 Mar. 1945. The University of Alberta was somewhat less extreme. It did not discriminate against Jewish medical school applicants who were resident in the province, but it refused admission to Jews from outside the province or the country except in "special" circumstances: R.C. Wallace to Sidney Smith, 13 Feb. 1936, President's Papers, 1928–36, 32/10/5.4, University of Manitoba: Correspondence, UAA. For confirmation of the Avukah Society's statistics on the ethnic origins of Manitobans, see *Census of Canada, 1941*, vol. 1 (Ottawa 1950), Table IV, 227. For a discussion of the history of anti-Semitism within Winnipeg, see Henry Trachtenberg, "The 'Old Clo Move': Politics and the Jews of Winnipeg 1882–1921," doctoral diss., York University 1984), 920–6. See also David Rome, *Clouds in the Thirties: On Anti-Semitism in Canada, 1929–1939* (Montreal: Canadian Jewish Congress 1979), for anti-Semitic incidents at the University of Montreal and in Quebec generally. On immigration policy, see Irving Abella and Harold Troper, *None Is Too Many: Canada and the Jews of Europe, 1933–1948* (Toronto: Deneau 1982).

63 For more on this, see chapter 6, 141, where the response of campuses to the rise of Naziism and the repression of Jews is discussed.

64 The case is discussed in the Board of Governors Minutes, 9 June 1932, DUA. The Tuberculosis Hospital in Halifax, the only one that would permit black doctors to train or practice, apparently had no spaces for the student doctor. Also, according to the associate dean of medicine at

McGill, apart from quotas on Jews, "the only other apparent discrimination against Americans is in respect to the negro. Because of hospital restrictions, particularly in obstetrics and gynaecology, we can take very few negroes ... though we occasionally make exceptions ... We have one American negro in our first year": J.C. Simpson to L.W. Douglas, 14 Jan. 1938, Jews: Matriculation RG2 C48, Office of the Principal, MUA. For an account of similar practices in London at the University of Western Ontario during the 1920s, see W. Sherwood Fox, *Sherwood Fox of Western* (Toronto: Burns and MacEachern 1964), 153–5.

65 W.J. Dunlop to President Falconer, 20 Oct. 1931, University Historian, A83–0036/002, Discrimination: Jewish Students, 1938–39, UTA.

66 Elaine Barnard, "A University at War: Japanese Canadians during World War II," *BC Studies* 35 (Autumn 1973): 36–55. Seven Japanese Canadian students forced to leave UBC were able to enrol at the University of Alberta between 1942 and 1944, but McGill accepted none until 1945.

67 At the University of Toronto, 1187 of 1506, or 79 per cent of students, stated specific career aspirations. Of those who did, 90.8 aspired to professional careers, 6.2 per cent to business, and 2.3 per cent to white-collar careers. In the 1930–31 graduating class in arts at the University of British Columbia, of the 78 women who stated their aspirations, 54 per cent chose education or teaching, 15 per cent librarianship, 7.7 per cent business, and 9 per cent graduate school. Of the 48 men who stated their aspirations, 41.7 per cent selected teaching, 14.6 per cent law, 8.3 per cent engineering, and 6.3 per cent medicine: *The Totem* (yearbook), 1930–31. For overall distribution, see Robin Harris, *A History of Higher Education in Canada*, 352.

68 Interview, 12 Feb. 1973, transcript in UBCA.

69 *Managra* 25, no. 6 (Apr. 1932): 10, UMA.

70 See, for example, Queen's University, *The Economic Welfare of Canadian Employees: A Study of Occupations, Earnings, Hours and Other Working Conditions, 1913–1937* (Kingston 1946), 7; Herb Hamilton, *Queen's* (Kingston 1977), 23; Dean's Papers, 41/12/11/424, "Prospective Employers of Graduates: Inquiries, Correspondence," UAA; John E Robbins Papers, MG 31 D91, vol. 1, Reminiscences, 1929–40, 7, NA.

71 Registration Records, Queen's University, 1935–36, QUA.

72 Interview with Grace Cullen (Queen's BA 1931), in *Hidden Voices*, QUA.

73 Alice H. Parsons, "Careers or Marriage," *Canadian Home Journal* (June 1938): 63–4, cited in Veronica Strong Boag, *The New Day Recalled: Lives of Girls and Women in English Canada, 1919–1939* (Toronto: Copp Clark 1988), 13.

74 Interviews with Gene (Morison) Hicks, 12 Aug. 1983; Jean Burnett, 19

Dec. 1985; and William Archibald (Dalhousie 1929–33), 12 Aug. 1983, all of whom confirmed the importance of the "Scottish" factor, as did Marion Cummer, correspondence, 12 May 1986.

75 Interview, 7 July 1984. Leonard Kitz, who attended Dalhousie, referred to his decision to go to university as an unquestioned "automatic reflex": interview, 9 Aug. 1983. For a discussion of the "Scottish myth" and higher education in the Maritimes, see John G. Reid, "Beyond the Democratic Intellect: The Scottish Example and University Reform in the Maritime Provinces, 1870–1933," in Paul Axelrod and John G. Reid, eds., in *Youth, University, and Canadian Society: Essays in the Social History of Higher Education* (Montreal: McGill-Queen's University Press 1989), 275–300.

76 Interview with W.E. Mann (University of Toronto 1938–42), 17 Dec. 1985.

77 H.S. Ferns, *Reading from Left to Right*, 33.

78 This study of UBC alumni from 1916 TO 1969 elicited 5210 responses, from 52,580 students in total. Over one-third of the alumni (forty-six) came to the university because it was "always assumed" they would go. Only 33.2 per cent of the classes of 1929–33 said that the opportunity for a better job was an important reason for enrolling, as opposed to 52.4 per cent of the 1944 class. The older classes were far more heavily influenced by parents' attitudes than were younger alumni. Among the alumni of 1929–33, 41.2 per cent replied that they were strongly influenced by their parents in their decisions, but after the Second World War the figure fell to 25 per cent (ninety-seven). From Peter Z.W. Tsong, *The UBC Alumni, 1916–1969: Thoughts of 12.6 per cent of the UBC Alumni* (Vancouver: Peter Tsong 1972).

79 DBS, *Annual Survey of Education* (Ottawa 1936), xxvii. Also, "There has been no tendency in post-war years for women to increase their enrolment in such professional lines of study as medicine, dentistry, pharamacy, law, theological or missionary courses … They have held in the main to Arts, including Science and Commerce, and to Education, Social Service and Public Health": ibid., xxvii. The treatment and perceptions of women are discussed more fully in chaps. 4 and 5. See also Veronica Strong-Boag, *The New Day Recalled*, chaps. 2–3, and Neatby, "Preparing for the Working World," 61–8.

80 John E. Robbins Papers, "Personal Reminiscences 1929–40," MG31 D91, NA.

81 Of the Queen's sample cited above, 53 per cent of male students stated intended occupations, compared to 35 per cent of women.

82 Interview, 14 Aug. 1978, in *Hidden Voices*, QUA.

83 Interview, 19 Dec. 1985.

84 *The Totem* 1930–31, UBCA.
85 Registration Records, University of Toronto, 1935–36, UTA, and various interviews.

CHAPTER THREE

1 Harry T. Logan, *Tuum Est: A History of the University of British Columbia* (Vancouver: University of British Columbia 1958), 81.
2 Robert Falconer, President's Address, 6 Jan. 1931, cited in *University of Toronto Monthly* 31, no. 5 (Feb. 1931): 220–1. For a fuller discussion of Falconer's views, see James G. Greenlee, *Sir Robert Falconer: A Biography* (Toronto: University of Toronto Press 1988), 123, 144–5.
3 Hugh M. Urquart, *Arthur Currie: The Biography of a Great Canadian* (Toronto: J.M. Dent and Sons Canada Ltd. 1950), 348.
4 C.G. Stone and F. John Garnett, *Brandon College: A History, 1899–1967* (Brandon: Brandon University 1969), 127.
5 See also Greenlee, *Robert Falconer: A Biography*, 123, 143, chap. 13; H.J. Cody (Toronto), President's Report, cited in *University of Toronto Monthly* 39, no. 4 (Jan. 1939): 111; R.C. Wallace (Queen's), in Frederick Gibson, *To Serve and Yet Be Free: Queen's University*, vol. 2, *1917–1961* (Montreal: McGill-Queen's University Press 1983), 159, 169; Walter Murray (Saskatchewan), in Michael Hayden, *Seeking a Balance: The University of Saskatchewan, 1907–1982* (Vancouver: University of British Columbia Press 1983), 23; W. Hamilton Fyfe, "The Object of a University Education," *University of Toronto Monthly* 32, no. 2, (Nov. 1931): 59.
6 President's Papers, University of Alberta 1928–36, Individual Problems: Correspondence (3281–4), Student and Alumni Affairs, UAA, includes considerable correspondence between the president and parents. A University of British Columbia student, who later became a professor of physics, recalled, "A university president in those days [1930s] was an important person, more so than now": Gordon Shrum with Peter Stursberg, ed. Clive Cocking, *Gordon Shrum: An Autobiography* (Vancouver: University of British Columbia Press 1986), 51. The president's custodial role with respect to students will be discussed in more detail in the next chapter.
7 Gibson, *Queen's University*, 2: 143–4.
8 Hayden, *Seeking a Balance*, 28–30. See also W. Sherwood Fox, *Sherwood Fox of Western: Reminiscences by William Sherwood Fox* (Toronto: Burns and MacEachern 1964), 24, 42. On Arthur Currie of McGill, see Stanley B. Frost, *McGill University: For the Advancement of*

Learning, vol. 2, *1895–1971* (Montreal: McGill-Queen's University Press 1984), 118–19.

9 See Charles M. Johnston, *McMaster University: The Early Years in Hamilton*, vol. 2, *1930–1957* (Toronto: University of Toronto Press 1981), passim; and John G. Reid, *Mount Allison University: 1914–1963*, vol. 2 (Toronto: University of Toronto Press 1984), passim.

10 The various contemporary efforts by intellectuals to reconcile faith and reason are explored in Ramsay Cook, *The Regenerators: Social Criticism in Late Victorian English- Canada* (Toronto: University of Toronto Press 1986), and A.B. McKillop, *Contours of Canadian Thought* (Toronto: University of Toronto Press 1987).

11 J.S. Thomson, in National Conference of Canadian Universities, *Proceedings 1939*, 114. Similar views were expressed by Carleton Stanley, president of Dalhousie. The two corresponded on the matter. See Thomson to Stanley, 16 Dec. 1938, 28 Dec. 1938; and Stanley to Thomson, 21 Dec. 1938; President's Papers, ser. II, B-138, USA. See also Carleton Stanley, President's Report 1933–34, 1–5, DUA.

12 R.M. Hutchins, *The Higher Learning in America* (New Haven: Yale University Press 1936, 1958).

13 NCCU, *Proceedings 1937*, 20–1; see also Malcolm Wallace, "Is the Arts Course Losing Ground?" 12–20. See comments of Leonard S. Klinck on the impact of specialization, *Ubyssey*, 6 Nov. 1931.

14 R.C. Wallace, Inaugural Address, *Queen's Journal*, 14 Oct. 1936.

15 R.C. Wallace, "Higher Education on the Stand," *Queen's Quarterly* 46, no. 3 (Autumn 1939): 261–6. See also H.J. Cody, "The Place of the University in National Life," *University of Toronto Quarterly* 4 (1934–35): 421–33. For a somewhat more pessimistic view, see J. Gordon Nelles, "What Canada Loses in the Arts Graduate," *Queen's Quarterly* 41 (Winter 1934): 71–80.

16 *McGill Daily*, 28 Feb. 1939.

17 "A University Deficiency," *Vancouver Sun*, 23 Sept. 1936.

18 Dalhousie University Calendar 1930–31, 10–12. See also McGill University Calendar 1935–36, 73, with similar admission requirements.

19 J.F. Leddy, "The Place of the Humanities in Secondary Education," in Watson Kirkconnell and A.S.P. Woodhouse, eds., *The Humanities in Canada* (Ottawa: Humanities Research Council of Canada 1947), 36; G.H. Henderson, "The Necessity of Compulsory Latin for Arts Matriculation," NCCU, *Proceedings 1937*, 34.

20 Calendar of the University of Saskatchewan 1929–30, 10.

21 Calendar of St Francis Xavier University 1935–36, 20.

22 University of Western Ontario, President's Report 1932–33, 38.

23 J.F. Leddy, "The Place of the Humanities in Secondary Education,"

30–1, 36; Patricia Jasen, "The English Canadian Liberal Arts Curriculum: An Intellectual History, 1800–1950," doctoral diss., University of Manitoba 1987, 162–4.

24 T.W.L. MacDermott, "Cooperation in University Matriculation," NCCU, *Proceedings* 1939, 74.

25 G.J. Trueman, "The Requirements for the B.A. Degree," NCCU, *Proceedings* 1934, 84.

26 University of Saskatchewan, President's Report 1933–34, 5. See also David Wood, dean of the Faculty of Education, A Study of the Causes of Student Failures in the First Year at University for the Academic Year 1937–38, Minutes of the Senate of the University of Manitoba, 11 Oct. 1938, UMA.

27 *Ubyssey*, 28 Jan. 1930.

28 Cited in Gibson, *Queen's University*, 2: 111.

29 "First Year Arts To Be Abolished," *University of Toronto Monthly* 30, no. 9 (June 1930): 404.

30 DBS, *Survey of Education, 1931–32* (Ottawa 1933).

31 For example, Saskatchewan demanded senior matriculation as a minimum entry requirement in 1934: Michael Hayden, *Seeking a Balance: The University of Saskatchewan, 1907–1982*, 176–8.

32 McGill University Calendar 1934–35, 103–4. See also Calendar of St Francis Xavier University 1935–36, 31–4.

33 Queen's University, Committee on Improvement of Students' Work, 12 Mar. 1930, 72, Faculty of Arts and Science, box 1, QUA.

34 Report of the Dean of the Faculty of Arts, in University of Manitoba, *Annual Report* 1935–36, 14.

35 Report of the Board of Governors and President of the University of Alberta 1934–35, 38–9, UAA.

36 W.E. McNeill, Report of Commission on University Entrance Examinations, NCCU, *Proceedings* 1942, 59.

37 A.S.P. Woodhouse, "English-Speaking Universities: Pass or General Courses," in *The Humanities in Canada*, 44.

38 Ibid. See also H.S. Ferns, *Reading from Left to Right: One Man's Political History* (Toronto: University of Toronto Press 1983), 32, where he describes the "flexibility" of the University of Manitoba curriculum. Students there could take courses in any order and write examinations without having to attend lectures.

39 Woodhouse, "English-Speaking Universities," 45.

40 R.S. Harris, *A History of Higher Education in Canada* (Toronto: University of Toronto Press 1976), 377–8; Jasen, "The English Canadian Liberal Arts Curriculum," 288–90.

41 A.S.P. Woodhouse, "English-Speaking Universities: Honours Courses," in

The Humanities in Canada, 59; Jasen, "The English Canadian Liberal Arts curriculum," 267.

42 Woodhouse, "English-Speaking Universities," 78–9; Harris, *A History of Higher Education in Canada*, 381–2.

43 Charles M. Johnston, *McMaster University*, 2: 35.

44 Arthur R.M. Lower, *My First Seventy-five Years* (Toronto: Macmillan 1967), 324; see also A.G. Bedford, *The University of Winnipeg: A History of the Founding Colleges* (Toronto: University of Toronto Press 1976), 223.

45 Report of the Board of Governors and President of the University of Alberta 1930–31, 52, UAA.

46 University of Western Ontario, President's Reports, 1932–33 to 1935–36, UWOA.

47 *Queen's Journal*, 2 Feb. 1937; *McGill Daily*, 15 Nov. 1933; Report of the Board of Governors and President of the University of Alberta 1935–36, 9, UAA. Carleton Stanley, "Dalhousie Today," *Dalhousie Review* 18 (1938): 219; Dalhousie University, President's Report 1931–32, 3.

48 *McGill Daily*, 15 Nov. 1933; *Gateway* (Alberta), 27 Oct. 1933; *Pharos* (Dalhousie yearbook) 1933, 53. As graduate Milton Shulman wrote in 1934, "Most students took the work seriously ... The Rhodes Scholar was more of a hero than the football star": "I'm a Graduate of '34," *Canadian Magazine*, Dec. 1934, 47.

49 *Montreal Star*, 7 Mar. 1934.

50 *Queen's Journal*, 1 Dec. 1931; Frederick Gibson, *Queen's University*, 2: 110.

51 Dalhousie University, President's Report 1933–34, 5, DUA.

52 Inauguration Address, 1 Oct. 1931, Board of Governors Minutes, 29 Oct. 1931, DUA; J.F. Macdonald, "Can First Class Honours Women Graduates Be Induced to Take Up Secondary School Teaching as a Life Work?" NCCU, *Proceedings* 1930, 102–14.

53 Gibson, *Queen's*, 2: 110.

54 Woodhouse, "Honours Courses," 73; Harris, *A History of Higher Education in Canada*, 381.

55 R.S. Knox, "The Educational Value of the Study of Literature," NCCU, *Proceedings* 1930, 56. See also *Dalhousie Gazette*, 29 Oct. 1930, which acknowledged – and criticized – the student view that subjects such as Latin were "useless and dead."

56 S.E.D. Shortt, *The Search for an Ideal: Six Canadian Intellectuals and Their Convictions in an Age of Transition, 1890–1930* (Toronto: University of Toronto Press 1976), chap. 5; Jasen, "The English-Canadian Liberal Arts Curriculum," 159; Paul Axelrod, "Moulding the

Middle Class: Student Life at Dalhousie University in the 1930s," *Acadiensis* 15, no. 1 (Autumn 1985): 97.

57 W. Kirkconnell, "The New Provinces," in *The Humanities in Canada*, 198; W.H. Alexander, "The Classics in a Liberal Education: Per Se and Per Alia," NCCU, *Proceedings* 1930, 47–56; Jasen, "The English-Canadian Liberal Arts Curriculum," 164–5.

58 Harris, *A History of Higher Education in Canada*, 384–5.

59 University of Western Ontario *Gazette*, 25 Feb. 1932. For a critical discussion of the traditionalism of English teaching at the University of Manitoba from the perspective of the university's most famous graduate, see Philip Marchand, *Marshall McLuhan: The Medium and the Messenger* (Toronto: Random House 1989), 15, 17.

60 University of Western Ontario calendar 1935–36, 123–8.

61 Patricia Jasen, "Arnoldian Humanism, English Studies, and the Canadian University," *Queen's Quarterly* 95, no. 3 (Autumn 1988): 564.

62 For examples of the dominance of English literature, of courses offered and books used, see McGill University calendar 1935–36, 129–32; St. Francis Xavier University calendar 1935–36, 57–9; University of British Columbia calendar 1930–31, 129–35.

63 Carl Berger, *The Writing of Canadian History: Aspects of English-Canadian Historical Writing since 1900*, 2nd edn (Toronto: Oxford University Press 1986), 1–8.

64 Ibid., 15.

65 Ibid., 156, 149–50; see also C.B. Macpherson, "The Social Sciences," in Julian Park, ed., *The Culture of Contemporary Canada* (Toronto: Ryerson Press 1957), 190–7.

66 Felix Walter, "Modern Language Teaching in Canadian Universities," NCCU, *Proceedings* 1932, 44 – the author was an associate professor of French at the University of Toronto. See also Harris, *A History of Higher Education in Canada*, 385.

67 Walter, "Modern Language Teaching," 45.

68 Ibid., 46.

69 Ibid., 49.

70 Harris, *A History of Higher Education in Canada*, 385.

71 John A. Irving, "Philosophy," in Park, ed., *The Culture of Contemporary Canada*, 246.

72 Ibid., 246; A.B. McKillop, *A Disciplined Intelligence: Critical Inquiry and Canadian Thought in the Victorian Era* (Montreal: McGill-Queen's University Press 1979), chap. 6; Leslie Armour and Elizabeth Trott, *The Faces of Reason: An Essay on Philosophy and Culture in English Canada, 1850–1950* (Waterloo: Wilfrid Laurier University Press 1981), chaps. 7–8.

73 Jasen, "The English-Canadian Liberal Arts Curriculum," 211–18,

Armour and Trott, *The Faces of Reason*, chaps. 11, 12.

74 Armour and Trott, *The Faces of Reason*, 433.

75 Irving, "Philosophy," 256.

76 Ibid., 258. See also Michael Gauvreau, "Philosophy, Psychology, and History: George Sydney Brett and the Quest for a Social Science at the University of Toronto, 1910–1940," Canadian Historical Association, *Historical Papers* 1988, 209–36.

77 Armour and Trott, *The Faces of Reason*, 403–4, 258–60.

78 Ibid., 419.

79 Rupert Lodge, "Philosophy as Taught at the University of Manitoba," *Culture* 2 (1941): 430–4, cited in Jasen, "The English-Canadian Liberal Arts Curriculum," 216.

80 Lodge inspired Marshall McLuhan to pursue his interest in philosophy, and remembered McLuhan as his "most outstanding student": Marchand, *Marshall McLuhan*, 15, 28. See also Armour and Trott, *The Faces of Reason*, chaps. 11–12, on the work of Wilfred Keirstead, John Macdonald, and Henry Wright.

81 Armour and Trott, *The Faces of Reason*, 514–16.

82 On the teaching of theology, see Harris, *A History of Higher Education*, 399–400; George Rawlyk and Kevin Quinn, *The Redeemed of the Lord Say So: A History of Queen's Theological College, 1912–1970* (Kingston: Queen's Theological College 1980), chaps. 2–4; Charles M. Johnston, *McMaster University*, 2: 66–7; John G. Reid, *Mount Allison University*, 2: chap. 9. On fine arts, see Harris, *A History of Higher Education*, 420–3; and Watson and Kirkconnell, *The Humanities in Canada*, 220–8.

83 On the influence and development in a Canadian context of idealism, empiricism, positivism, common-sense philosophy, and regeneration, see A.B. McKillop, *A Disciplined Intelligence*; McKillop, *Contours of Canadian Thought*; S.E.D. Shortt, *The Search for an Ideal; Six Canadian Intellectuals and Their Convictions in an Age of Transition, 1890–1930*; Ramsay Cook, *The Regenerators: Social Criticism in Late Victorian English Canada*; Jasen, "The English-Canadian Liberal Arts Curriculum," 95–113.

84 See R.C. Wallace, *A Liberal Education in a Modern World* (Toronto: University of Toronto Press 1932), 17, 44; and Greenlee, *Robert Falconer: A Biography*, 123.

85 Peter Hampton, "Schools of Psychology," *Queen's Quarterly* 46, no. 3 (1939): 289.

86 Gauvreau, "Philosophy, Psychology, and History: George Sydney Brett and the Quest for a Social Science at the University of Toronto, 1910–1940," 226.

87 See, for example, Joseph Kett, especially on the work of Stanley Hall,

in *Rites of Passage: Adolescence in America, 1770 to the Present*
(New York: Basic Books 1977), chap. 5; Leila Gay Mitchell McKee,
"Voluntary Youth Organizations in Toronto, 1880–1930," doctoral diss.,
York University 1982, chaps. 2, 5, 6; Jasen, "The English Canadian
Liberal Arts Curriculum," 211–25; See also Mary J. Wright and C.
Roger Myers, eds., *History of Academic Psychology in Canada*
(Toronto: C.J. Hogrefe Inc. 1982), for discussion of curriculum and
research developments at individual universities.

88 Jasen, "The English Canadian Liberal Arts Curriculum," 220, 223;
Thomas M. Nelson, "Psychology at Alberta," in *History of Academic
Psychology*, 198. Courses at Alberta included legal and industrial
psychology. Norman J. Symons, a psychology professor and an avowed
Freudian, was forced to resign from King's College in Halifax in 1929
under somewhat mysterious circumstances. The case is discussed in
Henry Roper, "Religion and Intellectual Freedom on the Dalhousie
Campus in the 1920s: The Case of Norman J. Symons," paper presented
to conference, The Past and Future of Liberal Education, Mount Allison
University, Sackville, New Brunswick, April 1989.

89 Gauvreau, "Philosophy, Psychology and History," 229, 232, 235.

90 University of Manitoba Annual Report 1935–36, 36, UMA.

91 The test was being given at 527 colleges on the continent: University of
Western Ontario *Gazette*, 13 Dec. 1937. It had first been given to
medical students in 1934.

92 University of British Columbia calendar 1934–35, 135–6. See also
Dalhousie University calendar 1935–36, 83; University of Alberta
calendar 1935–36, 153–4; University of Saskatchewan calendar 1934–
35, 157; St Francis Xavier University calendar 1934–35, 55–8;
University of Toronto calendar 1935–36, 30; R.S. Harris, *A History of
Higher Education in Canada*, 417–18.

93 "Education in Psychology," by W., *Trail* (alumni magazine), ca 1935, 11.

94 Jasen, "The English-Canadian Liberal Arts Curriculum," 226.

95 Macpherson, "The Social Sciences," 185.

96 Harris, *A History of Higher Education*, 388.

97 Ian Drummond, *Political Economy at the University of Toronto: A
History of the Department, 1888–1982* (Toronto: University of Toronto
Governing Council 1983), 64–5.

98 Doug Owram, *The Government Generation: Canadian Intellectuals and
the State* (Toronto: University of Toronto Press 1986), 195, 201–2.

99 H.S. Ferns, *Reading from Left to Right: One Man's Political History*,
41; interview with Lawrence Read (ex-Dalhousie student), 8 Sept. 1983.
At McGill, according to ex-student David Lewis, political economist
Stephen Leacock taught his subject from an orthodox perspective, while
J.C. Hemmeon was more progressive, though not radical. See David

Lewis, *The Good Fight: Political Memoirs, 1909–58* (Toronto: Macmillan 1981), 24–5.
100 Owram, *The Government Generation*, 194–5; Carl Berger, *The Writing of Canadian History*, chap. 4; Macpherson, "The Social Sciences," 201–4; Drummond, *Political Economy*, 66.
101 Owram, *The Government Generation*, 213–18.
102 Ibid., chaps. 10–11; Michiel Horn, *The League for Social Reconstruction: Intellectual Origins of the Canadian Left* (Toronto: University of Toronto Press 1980). Two well-known Canadian followers of Keynes were Robert Bryce, who attended Harvard from 1935 to 1937 and returned to Canada in 1938 to work for the federal government, and Mabel Timlin, an economist at the University of Saskatchewan who lectured "all over North America": J.S. Thomson, *Yesteryears at the University of Saskatchewan, 1937–1949* (Saskatchewan: University of Saskatchewan 1969), 22–3; On Bryce, see John Kenneth Galbraith, *A Life in Our Times: Memoirs* (Boston: Houghton-Mifflin 1981), 90.
103 University of British Columbia calendar 1938–39, 113–18.
104 Cited in "A Safe Education," *Gateway*, 4 Mar. 1932. This view is consistent with that of graduate Milton Shulman, who wrote, "British, Canadian, and American economic history showed me the results of the American and Industrial Revolutions, but didn't explain the left wing, the depression, inflation, the gold standard, the things I actually wanted to understand ... In our last year the authorities thought us old enough to handle such dangerous explosives as Marx and Malthus": Milton Shulman, "I Am a Graduate of '34," *Canadian Magazine*, Dec. 1934, 47.
105 Barry Ferguson and Doug Owram, "Social Scientists and Public Policy from the 1920s through World War II," *Journal of Canadian Studies* 15, no. 4 (Winter 1980–81): 9.
106 Ibid., 9–10; Michiel Horn, "Academics and Canadian Social and Economic Policy in the Depression and War Years," *Journal of Canadian Studies* 13, no. 4 (Winter 1978–79): 3–10. For Innis's views, see "The Role of Intelligence: Some Further Notes," *Canadian Journal of Economics and Political Science* 1 (1935): 280–7. On "social citizenship," see Jasen, "The English-Canadian Liberal Arts Curriculum," 122–30.
107 Ferguson and Owram, "Social Scientists," 11.
108 Fred E. Griffin, "Business Looks at the Commerce Course," The *Manitoba Arts Review* 1, no. 2 (Fall 1938): 24–5.
109 W. Sherwood Fox, *Sherwood Fox of Western* (Toronto: Burns and MacEachern 1964), 144–5. See also Sherwood Fox on the value of business training, University of Western Ontario *Gazette*, 5 Feb. 1931.

110 *Queen's Journal*, 13 Feb. 1933.
111 "The New Criticism of Commerce," *University of Toronto Monthly* 33, no 2 (Nov 1932): 63; similar views are expressed in an untitled paper prepared for the press on the purposes and values of the new program in commerce at Dalhousie: President's Papers, Newspapers: Correspondence, Articles, 10 Dec. 1928, DUA; J. Friend Day, "Commercial Education in the University," *Graduate Chronicle* (UBC), Apr. 1931, 12; University of Western Ontario *Gazette*, 20 Oct. 1934; and comments of C.A. Ashley, University of Toronto, cited in Ian Drummond, *Political Economy*, 68.
112 Charles N Cochrane, "The Question of Commerce Courses in Universities," NCCU, *Proceedings* 1932, 62, 63, 69.
113 Frank Underhill, "Commerce Courses and the Arts Faculty," NCCU, *Proceedings* 1930, 79. Stephen Leacock's equally acerbic comments about commerce training were cited in the University of Western Ontario *Gazette*, 6 Mar. 1935.
114 Drummond, *Political Economy*, 55; Fred E. Griffin, "Business Looks at the Commerce Course," *Manitoba Arts Review* 1, no. 2 (Fall 1938): 24–5.
115 *Gateway*, 19 Mar. 1937.
116 N.F. Pullen, *Ubyssey*, 19 Feb. 1937.
117 See R.C. Wallace to approximately eighty employers in Alberta, 25 June 1935, and responding correspondence by forty-six company officials: Dean's Papers, Faculty of Arts, 1914–19, 41/12/11/424, UAA.
118 *Ubyssey*, citing Mr Salter Carson, BC manager of Henry Birks and Sons, 23 Feb. 1937. See also *McGill Daily*, editorial, cited in *Queen's Journal*, 14 Oct. 1931, which noted the competition that students entering business faced from those without university education.
119 On the earlier emergence of business education and a business culture in the U.S., see Lawrence R. Veysey, *The Emergence of the American University* (Chicago: University of Chicago Press 1965), 113; Burton Bledstein, *The Culture of Professionalism: The Middle Class and the Development of Higher Education in America* (New York: W.W. Norton and Co. 1976), 318–31; John S. Brubacher and Willis Rudy, *Higher Education in Transition: The History of American Colleges and Universities, 1663–1976* (New York: Harper and Row 1976), 292–302. On Canada, see Paul Axelrod, *Scholars and Dollars: Politics, Economics, and the Universities of Ontario, 1945–1980* (Toronto: University of Toronto Press 1982), 101–10.
120 Jasen, "The English-Canadian Liberal Arts Curriculum," 239.
121 University of Alberta calendar 1935–36, 202–4.
122 University of Western Ontario Faculty of Arts calendar 1935–36, 117–21.

123 J.A. Corry, *My Life and Work: A Happy Partnership* (Kingston: Queen's University 1981), 73–4.

124 Ibid., Macpherson, "The Social Sciences," 209–14; Drummond, *Political Economy*, 69.

125 Macpherson, "The Social Sciences," 214.

126 Ibid., 209.

127 Significant publications of the period included three books by R. McGregor Dawson: *The Civil Service of Canada* (1929), *Constitutional Issues in Canada* (1933), and *The Development of Dominion Status 1900–1936* (1937). They also included R.A. MacKay, *The Unreformed Senate of Canada* (1926); R.M. MacIver, *Canada* (1932); and W.P.M. Kennedy, *The Constitution of Canada: An Introduction to Its Development and Law* (London: Oxford 1922). Diccy's *Introduction to the Study of the Law of the Constitution*, originally published in 1889, was a popular British source.

128 R.M. MacIver, "The Department of Social Service as a Branch of the University," *University of Toronto Monthly* 19 (Feb. 1919): 100, cited in Jasen, "The English Canadian Liberal Arts Curriculum," 240.

129 Marlene Shore, *The Science of Social Redemption: McGill, the Chicago School, and the Origins of Social Research in Canada* (Toronto: University of Toronto Press 1987), 25.

130 Ibid., 95–120.

131 Ibid., chap 5.

132 London: Oxford 1940.

133 Jasen, "The English-Canadian Liberal Arts Curriculum," 243.

134 Ibid., 245.

135 Shore, *The Science of Social Redemption*, 265–6; Frost, *McGill University*, 2: 201–5. See also Allan Irving, "Leonard Marsh and the McGill Social Science Research Project," *Journal of Canadian Studies* 21, no. 2 (Summer 1986): 6–26.

136 S.D. Clark, "Sociology in Canada: An Historical Overview," *Canadian Journal of Sociology* 1, no. 2 (1975): 225–34.

137 This view on curricululm developments between the wars can be inferred from Patricia Jasen's excellent thesis, which has been cited throughout this chapter. Of course, academics such as Carleton Stanley and J.S. Thomson, also cited above, believed that the liberal arts, the university, and Western civilization were all in decline. In a provocative critique Clarence Karr chides both Canadian intellectual historians and the subjects they study for over-emphasizing "conflict" and "crisis" in their analyses of Canadian intellectual and cultural life from the late nineteenth to the mid-twentieth century. See his "What Happened to Canadian Intellectual History?" *Acadiensis* 18, no. 2 (Spring 1989): 158–74.

CHAPTER FOUR

1 See, for example, William J. Goode, "Community within a Community: The Professions," *American Sociological Review* 22 (1957): 194–200.

2 A recent book that reflects these traditional themes, yet remains curiously untouched by the critical literature cited below, is Kenneth M. Ludmerer, *Learning to Heal: The Development of American Medical Education* (New York: Basic Books 1985).

3 Randall Collins, *The Credential Society: An Historical Sociology of Education and Stratification* (New York: Academic Press 1979); M.S. Larson, *The Rise of Professionalism: A Sociological Analysis* (Berkeley: University of California Press 1977); Nicholas Abercrombie and John Urry, *Capital, Labour and the Middle Classes* (London: George Allen and Unwin 1983); George Rosen, *The Structure of American Medical Practice, 1875–1941* (Philadelphia: University of Pennsylvania 1983); David Noble, *America By Design: Science, Technology, and the Rise of Corporate Capitalism* (New York: Knopf 1977); Paul Starr, *The Social Transformation of American Medicine* (New York: Basic Books 1982); Burton Bledstein, *The Culture of Professionalism: The Middle Class and the Development of Higher Education in America* (New York: W.W. Norton and Co. Inc. 1976).

4 M.S. Larson, *The Rise of Professionalism*, xvii.

5 Rosen, *The Structure of American Medical Practice*, 65; A. Lawrence Lowell et al., *Final Report of the Commission on Medical Education* (New York: Office of the Director of the Study 1932), 91; Paul Starr, *The Social Transformation of American Medicine*, 118.

6 R.S. Harris, *A History of Higher Education in Canada, 1663–1960* (Toronto: University of Toronto Press 1976), 267–8; Starr, *The Social Transformation of American Medicine*, 105, 117–20; Ludmerer, *Learning to Heal*, chap. 9. As Starr notes, the accessibility of medicine to women, blacks, immigrants, and Jews, whose growing presence in the profession was believed to diminish doctors' professional image and status, was one casualty of the changes introduced at the beginning of the twentieth century (123–4). See also Gerald E. Markowitz and David Karl Rosner, "Doctors in Crisis: A Study of the Use of Medical Educational Reform to Establish Modern Professional Elitism in Medicine," *American Quarterly* 25 (March 1973): 95.

7 Rosen, *The Structure of American Medical Practice*, 40; S.E.D. Shortt, "'Before the Age of Miracles': The Rise, Fall, and Rebirth of General Practice in Canada, 1890–1940," in Charles Roland, ed., *Health, Disease and Medicine: Essays in Canadian History* (Hamilton: Hannah Institute 1984), 128–9.

8 William Johnston, *Before the Age of Miracles: Memoirs of a Country*

Doctor (Toronto: Fitzhenry and Whiteside 1972), 106 7.

9 W.B. Parson, "Medicine in the Thirties," *Canadian Doctor* 46, no. 1 (Jan. 1980): 69–70. Also Shortt, "Before the Age of Miracles," 128–9. For an account of the trials, tribulations, and rewards of being a country doctor (in Cape Breton), see D. Lamont MacMillan, *Memoirs of a Canadian Doctor* (Markham, Ont.: Paperjacks 1977). MacMillan graduated from Dalhousie in 1928. See also John Duffy, "American Perceptions of the Medical, Legal and Theological Professions," *Bulletin of the History of Medicine* 58, no. 1 (Spring 1984): 13: "Although the rising standard of living with its concomitant improvements in sanitation, water, and food supplies played the major role in reducing morbidity and mortality rates, the medical profession, through developments in microbiology and other fields, received most of the credit for improved health."

10 Mary Vipond, "A Canadian Hero of the 1920s: Dr. Frederick G. Banting," *Canadian Historical Review* 63, no. 4 (Dec. 1982): 482. See also Robert Falconer: "Through the scientific spirit, facts are drawn from a vast range of experience and are carefully observed, and are impartially weighed," Address to Graduates, 9 June 1910, *University of Toronto Monthly* 4, no. 9, (July 1910): 503–14, cited in Sandra Frances McRae, "'The Scientific Spirit' in Medicine at the University of Toronto, 1880–1910," doctoral diss., University of Toronto 1987, 299.

11 Rosen, *The Structure of American Medical Practice*, 62.

12 Ibid., 47; Morris J. Vogel, *The Invention of the Modern Hospital: Boston, 1870–1930* (Chicago: University of Chicago Press 1980); Starr, *The Social Transformation of American Medicine*, 145–6.

13 Shortt, "Before the Age of Miracles," 140.

14 Across the continent the percentage was 36.1. See also H.R. Clouston, "The Medical Curriculum as Viewed by a Country General Practitioner," *Canadian Medical Association Journal* 28 (Mar. 1933): 317–20.

15 *Final Report of the Commission on Medical Education*, 24.

16 Ibid., 124–5. On fee-splitting, see H. Alan Skinner, "Education and Medical Learning," *Canadian Medical Association Journal* 28 (Apr. 1931): 430. He also criticized rote learning. "If the student is to be taught only two things let us be sure that these be logic and the scientific method; then the facts will take care of themselves": 431.

17 C.F. Martin in *Canadian Doctor* 2, no. 5 (May 1936): 12.

18 *Final Report of the Commission on Medical Education*, 24. See also A.C. Corcoran, "The Student Looks at Medical Education," *Canadian Medical Association Journal* 28 (June 1933): "The student in the wards sometimes regards the patient as a more or less depersonalized disease, whose vitality is useful chiefly for the purpose of taking the history and

of illustrating the course of pathological process not yet stilled in a preservative nor frozen on printed page": 664.

19 Oswald Hall, "The Informal Organization of the Medical Profession," *Canadian Journal of Economics and Political Science* 12 (1946): 36.

20 Hall, "The Informal Organization," 42.

21 Ibid., 36..

22 *Final Report of the Commission on Medical Education*, 272.

23 Hall, "The Informal Organization," 34, 39.

24 John Avery (acting dean of medicine) to President Kerr, President's Papers 1936–42, 3386–10, Student Associations, Clubs: Medical Student Undergraduate Society, UAA.

25 Hall, "The Informal Organization," 39.

26 Ibid., 34, 37.

27 Ibid., 34.

28 Editorial, *University of Toronto [Undergraduate] Medical Journal* 13, no. 5 (March 1936): 147–8; see also J.C. Gray, "Vocational Training for Women," ibid. 11, no. 4 (Feb. 1934): 115–17.

29 Hall, "The Informal Organization," 31.

30 *Queen's Journal*, 21 Mar. 1939.

31 McGill Medical Banquet, and other documents, MG 2023, MUA.

32 J.H. Goodes, "Organized Medicine," *University of Western Ontario Undergraduate Medical Journal*, 7, no. 4 (1937): 173.

33 Robert Bothwell and John R. English, "Pragmatic Physicians: Canadian Medicine and Health Care Insurance, 1910–1945,' in S.E.D. Shortt, ed., *Medicine in Canadian Society: Historical Perspectives* (Montreal: McGill-Queen's University Press 1981), 479–93. The BC plan was not passed. See also H.E. MacDermot, *History of the Canadian Medical Association* (Toronto: Murray 1958), who traces debates over the issue of state health insurance.

34 James Stevenson, "Unity and Strength," *Canadian Doctor* 11 (May 1936): 15.

35 J.H. Goodes, "Organized Medicine," 173.

36 A survey of Hamilton doctors found that betweeen 1929 to 1932, the percentage of doctors engaged in remunerative work slipped from 77.5 per cent to 50 per cent: Bothwell and English, "Pragmatic Physicians," 482.

37 The CMA plan would have provided free medical services to those with incomes under $2400: Bothwell and English, 484.

38 C. David Naylor, "Canada's First Doctors' Strike: Medical Relief in Winnipeg, 1932–4," in Michiel Horn, ed., *The Depression: Responses to Economic Crisis* (Toronto: Copp Clark Pitman 1988), 105.

39 Colin M. MacLeod, *McGill Medical Undergraduate Journal* 1, no. 2 (Jan. 1932): 12.

40 R.A. Falconer, "The Last Quarter of a Century of the Faculty of Medicine," *University of Toronto Medical Journal* 9, no. 1 (Nov. 1931): 5–7.

41 Falconer, "The Last Quarter," 7.

42 *University of Toronto Medical Journal* 8, no. 4 (Feb. 1931): 112–13; see also 7, no. 2 (Dec. 1930): 30; and 8, no. 5 (Mar. 1931): 147. See also "From the Student's Viewpoint," *University of Western Ontario Undergraduate Medical Journal* 11, no. 4 (1934): 99; C. Corcoran, "The Student Looks at Medical Education," *Canadian Medical Association Journal* 28 (June 1933): 662–5; H. Alan Skinner, "Education and Medical Learning," *Canadian Medical Association Journal* 28 (Apr. 1933): 431–2; Ludmerer, *Learning to Heal*, 253–4.

43 *Final Report of the Commission on Medical Education*, 174.

44 Ibid., 143.

45 Ibid., 176; Editorial, *University of Western Ontario Undergraduate Medical Journal* 7 no. 2 (1937): 81.

46 Martin Kaufman, "American Medical Education," in Ronald L. Numbers, ed., *The Education of American Physicians: Historical Essays* (Berkeley: University of California Press 1980), 22. See also C.F. Martin, "Medical Education and Medical Practice," *Bulletin of the New York Academy of Medicine*, Dec. 1930.

47 Dr H.B. Van Wyck, "Address to the Graduating Year," *University of Toronto Medical Journal* 7, no. 1 (May 1930): 220–2, while a student, expressed uncertainty about how well medical schools succeeded in producing "cultured gentlemen versed in the scientific method." A.C. Corcoran, "The Student Looks at Medical Education," *Canadian Medical Association Journal* 28 (June 1933): 662.

48 James Miller, "The Teaching of the Preliminary and of the Basal Medical Sciences," *Canadian Medical Association Journal* 27 (May 1933): 550.

49 Clement C. Clog, "Medical Education in the United States," *McGill Medical Undergraduate Journal* 1, no. 1 (Nov. 1931): 26. See also statistics on admission to the University of Manitoba Medical School in chap. 2.

50 McGill University calendar 1935–36.

51 H.P. Macey, "The McGill Medical School of the Past, 1825–1920," *McGill Medical Undergraduate Journal* 1, no. 1 (Nov. 1931): 8.

52 For other accounts of the McGill system, see *McGill Medical Undergraduate Journal* 5, no. 3 (Mar. 1936): 4; C.R. Drew, "A Discussion of the Experiment in Medical Education at McGill," ibid. 7, no. 2 (Jan. 1937): 37–47; *Canadian Medical Association Journal* 34, no. 3 (Mar. 1936): 340.

53 See H.V. Nelles, "Introduction," in T.C. Keefer, *Philosophy of Railroads* (Toronto: University of Toronto Press 1972), ix–lvii.

54 J. Rodney Millard, *The Master Spirit of the Age: Canadian Engineers and the Politics of Professionalism* (Toronto: University of Toronto Press 1988), chap. 1 and passim; David Noble, *America By Design: Science, Technology, and the Rise of Corporate Capitalism* (New York: Alfred Knopf 1977), 39–41.

55 *EJ.* 16, no. 3 (Mar. 1933): 137; see also "Number of Engineers and Related Professions Employed by Industry and Public Service Corporations, 1941," DBS, *Supply and Demand of the Professions in Canada* (Ottawa 1945), 28, 13. Some two thousand of these were in active wartime service. See also 1937 report of same title, 21.

56 Dean C.H. Mitchell, "Applied Science and Engineering: Its Relation to Everyday Life," *University of Toronto Monthly* 38, no. 7 (Apr. 1938): 177–9.

57 *EJ.* 13, no. 2 (Feb. 1930): 126; "The Professional Status of the Engineer," *EJ.* 14, no. 2 (Feb. 1931): 120–1; "Engineering as a Profession," editorial in *EJ.* 17, no. 8 (Aug. 1934): 371; see also Noble, *America By Design*, 29–31, 310.

58 Noble, *America By Design*, 310. See also Millard, *The Master Spirit of the Age*, chap. 3; *EJ.* 16, no. 3 (Mar. 1933): 137.

59 "Report of the Committee on Development of the Engineering Institute of Canada," *EJ.* 15, no. 10 (Oct. 1932): 483–90.

60 "Engineering as a Profession," *EJ.* 17, no. 8 (Aug. 1934): 370; Millard, *The Master Spirit of the Age*, chap. 9.

61 DBS, *Higher Education in Canada, 1936–1938* (Ottawa 1939), 28.

62 "The Professional Status of the Engineer," *EJ.* 14, no. 2 (Feb. 1931): 121; also *EJ.* 16, no. 3 (Mar. 1933): 137; "Report of Committee on Unemployment," *EJ.*, 16, no. 10 (Oct. 1933): 138; DBS, *Supply and Demand in the Professions* (Ottawa 1945), 36. These statistics refer to the salaries of male professionals and are based on my averaging of 1931 and 1941 figures. Dentists earned $1961 each annually, clergymen $1333, and social-welfare workers $1678.

63 "Engineering as a Profession," *EJ.* 17, no. 8 (Aug. 1934): 370. As Randall Collins has argued, "The strength of doctors and lawyers vis-à-vis their clients is precisely in the fact that their cures or legal manoeuvres are not necessarily efficacious, and hence they are held much less accountable for their failures. Engineers' and technicians' work is productive labor, that of doctors and lawyers is primarily political labor. The one produces real outcomes; the other tends to manipulate appearances and beliefs": *The Credential Society*, 175.

64 Millard, *The Master Spirit of the Age*, 37–8. Quotation from an article on the role of the EIC by Past President H.H. Vaughan, *EJ.* 20, no. 8 (Aug. 1937): 671.

65 *EJ.* 13, no. 1 (Jan. 1930): 71.

66 *EJ.* 12, no. 2 (Mar. 1930): 212.

67 Millard, *The Master Spirit of the Age* , 146.

68 "A Report of the Commmittee on Development of the Engineering Institute of Canada," *EJ.* 15, no. 10 (Oct. 1932): 483.

69 *EJ.* 13, no. 3 (Mar. 1930): 189–91.

70 P.M. Sauder, "The Need for an Active Associations' Dominion Council," *EJ.* 19, no. 2 (Feb. 1936): 113.

71 *EJ.* 21, no. 3 (Mar. 1938): 152–3.

72 *EJ.* 20, no. 7 (Jul. 1937): 583–4. The discussions leading up to the vote in 1937 were recorded in great detail in several issues of *EJ.*

73 Noble, *American By Design*, 39.

74 Harris, *A History of Higher Education*, 403.

75 DBS, *The Canada Year Book 1941* (Ottawa 1941), 892.

76 University of British Columbia calendar 1938–39, 161–2.

77 Ibid., 165–6. See also University of Toronto calendar, Faculty of Applied Science and Engineering 1938–39, 25.

78 Frank Underhill, "Commerce Courses and the Arts Faculty," NCCU, *Proceedings* 1930, 80.

79 *EJ.* 13, no. 2 (Mar. 1930): 183–4.

80 R.L. Sackett, "Character Building," *Journal of Engineering Education* 17, no. 3 (Nov. 1936): 187–92.

81 Daniel W. Mead, "Instruction as Professional Life and Conduct," *Journal of Engineering Education* 27, no. 1 (Sept. 1936): 31–6.

82 "A Report of the Committeee on Development of the Engineering Institute of Canada," *EJ.* 15, no. 10 (Oct.1932): 483–90, and *EJ.* 16, no. 12 (Dec. 1933): 532.

83 *EJ.* 17, no. 3 (Mar. 1934): 153.

84 R.G Segsworth, "The Thirties," in Robin S. Harris and Ian Montagnes, eds., *Cold Iron and Lady Godiva: Engineering Education at Toronto, 1920–1970* (Toronto: University of Toronto Press 1973), 69.

85 "What Kinds of Men Are Needed in Engineering Industries?" (author not identified), in Report to Sir A.W. Currie, principal of McGill University, from Faculty of Applied Science, Apr. 1931, RG2 C36, Principal's Papers, MUA.

86 University of Toronto calendar, Faculty of Applied Science and Engineering 1938–39, 25. See also Noble, *America By Design*, 312–16, which discusses the emergence of this view in the United States.

87 *EJ.* 13, no. 9 (Sept. 1930): 539–42.

88 Harris, *A History of Higher Education*, 156–60, 264–6, 400–1; Brian D. Bucknall, C.H. Baldwin, J. David Lakin, "Pedants, Practitioners and Prophets: Legal Education at Osgoode Hall to 1957," *Osgoode Hall Law Journal* 6, no. 1 (Oct. 1968): 137–229; Curtis Cole, "A Hand to Shake the Tree of Knowledge: Legal Education in Ontario, 1871–1923,"

Interchange 17, no. 3 (1986): 15–27; C. Ian Kyer and Jerome E. Bickenbach, *The Fiercest Debate: Cecil Wright, the Benchers, and Legal Education in Ontario, 1923–1957* (Toronto: University of Toronto Press 1987), intro., chap. 1; John Willis, *A History of Dalhousie Law School* (Toronto: University of Toronto Press 1979); Michael Hayden, *Seeking a Balance*, 129–31; Stanley B. Frost, *McGill University*, 2: 153–8.

89 Harris, *A History of Higher Education*, 401.

90 Bucknall et al., "Pedants, Practitioners and Prophets," 186.

91 F.R. Scott, "The Future of the Legal Profession," *Alarm Clock*, Jan. 1933, reprinted in Michiel Horn, ed., *A New Endeavour: Selected Political Essays, Letters, and Addresses* (Toronto: University of Toronto Press 1986), 10, 13.

92 Kyer and Bickenbach, *The Fiercest Debate*, 110.

93 Ibid., 108.

94 *Canadian Bar Review* 11, no. 9 (June 1933): 629. For a discussion of similar debates and developments within American legal education, see Robert Stevens, *Law School: Legal Education in America from the 1850s to the 1980s* (Chapel Hill and London: University of North Carolina Press 1983), esp. chaps. 8–11.

95 Kyer and Bickenbach, *The Fiercest Debate*, 115–16. See also J.A. Corry, *My Life and Work: A Happy Partnership* (Kingston: Queen's University 1981), 62; and Michael Hayden, *Seeking a Balance*, 130–1, on Saskatchewan; John Willis, *A History of Dalhousie Law School*, 131–3; John E. Read, "Fifty Years of Legal Education at Dalhousie," *Canadian Bar Review* 11, no. 6 (June 1933): 392–5; Stanley Frost, *McGill*, 2: 156; Report of the Manitoba Law School, University of Manitoba Annual Report 1935–36, 124.

96 Jerome Frank, general counsel for the Agricultural Adjustment Administration, *Canadian Bar Review*, 12, no. 12 (Feb. 1934): 105.

97 *The Fiercest Debate*, 129.

98 *The Fiercest Debate*, chap. 2.

99 Bucknall et al., "Pedants, Practitioners and Prophets," 196–7; *The Fiercest Debate*, 113–14. The authors do express surprise at the inconsistency of this in light of the profession's desire to reduce the glut of lawyers on the market.

100 The report was printed in the *Canadian Bar Review*, from which the following quotations, unless otherwise indicated, are drawn: "Education for the Bar: Report of the Special Committee of Students of Osgoode Hall," *Canadian Bar Review* 12, no. 2 (Mar. 1934): 144–60.

101 Willis, *A History of Dalhousie Law School*, 131.

102 *The Fiercest Debate*, 144–5.

103 Harris, *A History of Higher Education*, 408. The five schools were Dalhousie, McGill, Montreal, Toronto, and Alberta. See W.J. Gies,

Dental Education in the United States and Canada, Carnegie
Foundation for the Advancement of Teaching, bulletin no. 19 (New York
1926); DBS, *Supply and Demand in the Professions* (Ottawa 1945), 16.
See also the May 1965 issue (31, no. 5) of the *Canadian Dental
Association Journal*, which includes brief historical articles on Canada's
dental schools.

104 D.W. Gullet, *A History of Dentistry in Canada* (Toronto: University of
Toronto Press 1971), 187.

105 Gullet, *A History of Dentistry*, 187–8; DBS, *Supply and Demand in the
Professions* (1945), 36.

106 Gullet, *A History of Dentistry*, 191.

107 Harris, *A History of Higher Education*, 405.

108 University of Saskatchewan, President's Report 1931–32, 24–34, USA.
See also University of Manitoba Annual Report 1935–36, 80–7, UMA;
also DBS, *Supply and Demand in the Professions* (1937), 6, and report
of same title (1945), 14.

109 Interview with Olga Volkhoff, 2–2, 12, UBCA.

110 Report of the President, University of Manitoba Annual Report
1935–36, 5.

111 In Report of the Board of Governors and President of the University of
Alberta 1931–32, 52–3, UAA.

112 Harris, *A History of Higher Education*, 280, citing A.S. Morton,
Sakatchewan: The Making of a University (Toronto: University of
Toronto Press 1959), 37.

113 James Sutherland Thomson, *Yesteryears at the University of
Saskatchewan, 1937–1949* (Saskatoon: University of Saskatchewan
1969), 17–19.

114 For accounts of the development of agricultural education in eastern
Canada, at Guelph and McGill, see J.F. Snell, *Macdonald College of
McGill University: A History from 1904–1955* (Montreal: McGill
University 1963), and A.M. Ross, *The College on the Hill* (Guelph:
University of Guelph 1974).

115 See exchange of correspondence between J.S. Thomson, president of the
University of Saskatchewan, and Carleton Stanley, president of
Dalhousie, 16 Dec., 28 Dec. 1938, Presidential Papers II, B-138, USA;
R.M. Wallace, principal, University College, University of Toronto,
"Culture: The Essential Background of Science," *University of Toronto
Monthly* 30, no. 9 (June 1930): 413–18.

116 See Harris, *A History of Higher Education*, 404–6; J.W.B. Sisam,
Forestry Education at Toronto (Toronto: University of Toronto Press
1961); H.E. Videto, "The Growth of Forestry at the University of New
Brunswick," in A.G. Bailey, ed., *The University of New Brunswick
Memorial Volume* (Fredericton 1950), 87–97; G. Sonnedecker, E.W.

Steib, D.R. Kennedy, *One Hundred Years of Pharmacy in Canada*
(Toronto: Canadian Academy of the History of Pharmacy 1969);
Commission on Pharmaceutical Services, *Pharmacy in a New Age*
(Toronto: Canadian Pharmaceutical Association, 1971).

117 R.C. Wallace, *Edmonton Journal*, 8 Oct. 1936.

118 1 June 1932.

119 J.F. Macdonald "Can First Class Honours Women Graduates be Induced
To Take Up Secondary School Teaching as a Life Work?" NCCU,
Proceedings 1930, 106–7; Carleton Stanley, Inauguration Address,
9 Oct. 1931, Board of Governors Minutes, 29 Oct. 1931, DUA. "After a
certain age," Stanley wrote, "boys can be educated only by men": NCCU,
Proceedings 1930, 25.

120 NCCU, *Proceedings 1930*, 277. See also Charles M. Johnston and John
Weaver, *Student Days: An Illustrated History of Student Life at
McMaster University from the 1890s to the 1980s* (Hamilton:
McMaster University Alumnni Association 1986), 50. These were not
peculiarly Canadian attitudes. See Peter N. Stearns, *Be a Man! Males in
Modern Society* (New York: Holmes and Meier 1979), 105.

121 B.S. to Robert Stamp, private collection, 2 Jan. 1981. "Had registration
in the Faculty of Medicine at Queen's been open to women in 1935 to
1939, I would have become a physician," recalled Eleanor Clarke Hay,
who obtained a doctorate in pharmacology at McGill. See Hay,
"Change and Changing," in Joy Parr, ed., *Still Running…: Personal
Stories by Queen's Women Celebrating the Fiftieth Anniversary of the
Marty Scholarship* (Kingston: Queen's University Alumnae Association
1987), 41.

122 Alan Morley, "Are Women Good Scientists?" *Vancouver Sun*, 23 Dec.
1935.

123 *Ubyssey*, 8 Nov. 1935. See also Judith Fingard, "Gender and Inequality
at Dalhousie: Faculty Women before 1950," *Dalhousie Review* 64, no. 4
(Winter 1984–85): 687–703.

124 DBS, *Supply and Demand in the Professions in Canada* (1945), 56.

125 In the social-welfare area, men earned substantially more than women.
In 1931, male social workers earned $1678, versus $1086 for women;
male librarians earned $2046, compared to $1115 for women: DBS,
Higher Education in Canada, 1936– 38 (Ottawa 1939), 32. On teaching
salaries, see ibid., 8. See also DBS, *Supply and Demand in The
Professions, 1945*, 11, 31. It notes that teachers' salaries had suffered
"severe reductions" since 1930, averaging in 1936 $579 for rural
teachers and $1095 for urban teachers, with major regional variations.
Paid only $808 annually, nurses were among the lowest-paid
professionals in the country.

126 See Diana Pedersen, "'The Scientific Training of Mothers': The

Campaign for Domestic Science in Ontario Schools, 1890–1913," in R.
Jarrell and Arnold A. Roos, eds., *Critical Issues in the the History of
Canadian Science, Technology and Medicine* (Thornhill, Ont.: HSTC
Publications 1983), 178–94; Barbara Riley, "Six Saucepans to One:
Domestic Science vs the Home in British Columbia 1900–1930," in
Barbara K. Latham and R.J. Pazdro, eds., *Not Just Pin Money: Selected
Essays on the History of Women's Work in British Columbia* (Victoria:
Camousan College 1984), 184–93.

127 See St Francis Xavier University calendar 1935–36, which lists the
courses offered. See also DBS, *Supply and Demand in the Professions*
(1945), 12, which notes more "progressive attitudes towards nutrition."

128 "UBC to Get Home Economics This Fall," *Alumni Chronicle*, July 1943.

129 "Why a College Course?" *Managra* 25, no. 6 (Apr. 1932).

130 James Struthers, "'Lord Give Us Men': Women and Social Work in
English Canada, 1918–1953," Candian Historical Association,
Historical Papers 1983: 101. See also John Donald MacQueen Bliss,
"A History of the School of Social Work of the University of British
Columbia, 1929–54," MSW thesis, University of British Columbia 1954.

131 Margaret Ray, "What Becomes of the University Woman?" *University of
Toronto Monthly* (Jan. 1930): 136. In a debate on co-education at the
University of Manitoba, a student, Gerda Hiebert, argued that better-
educated and professional women were indirectly contributing to family
life. "Women no longer need to marry for a meal ticket, therefore they
can choose, and make their marriage a career": *Manitoban*, 21 Feb.
1930.

132 Cited in *Gateway*, 18 Dec. 1931.

133 *Queen's Journal*, 3 Mar. 1933, 6 Dec. 1935.

134 Wallace to H.P. Whidden, 7 Feb. 1933, President's Papers, University of
Alberta, 1928–36, McMaster University: Correspondence, 3.2.10.5–6,
UAA. See also C.G.S Stone and F. Joan Garnett, *Brandon College: A
History 1899–1967* (Brandon: Brandon University 1969); University of
Western Ontario, President's Report 1933–34, 17; and W.F. Tamblyn,
These Sixty Years (London: University of Western Ontario 1938), 109.

135 Report of the President, University of Manitoba Annual Report 1935–
36, 5; University of Manitoba Students' Union, Report of the Student
Commission of the University of Manitoba 1932–33, 18, UMA.

136 *Ubyssey*, 16 Feb. 1934.

137 W.M., *Dalhousie Gazette*, 3 Dec. 1937.

138 *Gateway*, 5 Feb. 1937.

139 Report of the Student Commission of the University of Manitoba, 15.

140 Cited in Rupert F. Legget, "The Lecture System," *Queen's Quarterly* 46,
no. 2 (1938): 208–9.

141 Hayden, *Seeking a Balance*, 186. See also *Queen's Journal*, 22 Nov.

1935, which describes the "ideal" lecturer. Various interviewees recalled popular and unpopular professors across the country, and personal anecdotes can be found in Michael Taft, *Inside These Greystone Walls: An Anecdotal History of the University of Saskatchewan* (Saskatoon: University of Saskatchewan 1984), 162–3.

142 "Satiric Humour of Stephen Leacock Scorches Campus," *Ubyssey*, 8 Jan. 1937.

143 "Soon I shall be educated. Ain't it grand?" from *Gateway*, reprinted in *Queen's Journal*, 25 Jan. 1938.

144 McGill University calendar 1935–36, 480, outlines formal dress requirements. See also Taft, *Inside These Greystone Walls*, 205.

145 Report of the Student Commission of the University of Manitoba, 25.

CHAPTER FIVE

1 "School and College," 2, 6: speech to the meeting of the National Conference of Canadian Universities, June 1936, President's Office Papers, DUA. His views were shared by Hamilton Fyfe, the principal of Queen's University; see Frederick Gibson, *'To Serve and Yet Be Free': Queen's University*, vol. 2, *1919–1961* (Montreal: McGill-Queen's University Press 1983), 109–10.

2 Sidney Smith, president, University of Manitoba, President's Report 1934–35, I, UMA.

3 *Queen's Journal*, 1 Oct. 1935, 15 Nov. 1932.

4 Such charges were made by M.P. for Brome Missisquot, F.H. Pickel, House of Commons *Debates*, 2 Apr. 1935, 2436. And in his convocation address in 1930, R.W. Boyle referred to similar public perceptions, which he admitted were distortions about the reality of student life: Convocation Address, *The Trail*, publication of the Alumni Association, University of Alberta, Oct. 1930, 32, UAA.

5 Paula Fass, *The Damned and the Beautiful: American Youth in the 1920s* (New York: Oxford 1977).

6 *Gateway*, 16 Oct. 1934. For other examples, see *Dalhousie Gazette*, 17 Feb. 1928; University of Western Ontario *Gazette*, 9 Oct. 1930; *Gateway*, 20 Nov. 1930; *Queen's Journal*, 10 Mar. 1931; *Ubyssey*, 19 Feb. 1937.

7 *Sheaf*, 3 Nov. 1932. According to Edward Fox, an exchange student from the University of Western Ontario attending the University of British Columbia, a shortage of funds during the Depression had contributed to the disappearence from the campus of the "college type": *Ubyssey*, 29 Sept. 1933.

8 Cited in *Sheaf*, 25 Feb. 1932.

9 See W.H. Cowley and Willard Waller, "A Study of Student Life: The

Appraisal of Student Traditions as a Field of Research," *Journal of Higher Education* 6, no. 3 (Mar. 1935): 132–42; Helen Lefkowitz Horowitz, *Campus Life: Undergraduate Cultures from the End of the Eighteenth Century to the Present* (New York: Alfred A Knopf 1987), chap. 2; David Allmendinger, *Paupers and Scholars: The Transformation of Student Life in Nineteenth Century New England* (New York: St Martin's Press 1975), chaps. 6–8. There is less information about student life in late nineteenth-century Canada. But see John G. Reid, *Mount Allison University, 1843–1963*, 2 vols. (Toronto: University of Toronto Press 1984), passim; Hilda Neatby, *'And Not To Yield': Queen's University*, vol. 1, *1841–1917* (Montreal: McGill-Queen's University Press 1978), passim; and W.G. MacElhinney, "The Engineering Society," in R.S. Harris and Ian Montagnes, eds., *Cold Iron and Lady Godiva: Engineering Education at Toronto, 1920–1972* (Toronto: University of Toronto Press 1973), 23–6.

10 *Ubyssey*, 1 Mar. 1935, editorial. For a discussion of the role of student government, see Report of the President of the Students' Council, University of Alberta, 1934–35, Arthur Bierwagon, president, Student Council Minute Book 1934–35, UAA. See also the objects of the Alma Mater Society, University of British Columbia, as described in Constitution of the Alma Mater Society, 1 May 1934, University of British Columbia Alma Mater Society Records 1933–34, folder 1–1, UBCA.

11 University of Western Ontario, President's Report 1930–31, 22, UWOA. Sherwood Fox was president. At the University of Saskatchewan, "The purpose of the Students' Representative Council shall be to promote the general interests of the students; to constitute a recognized medium of communication between the University authorities, the public and the students; and except where otherwise provided, to supervise and control all student organizations and the conduct and activities of students in connection with the University": *Sheaf*, 9 Oct. 1930.

12 The list of student activities can be found in annual yearbooks, student newspapers, and archive records: see, for example, *Evergreen and Gold* (University of Alberta yearbook), 1934–35; *Old McGill* (McGill yearbook), 1939–40; and Student Activities: Committee on Student Organizations, 1935–36, RG2 C52, MUA. Although they tended to face more restrictions on their social activities, students in religious colleges, such as Wesley, McMaster, and Mount Allison, shared the common student culture. See A.G. Bedford, *The University of Winnipeg: A History of the Founding Colleges* (Toronto: University of Toronto Press 1976), 203; C.M. Johnston and John Weaver, *Student Days: An Illustrated History of Student Life at McMaster University from the 1890s to the 1980s* (Hamilton: McMaster University Alumni

Association 1986), chap. 4; Reid, *Mount Allison University,* 2: 109–12. Student activities are discussed in more detail below.

13 Keith Walden, "Hazes, Hustles, Scraps and Stunts: Initiations at the University of Toronto, 1880–1925," in Paul Axelrod and John G. Reid, eds., *Youth, University, and Canadian Society: Essays in the Social History of Canadian Higher Education* (Montreal: McGill-Queen's University Press 1989), 112.

14 *Queen's Journal,* 4 Oct. 1929.

15 Johnston and Weaver, *Student Days,* 45; Michael Taft, *Inside These Greystone Walls: An Anecdotal History of the University of Saskatchewan* (Saskatoon: University of Saskatchewan 1984), 35–41; *Queen's Journal,* 28 Nov. 1930, where Professor Prince explains the purpose of initiation.

16 *Ubyssey,* 28 Sept. 1937; *Queen's Journal,* 7 Oct. 1932; *McGill Daily,* 11, 17 Oct. 1930; Axelrod, "Moulding the Middle Class: Student Life at Dalhousie University in the 1930s," *Acadiensis* 15, no. 1 (Fall 1985): 105. On the invasion of theatres, see Keith Walden, "Respectable Hooligans: Male Toronto College Students Celebrate Hallowe'en, 1884–1910," *Canadian Historical Review* 68, no. 1 (Mar. 1987): 1–34.

17 Three UBC students found intoxicated at a university function were fined twenty-five dollars by the Students' Council and barred from university dances for the rest of the term: *Ubyssey,* 4 Feb. 1930. See also Minutes of Meeting of the Discipline Committee, 17 Jan. 1935, in Faculty Committee on Student Affairs Records, UBCA; and report on activities of Alma Mater Society Court, *Queen's Journal,* 27 Feb. 1931.

18 Dorothy McMurray, *Four Principals of McGill* (Montreal: Graduates Society of McGill University 1974), 21–2. Report of the Provost (J.M. MacEachen), in Report of the Board of Governors of the University of Alberta 1931–32, 24–32, UAA, provides a detailed account of the advantages and strains involved in student self-discipline. Dean K.W. Taylor of McMaster noted, "the delegation of the students themselves of the control of general student discipline is the oldest and most general form of student self-government ... [and] has proved highly satisfactory": NCCU, *Proceedings* 1939, 28–33.

19 University of Saskatchewan calendar 1929–30, 22, USA.

20 Gerald Friesen, "Principal J.H. Riddell: The Sane and Safe Leader of Wesley College," in Dennis L. Butcher et al., eds., *Prairie Spirit: Perspectives on the Heritage of the United Church of Canada in the West* (Winnipeg: University of Manitoba Press 1985), 258.

21 R.C. Wallace to A. Matheson, 27 Sept. 1929, President's Papers, 1928–36, University of Alberta, Student and Alumni Affairs, Initiation: Correspondence, 3281.5, UAA; Arthur Currie to Bill Pender et al., 6 Mar. 1930, in which he said there was no proof that McGill students

were involved in the disruption of Lowe's theatre, and the university therefore could not assume liability for the damage caused: Principal's Papers: Students, RG2 C52, MUA. See also J.S.Thomson to G. McDonald, 23 Mar. 1939, in which the president seeks more information from police about the allegedly unruly behaviour of some Saskatchewan students: Presidential Papers, ser. II, B-53, USA. For a discussion of efforts at Saskatchewan to control raffles, lotteries, and gambling following unfavourable public reports of these activities, see Charles A. Rowles to J.S. Thomson, 4 Feb. 1938, and Thomson to Rowles, 7 Feb. 1938, Presidential Papers, ser. II, B-177, USA.

22 Carleton Stanley to Judson Conrad, 2 Oct. 1939, Correspondence: Student Misdemeanours, President's Office Papers, DUA.

23 C.G. Stone and F. Joan Garnett, *Brandon College: A History, 1899–1967* (Brandon: Brandon University 1969), 137.

24 Walter H. Johns, *A History of the University of Alberta* (Edmonton: University of Alberta Press 1981), 141–5.

25 Appeal Book, Supreme Court of Alberta, Appellate Division, Between Charles J.A. Powlett and Charles H.A. Powlett and the University of Alberta, the Governors of the University of Alberta, and the Senate of the University of Alberta, Oct. 1933. Copy in Hon. J.H. Hyndman Papers, MG 30 E 182, transcript, vol. 2, 492–525, NA.

26 Ibid., vol. 3, 1210–16.

27 Students at St Francis Xavier University in Antigonish, Nova Scotia, had to promise on their registration forms not to "favour or take part in the initiation or hazing of other students": St Francis Xavier University calendar 1935–36, 126. See also Johns, *A History of the University of Alberta*, 141–2; *Maclean's*, 1 Sept. 1934, 34; *Sheaf*, 9 Nov. 1934; *Gateway*, 23 Jan. 1934; *Manitoban*, 31 Oct. 1933; *Globe*, 31 Oct. 1933; *Varsity*, 27, 30 Sept. 1935. Initiations even returned to Alberta: interview with Wilfred Bowker, 7 July 1984. For comparative anecdotal accounts of initiation, see Harry Bruce, "Hazing Just Isn't What It Used To Be," *Dalhousie Alumni Magazine*, Fall 1986, 25–7.

28 Paula Fass, *The Damned and the Beautiful*, 142–57; G. Kurt Piehler, "Phi Beta Kappa: The Invention of an Academic Tradition," *History of Education Quarterly* 28, no. 2 (Summer 1988): 207–29; James McLachlan, "The 'Choice of Hercules': American Student Societies in the Early Nineteenth Century," in Lawrence Stone, ed., *The University in Society*, vol. 2 (Princeton: Princeton University Press 1974), 449–94; John Gillis, *Youth and History* (New York: Academic Press), 77–91; Lefkowitz Horowitz, *Campus Life*, 26–9.

29 *Queen's Journal*, 6 Feb. 1934; also Gibson, *Queen's University*, 2: 105; extracts from "Undergraduates – A Study of Morale in Twenty-three American Colleges and Universities," 1928, copy in President's

Papers, 1928–36, University of Alberta, General: Reference Material, 3287.2, UAA. Figures on McGill and Toronto drawn from appendix to this report. See also Margaret Fisher Wendell, "I'd Abolish Sororities!" *Chatelaine*, Mar. 1933, 24, 36.

30 Memorandum by W.A.R. Kerr, President's Papers, 1928–36, General: Reference Material, 3287.2, UAA.

31 Chester Prevey, John Corley, and several others to R.C. Wallace, n.d., ca Mar. 1935, who successfully petitioned the University of Alberta for recognition of a chapter of Psi Epsilon: Presidents Paper's, 1928–36, General: Correspondence: Reports, 3287.1, UAA. See also "Sororities Have a Place," *Chatelaine*, June 1933, 13, 26.

32 Arthur Currie to A.S. Mackenzie, 3 Dec. 1924, Student Activities: Fraternities and Sororities, RG2 C52, Principal's Papers, MUA.

33 President's Papers, 1936–42, University of Alberta, Fraternities, Sororities: General Correspondence, 3387.1, UAA; Minutes of Administrative Council, 17 Sept. 1932, Administrative Council Box, UWOA; Carleton Stanley to Sherwood Fox, 21 Feb. 1935, Correspondence: Fraternities' File, President's Office Papers, DUA.

34 In 1936–37, 34 per cent of University of Western Ontario women were members of one of the three sororities: University of Western Ontario, President's Report 1936–37, 41. Approximately 16 per cent of the student body at Alberta were fraternity members in 1934–35: *Evergreen and Gold*, 1934–35. About 20 per cent of Dalhousie students belonged: *Pharos*, 1938. At the University of British Columbia, 31 per cent of women belonged to sororities and 23 per cent of men to fraternities: *Totem*, 1938. At McGill in 1931 there were 554 fraternity members, representing approximately 18 per cent of the student body: H.M. Jaquays to Arthur E. Morgan, 5 Sept. 1935, Student Activities: Frats and Sororities, RG2 C52, MUA.

35 University of Western Ontario, President's Report, 1931–32, 29; and 1937–38, 21. See also W. Sherwood Fox to Pi Beta Phi Fraternity, 8 June 1934, Administrative Council Box: Correspondence File, 1932–35, UWOA; and W. Sherwood Fox to Carleton Stanley, 14 Feb. 1935, and Stanley to Fox, 21 Feb. 1935, discussing the way in which fraternities at their respective institutions had been kept in check: President's Office Papers: Correspondence: Fraternities File, DUA.

36 President's Papers, 1928–36, Phi Kappa Pi, 3287.3 (4); Archer Davis, president of Phi Delta Theta, to R.C. Wallace, 7 Nov. 1932; also Phi Delta Theta, 3287.3 (3), UAA; Rules for Entertainment of Prospective Members of Sororities, General Correspondence: Reports, 3287.1 ca 1929, UAA; Constitution of the Western Ontario Chapter of the Delta Upsilon Fraternity, 10 Apr. 1933; Student Affairs Box, Student Clubs, UWOA; Evelyn M. Eaton to Robert Stamp, 3 Apr. 1981 (on frat rules on

drinking); Intrafraternity Council of McGill University, Rushing Rules 1937–38, Student Activities, Fraternities and Sororities, RG2 C52, MUA.

37 The constitution of the Phi Nu fraternity at McGill said, "No man of Hebrew blood may be a member": Student Activities: Fraternities and Sororities, RG2 C52, MUA. The Phi Kappa Pi fraternity at the University of Alberta restricted membership to students of "British nationality" Secretary-treasurer of Phi Kappa Pi to R.C. Wallace, 11 Feb. 1930, President's Papers, 1928–36, Phi Kappa Pi, 3287.3 (4), UAA.

38 The letter is from an unlikely source: W.H. Alexander, a well-known socialist. He wrote to the international office of the Pi Beta Phi fraternity, ca May 1934: Administrative Council Box: Administrative Council Correspondence, 1932–35, copy in UWOA. See also Wilfred Bovey to L.S. Lyon, 5 Feb. 1930, Student Activities: Fraternities and Sororities, RG2 C52, Principal's Papers, MUA; Ubyssey, 22 Mar. 1929. Also W.P.M. Kennedy to Robert Falconer, 5 Feb. 1929, who writes favourably of the fraternity boys he has taught over the years: University Historian, A83–0036/032, Student Organizations: Fraternities, UTA. Similar views were expressed by Ursulla N. MacDonnel, dean of women, University of Manitoba, about sororities on campus: University of Manitoba, President's Report 1935–36, 145.

39 Varsity, 26 Nov. 1935; Interview with University of Saskatchewan student Edith Fowke, cited in Taft, Behind These Greystone Walls, 58; interviews with Dalhousie students Jean Begg, 13 Aug. 1983, and Zilpha Linkletter, 11 Aug. 1983; and General Report, by Margaret E. Lowe, warden of Shirreff Hall, Shirreff Hall: General, President's Office Papers, DUA; Memorandum re Rules at the University of Alberta, Minute Book, Students' Council, 1935–36, UAA. According to Margaret Addison, the dean of women at University College, Toronto, residential life would imbue "young women with grace and charm, with poise and dignity, and with the ability to act unselfishly and assume their responsibilities in home and public life more intelligently and effectively": Walter T. Brown, In Memoriam: Margaret Addison, 1868–1940 (Toronto, Victoria University: Clarke Irwin and Co. 1941), 14.

40 Johnston and Weaver, Student Days, 50–1; Florence E. Dodd (adviser to women students) to Mr T.M. Carlyle, 19 Jan. 1934, President's Papers, 1928–36, General Correspondence: Reports, 3284.1, UAA.

41 Axelrod, "Moulding the Middle Class," 113; University of Western Ontario, President's Report, 1932–33, 21, UWOA; Report of the Dean of Women, in Report of the President, University of British Columbia 1931, 23; University of British Columbia calendar 1939–40, 33, UBCA. See also recollections of Elizabeth Leslie Stubbs, The Way We Were (Vancouver: UBC Alumni Association 1987), 21.

42 Interview with John W. Chalmers, (University of Alberta student,

enrolled in 1931), 4 July 1984. He recalled how residence students used to leave beer for the custodian in exchange for his silence about residence "beer parties." See also Memorandum re Dormitory Rules at the University of Alberta, Minute Book, Students' Council, 1935–36, UAA. St Michael's College residence in Toronto, however, more vigilantly controlled the evening activities of men. Interview, Carney Morris, 20 Sept. 1985.

43 Stephen Leacock, "The Need for Dormitories at McGill," ca 1930, MUA; interview, Arthur Hackett, 10 Jan. 1987; Hackett, a student at Victoria College in Toronto, testified to the closeness among residence students. See also Joan Brothers, "The Tradition of Residence," in Joan Brothers and Stephen Hatch, eds., *Residence and Student Life: A Sociological Inquiry in to Higher Education* (London: Tavistock Publications 1971), 25–47.

44 A.W. Mathews, *Athletics in Canadian Universities: The Report of the ACCU/CIAU Study of Athletic Programs in Canadian Universities* (Ottawa: AUCC 1974), 5–8, 39–40.

45 More than half the student body at U of T attended intercollegiate games at Varsity Stadium (Robin Harris, "The Depression, 1932–1939," chap. 5, University Historian, A83–0036/001, UTA). A rugby game between Dalhousie and a team from the armed services evidently drew four thousand fans, "including every man, woman, and child connected with the university": *Dalhousie Gazette*, 5 Nov. 1929.

46 On the history of Canadian sport, see Alan Metcalfe, *Canada Learns To Play: The Emergence of Organized Sport, 1807–1914* (Toronto: McClelland and Stewart 1987). On the development and commercializaton of American university sports, see Paula Fass, *The Damned and the Beautiful*, 182; Robert Cooley Angel, *The Campus: A Study of Contemporary Life in the American University* (New York: D. Appleton 1928), and Calvin B.T. Lee, *The Campus Scene, 1900–1970: Changing Styles in Undergraduate Life* (New York: Mckay 1970), 7. See also Robert Knight Barney, "Physical Education and Sport in North America," in Earle F. Zeigler, ed., *History of Physical Education and Sport* (Englewood Cliffs, NJ: Prentice Hall 1979), 171–227; Frank Cosentino and Maxwell L. Howell, *A History of Physical Education in Canada* (Toronto: General Publishing Company 1971); Ronald Lappage, "The Canadian Scene and Sport, 1921–1939," in Maxwell L. Howell and Reet A. Howell, eds., *History of Sport in Canada* (Champaign, Illinois: Stipes Publishing 1981), 236–316; Guy Lewis, "The Beginning of Organized Collegiate Sport," *American Quarterly* 22 (Summer 1970): 222–9; Guy Lewis, "Sport, Youth Culture and Conventionality, 1920–1970," *Journal of Sport History* 4, no. 2 (1977): 129–50.

47 Garry John Burke, "An Historical Study of Intercollegiate Athletics at

the University of Western Ontario, 1908–1945," MA thesis, University of
Western Ontario 1979, 241, 314. In his autobiography, Sherwood Fox,
the president of Western, admitted that the promotion of football was
designed to enhance the university's image in the region and province:
W. Sherwood Fox, *Sherwood Fox of Western* (Toronto: Burns and
MacEachren 1964), 160.

48 Metcalfe, *Canada Learns to Play*, 71, 106, 124–6.

49 *Gateway*, 16 Oct. 1934.

50 Currie cited in the *Queen's Journal*, 11 Mar. 1932; *Sheaf*, 22 Jan. 1931.
See also *Edmonton Journal*, 8 Oct. 1936, where W.A. Kerr, president of
the University of Alberta, expressed similar sentiments, and for a
pessimistic view, T.L. MacDermott, "The Tendency of Athletics in
Canadian Colleges: Do They Lower Regard for Intellectual Development?" NCCU, *Proceedings* 1930, 119–27. According to *Ubyssey*,
31 Jan. 1940: "It may be safely said that athletics as conducted at U.B.C.
complements the curriculum, and instills in all who partake of it,
something akin to a moral code that is of the highest value in a
student's contact with knowledge and education in university, and in his
application of that learning in future years." This contrasts with the
situation in the United States, "where athletics is so dominated by
materialism that it has ceased to become a spontaneous outburst of the
students towards a search for health and mental betterment." The
Carnegie Foundation, which investigated intercollegiate athletics in
North America, placed a slightly different interpretation on the failure
of Canadian universities to subsidize university athletes. "A far larger
proportion of university athletes come from the more prosperous classes
and are maintained entirely by their families. The needy athlete is
comparatively rare, and even when he exists he does not expect special
consideration": cited in *Queen's Journal*, 1 Nov. 1929. That Canadian
tuition fees were far lower than those in private American universities
allowed the exceptional athletes to attend university and compete
without requiring subsidization.

51 Ellen Gerber, "The Controlled Development of Collegiate Sport for
Women, 1923–1936," *Journal of Sport History* 2, no. 1 (Spring 1975):
1–28; Burke, "An Historical Study," 301, 316. Play Days were
introduced at UBC: Report of the Dean of Women in Report of the
President of the University of British Columbia, 31 Aug. 1933, 25.
Helen Lenskyj, "Femininity First: Sport and Physical Education for
Ontario Girls, 1890–1930," *Canadian Journal of Sport History* 13, no.
2 (Dec. 1982): 4–17; Helen Lenskyj, "The Role of Physical Education in
the Socialization of Girls in Ontario, 1890–1930," doctoral diss.,
University of Toronto 1983, 227–8. Interview with S. Marion Ross (BA
Queen's 1939), 17 July 1978, describes limited facilities for women: in

Hidden Voices: The Life Experiences of Women Who Have Worked and Studied at Queen's University (Kingston 1980), QUA. See also *Queen's Journal*, 20 Jan. 1933. For an enlightening discussion of changing approaches to women's athletics in late nineteenth-century Canada, see Michael Smith, 'Graceful Athleticism or Robust Womanhood: The Sporting Culture of Women in Victorian Nova Scotia, 1870–1914,' *Journal of Canadian Studies* 23, nos. 1, 2 (Spring 1988): 120–37.

52 Burke, 302; women's athletics received $929 annually, compared to $17168 for men. Marginal improvements were made in the next four years. In 1939 women's sports received 11 per cent of the funds, though in 1940 the figure slipped back to 7.5 per cent. On Hart House, see Nancy Kiefer, "The Impact of the Second World War on Female Students at the University of Toronto, 1939–1945," MA thesis, University of Toronto 1984, 83–5. See also Margaret Gillett, *We Walked Very Warily: A History of Women at McGill* (Montreal: Eden Press 1981), 245–6.

53 Scott Wade and Hugh Lloyd, *Behind the Hill* (Fredericton: Students Representative Council and the Associated Alumni and Senate of UNB 1967), 97; at Western, in 1938–9, only 10.6 per cent of men and 21.5 per cent of women did not participate in athletic activities: University of Western Ontario, President's Report 1938–39, 39–40.

54 Report of the University Health Services, in Report of the President 1937, University of British Columbia, 46; UBC Calendar, 1939–40, 31, UBCA; see also Helen Lenskyj, "The Role of Physical Education in the Socialization of Girls in Ontario, 1890–1930," 57. In Alberta, according to *Gateway*, 19 Jan. 1937, six thousand Edmonton school-children had been afflicted, and the university infirmary was full. See also Malcolm MacLeod, "Parade Street Parade: The Student Body at Memorial University College, 1925–1949," in Axelrod and Reid, eds., *Youth, University, and Canadian Society*, 59.

55 Students at the University of Manitoba and Dalhousie campaigned for compulsory physical education classes for freshmen: *Manitoban*, 9 Mar. 1934; *Dalhousie Gazette*, 18 Oct. 1934. The *Queen's Journal*, however, denounced the practice in a 27 Jan. 1933 editorial. According to Sherwood Fox, "Universities have learned that unless they make some provision for the health of their students, the students fall far short of doing their best academic work": President's Report, 1933–34, University of Western Ontario, 57, and 1934–35, 4–41, UWOA, which detail various athletic activities in which students were engaged. Traditional academics, like Carleton Stanley, however, felt that the university was simply pandering to yet another modern trend: *Dalhousie Gazette*, 23 Nov., 1 Dec. 1932. University of British Columbia students requested a full-time instructor in physical training, who was appointed in Jan. 1936: H.T. Logan, *Tuum Est: A History of the University of*

British Columbia (Vancouver: UBC 1958), 133.

56 Gordon H. Thompson to Professor C.H. Mercer, Senate Gymnasium
Commitee, 15 Mar. 1938; G. Fred Day to Col. W.E. Thompson,
Secretary of the Board of Governors, 15 Mar. 1938, President's Office
Papers: Correspondence: Athletics and Physical Education, DUA; *Halifax
Citizen*, 18 Mar. 1938. Board of Governors' Minutes, 19 Aug. 1939,
announce that a replacement for Korning is being sought.

57 *Manitoban*, 19 Jan. 1932, 10 Nov. 1938; *Gateway*, 28 Feb. 1936;
Queen's Journal, 25 Nov. 1938.

58 University of Western Ontario *Gazette*, 19 Mar. 1931, 20 Feb. 1934;
Manitoban, 10 Nov. 1938; *Sheaf*, 2 Dec. 1938; Vancouver *Daily
Province*, 18 Jan. 1939.

59 *Queen's Journal*, 4 Mar. 1930, 31 Jan. 1931.

60 Senate Minutes, Dalhousie University, 23 Mar. 1933, DUA. On the
situation of poorer students, see interview with Jack Pringle (University
of Saskatchewan BA 1938), cited in Taft, *Inside These Greystone Walls*,
42.

61 Gerald Friesen, "Principal J.H. Riddell," 257–8; Bedford, *The University
of Winnipeg*, 214–15; Weaver and Johnston, *Student Days*, 45.

62 *Queen's Journal*, 12 Jan. 1937, 1 Nov. 1938; *Dalhousie Gazette*, 14 Jan.
1938.

63 *Queen's Journal*, 30 Nov. 1937, 7 Dec. 1937.

64 *Sheaf*, 8, 18 Nov. 1938; 3 Feb. 1939; *Gateway*, 28 Nov. 1939; *Queen's
Journal*, 22, 25 Nov. 1938.

65 An example of the paternalism of universities was the decision by the
Queen's University Library to keep E. Van de Velde's book, *Ideal
Marriage*, off the shelves and under lock and key. Students had to ask to
borrow it. H.S. Ferns describes this and his own sexual innocence in
Reading from Left to Right, 57. On the University of Toronto petting
incident, see the *Globe*, 1, 4 Feb. 1929; plus campus responses
elsewhere: *The Sheaf*, 31 Jan. 7, 14 Feb. 1929.

66 Dorothy Dunbar Bromley and Florence Haxton Britten, *Youth and Sex:
A Study of 1300 College Students* (New York: Harper and Brothers
1938), chaps. 1–2; quotation from "Youth in College," *Fortune
Magazine*, June 1936, 101. See also Maxine Davis, *The Lost
Generation: A Portrait of American Youth Today* (New York:
Macmillan 1936), 83; Barbara Solomon, *In the Company of Educated
Women* (New Haven and London: Yale University Press 1985) 161–2.

67 See Dianne Dodd, "The Canadian Birth Control Movement: Two
Approaches to the Dissemination of Contraceptive Technology," *Scientia
Canadensis* 9, no. 1 (June 1985): 53–66; Angus McLaren and Arlene
Tigar McLaren, *The Bedroom and the State: The Changing Practices
and Politics of Contraception and Abortion in Canada, 1880–1980*

(Toronto: McClelland and Stewart 1986), chap. 1; D.N. Trimble, "Contraception in Its Modern Aspects," *University of Toronto Medical Journal* 14, no. 5 (1937): 234–40; Veronica Strong-Boag, *The New Day Recalled: Lives of Girls and Women in English Canada, 1919–1939* (Toronto: Copp Clark Pitman 1988), 88–9.

68 Various interviews and correspondence with the author, 1983–87. On the open recognition of the practices of necking and petting, see UWO *Gazette*, 13 Feb. 1934; *Queen's Journal*, 10 Feb. 1934. For a discussion of the ideology of "sexual containment" in the United States, see Elaine Tyler May, *Homeward Bound: American Families in the Cold War Era* (New York: Basic Books 1988), chap. 5.

69 Dodd, "The Canadian Birth Control Movement"; and McLaren and Tigar McLaren, *The Bedroom and the State*, chaps. 3–5.

70 *Queen's Journal*, 7 Jan. 1938; and Wallace to Virtue, 19 Oct. 1938; and see n 67. See also Strong-Boag, *The New Day Recalled*, 87; Beth Bailey, "Scientific Truth ... and Love: The Marriage Education Movement in the United States," *Journal of Social History* (Summer 1987): 711–32; and *McGill Daily*, 17 Oct. 1938. An editorial in the University of Western Ontario *Undergraduate Medical Journal* 8, no. 1 (1938): 41, calls for public education on the problem of syphilis.

71 *Varsity*, 13 Oct. 1938; *Gateway*, 27 Jan. 1939. This, of course, is why "sex education" received general approval. For the forward-thinking it was a form of progressive education; for conservatives it was an opportunity to preach to students the dangers of moral laxity. See also Isabel Dingman, "Your Teenage Daughter," *Chatelaine*, Oct. 1934, on the value of sex education. Alfred Henry Tyrer's *Sex, Marriage and Birth Control: A Guide Book to Sex Health, and a Satisfactory Sex Life in Marriage* (Toronto: Marriage Welfare Bureau 1943) was first published in 1936 and had been reprinted nine times by 1943. It advised engaged couples who longed for sexual intimacy to marry as soon as "a home, no matter how simple, can be provided, and then to practise conception control until such time as conditions justify an addition to the family" (124–5). Thus, even this most liberal of advice manuals, which extolled the pleasures of sex, would not endorse pre-marital intercourse.

72 A. Gladstone Virtue to W.A.R. Kerr, 13 Oct. 1938; Kerr to Virtue, 19 Oct. 1938; Virtue to Kerr, 26 Oct. 1938; Kerr to Virtue, 8 Nov. 1938, President's Papers, 1936–42, 3386.4; Student Associations: Clubs, *Gateway*, 3386.4, UAA.

73 Veronica Strong-Boag, introduction to Nellie McLung, *In Times Like These* (1915; Toronto: University of Toronto Press 1972), viii; Strong-Boag, *The New Day Recalled*, passim. To say that there was no widespread women's movement does not imply a complete absence of feminist consciousness. Women's organizations founded in the wake of

the First World War worked resolutely in the 1930s, if more quietly than earlier, to advance the economic and social positions of women. See Alison Prentice et al., *Canadian Women: A History* (Toronto: Harcourt Brace Jovanovich 1988), 263–88. See also Carol Bacchi, *Liberation Deferred? The Ideas of the English Canadian Suffragists, 1877–1918* (Toronto: University of Toronto Press 1982); Alice Klein and Wayne Roberts, "Besieged Innocence: The 'Problem' and the Problems of Working Women – Toronto, 1896–1914," in *Women at Work: Ontario, 1850–1930* (Toronto: Women's Press 1974), 211–60. The fond memories of university women are evident in correspondence and numerous interviews with women from Western, Queen's, Dalhousie, and Alberta. For examples of debates and editorials on coeducation, see *Ubyssey*, 14 Nov. 1929; *Dalhousie Gazette*, 8 Nov. 1934; *Manitoban*, 21 Feb. 1930, 25 Feb. 1936; *Queen's Journal*, 26 Jan. 1936, 22 Oct. 1937; *McGill Daily*, 26 Oct. 1939.

74 Gillett, *We Walked Very Warily*, 233, 237; and *McGill Daily*, 29 Jan. 1937. See also Johnston and Weaver, *Student Days*, 49–51, for examples of discrimination against women at McMaster. There too they were barred from many campus clubs, and until 1935 they were subjected to segregated seating in chapel. See also Judith Fingard, "They Had a Tough Row to Hoe," *Dalhousie Alumni Magazine* (Winter 1985): 29.

75 See *Sheaf*, 4 Feb. 1932; and *Gateway*, 5 Nov. 1937; UWO *Gazette*, 19 Feb. 1937; interview, Olga Volkhoff (UBCA); and *Ubyssey*, 23 Jan. 1931, 6 Feb. 1931. For examples of poems and jokes, see *Gateway*, 26 Jan. 1937; *Queen's Journal*, 26 Jan. 1932.

76 *Manitoban*, 19 July 1932. According to Fred Stone, an exchange student from McGill attending UBC, "the presence of women students at class meetings and in the Debating Union was a novelty for me": *Ubyssey*, 21 Oct. 1930.

77 William D. Tait (professor of psychology, McGill University), "Some Feminisms," 52–3; and J.A. Lindsay, "Sex in Education," 148–9; both in *Dalhousie Review* 10 (1930–31); *McGill Daily*, 26 Oct. 1939. There are many other examples of such thinking throughout the decade in both the popular and campus press: e.g., A.M. Pratt, "Co-education? – No!" *Maclean's*, 15 Oct. 1934, 16.

78 Thomas Goudge in *Dalhousie Gazette*, 11 Jan. 1929.

79 *Queen's Journal*, 4 Mar. 1932.

80 *Queen's Journal*, 8 Mar. 1934.

81 Gillett, *We Walked Very Warily*, 189; *Vancouver Sun*, 10 Nov. 1937; UWO *Gazette*, 19 Feb. 1937.

82 *Gateway*, 13 Nov. 1936.

83 By Alberta A. Townsend, Sept. 1932, 20, 56. Similar advice was offered by Alfred Henry Tyrer, who counselled wives to be clean and neat and

to avoid nagging and sulking: Tyrer, *Sex, Marriage, and Birth Control*, 211–36.

84 See, for example, Margaret MacDonald, "Manners for Girls," *Chatelaine*, Sept. 1932, 48. See also *Gateway*, 1 Oct., 5, 10 Nov. 1937, for advice to women on dress and deportment. The *Gateway*, 24 Oct. 1939, cited an American study that found "that college graduates, men and women, were more successful in marriage than grammar and high school graduates." And according to the *Sheaf*, 31 Jan. 1929, "A higher education enables a woman to be a more interested and interesting companion for her husband. A college career does not change the woman to a pedant; her education is social asset." See also Elizabeth Dundas Long, "That After-Luncheon Speech," *Chatelaine*, Oct. 1932, 21.

85 Report of the Dean of Women, in Report of the President of the University of British Columbia, Academic Year Ending 31 August 1935, 28, UBCA.

86 *Senate Minutes*, University of British Columbia, 23 Aug. 1935, UBCA. Such ideals were upheld by university women's clubs across the country. The University Women's Club of Edmonton, whose membership included wives of prominent citizens, declared its goal "to assist in giving to the women students of the University, a social life that will be both cultural and wholesome." See Marjorie W. Buckley, ed., *"As It Happened": The University Women's Club of Edmonton: The First Sixty Years* (Edmonton 1973), 8. They sponsored teas, scholarships, and charities, and participated in peace-related activities throughout the 1930s.

87 May 1934, 14.

88 Various interviews, 1983–87; *Hidden Voices: The Life Experiences of Women Who Have Worked and Studied at Queen's University*, plus transcripts, QUA; correspondence of the Class of 1939, University of Western Ontario, with Robert Stamp, 1980–81. On the American experience, see Barbara Solomon, *In the Company of Educated Women*, 169–70. She notes: "The young college graduate had confidence in her capabilities as a woman and as an individual ... Few students thought of themselves as oppressed or perceived feminism as a special cause. Even though they had flouted the prescribed rules of behavior, alumnae recalled that they absorbed gentility and manners while at college. Many doubtless would have agreed with 1935 Fisk alumna, Mary L. Martin, who explained: 'Our college professors taught us to be women with all the social graces and these alone prepared us for leadership in our communities.' According to Diana Trilling (1925), 'we learned together how to become ladies.' Strong and capable herself, the graduate felt that a woman probably could have it all, whatever she wanted; she took for

granted her feminist legacy and no longer took up her sex as a cause" (170–1). See also Ruth S. Cavan and Jordan T. Cavan, *Building a Girl's Personality: A Social Psychology of Later Girlhood* (New York: Abingdon Press 1932).

89 *Sheaf*, 15 Feb. 1938.

90 *Vancouver Sun*, 10 Dec. 1937. See also *Gateway*, 4 Feb. 1936.

91 *Sheaf*, 18 Feb. 1937. For an interesting discussion of the spending and saving habits of the middle class, see Daniel Horowitz, "Frugality or Comfort: Middle-class Styles of Life in the Early Twentieth Century," *American Quarterly* 37 (1985): 239–59.

92 *Queen's Journal*, 28 Oct. 1930, 30 Sept. 1932.

93 5 June 1935, 22.

94 *Queen's Journal*, 18 Mar. 1937.

95 *Canada Year Book* 1939, 620.

96 R. Bothwell, I. Drummond, J. English, *Canada: 1900–1945* (Toronto: University of Toronto Press 1987), 290.

97 Robert Sklar, *Movie-Made America: A Social History of American Movies* (New York: Random House 1975), 46; Roy Rosenzweig, *Eight Hours for What We Will: Workers and Leisure in an Industrial City, 1870–1920* (Cambridge: Cambridge University Press 1983), chap. 8.

98 Sklar, *Movie Made America* 175 and passim. An illustration of the period genres can be found in Jerry Vermilye, *The Films of the Thirties* (Syracuse, NJ: Citadel Press 1982). See also Ann Lloyd and David Robinson, eds., *Movies of the Thirties* (London: Orbis 1983): "In the United States, out of the thousands of films made during the decade, not a dozen so much as touched upon the Depression, the Spanish Civil War or any of the cataclysmic developments in Europe" (7). On the Production Code, see 84–5. On the sanitized treatment of youth in films, see David M. Considine, *The Cinema of Adolescence* (Jefferson, NC and London: McFarland 1985), 9, and chap. 2.

99 J. Thompson and A. Seager, *Canada 1929–1939: Decades of Discord* (Toronto: McClelland and Stewart 1985), 179.

100 8 Nov. 1932; see also *Gateway*, 22 Jan. 1931; *Dalhousie Gazette*, 20 Jan. 1939.

101 According to Pierre Berton, fifty-seven such features including Canadian content were made by Hollywood in the 1930s. They were preoccupied with distorted images of Indians, the RCMP, and northern geography. See *Hollywood's Canada: The Americanization of Our National Image* (Toronto: McClelland and Stewart 1975), 263–5 and passim.

102 Canadian Youth Commission, *Youth, Marriage, and the Family* (Toronto: Ryerson Press 1948), 20.

103 On the particular appeal of Hollywood films to youth, and their essentially conservative themes, see Elaine Tyler May, *Homeward*

Bound: American Families in the Cold War Era, 41–7.

104 Thompson and Seager, *Canada: 1922–1939*, chap. 8; and Bothwell, Drummond, and English, *Canada: 1900–1945*, chap. 17.

105 *Dalhousie Gazette*, "Student Government History," 18 Mar. 1976.

106 Bothwell et al., 288–9.

107 Carleton Stanley to Hans Mohr, 25 Jan. 1932, President's Office Papers: Correspondence: Broadcasting File, DUA; *Dalhousie Gazette*, 10, 17, 24 Feb. 1932. See also *Globe*, 21 Oct. 1932; and C.G. Stone and F. Joan Garnett, *Brandon College: A History 1899–1967*, 136. Radio broadcasts were introduced at Brandon in 1930. See E.A. Corbett, "The Use of Radio by the University," NCCU, *Proceedings 1932*, 55–60, for a description of extension education through university radio broadcasts. The University of Alberta operated its own radio station and in 1935–36 broadcast 433 radio talks and 29 radio plays, symphony hours, and organ recitals. Cited in Report of the Radio Broadcasting Committee, in University of Manitoba Annual Report 1935–36, 134–5, UMA.

108 *Totem* (UBC Yearbook) 1937, 176; *Dalhousie Gazette*, 24 Jan. 1936. *Chatelaine*, Apr. 1934, 28, reported that Greta Garbo, the highest-paid actor in 1934, earned nine thousand dollars a week.

109 *Queen's Journal*, 21 Feb. 1938; *Ubyssey*, 11 Feb. 1938; *Manitoban*, 28 Jan. 1938; UWO *Gazette*, 4 Feb. 1938.

110 Mary L.Bollert, the dean of women at the University of British Columbia, noted in 1931 that "requests for assistance in procuring part-time employment during the academic year and full time during the vacation were almost twice as many as during any previous year. Unfortunately, work was obtainable in inverse ratio": Report of the President of the University of British Columbia, Year Ending 31 August 1931, 24, UBCA. According to the students' adviser at Western in 1936, "an increasing percentage of women are finding it necessary to supplement their sources of income with self-help of various kinds": University of Western Ontario, President's Report 1935–36, 49. Also Donna-Jeanne (Raymer) Andrews (UWO) to Robert Stamp, 24 Nov. 1980; interview with Doug Cherry (University of Saskatchewan), 11 July 1984; correspondence to author from Marion Cummer (University of Toronto and Ontario College of Education), 8 Jan. 1986; correspondence to author from Gordon Henry (Ontario Agricultural College), 6 Jan. 1986.

111 Interview with Rose Mary Gibson (Queen's University), in *Hidden Voices*, 24 July 1978.

112 University of Western Ontario, President's Report, 1935–36, 49.

113 H.S. Ferns, *Reading from Left to Right: One Man's Political History*, 26.

114 Philip Marchand, *Marshall McLuhan: The Medium and the Messenger*

(Toronto: Random House 1989), 22. They travelled in the summer of
1932. One account of such a European trip was printed in *Queen's
Journal*, 29 Sept. 1936: "We are sea sick, uncomfortably dirty, and
badly fed ... We are considered to be inferior to the nigger stokers. Why
do we do it? Because it is a cheap method of getting to England and
back and because it is one job you can't walk out on."

115 Harold MacAdam and Max Sheppard, "A Study of the Part-Time
Employment of Undergraduates of the University of Western Ontario,
2 May 1940," UWOA.

116 A similar point is made by Thomas W. Gutowski in "Student Initiative
and the Origin of the High School Extracurriculum: Chicago, 1880–
1915," *History of Education Quarterly* 28, no. 1 (Spring 1988): 49–72.

117 *Manitoban*, reprinted in *McGill Daily*, 13 Feb. 1931.

118 "For the most part," contended the ever-sceptical Carleton Stanley, "the
life of our students is wholesome. There is a refreshing absence of
professionalism in athletics, college journalism and college politics ...
I am convinced that the common sense which marks our student body
as a whole, and the high seriousness of our best students, will presently
result in sanity and balance": Dalhousie University, President's Report,
1931–32, 2, DUA.

CHAPTER SIX

1 See Alexander DeConde, ed., *Student Activism: Town and Gown in
Historical Perspective* (New York: Charles Scribner's Sons 1971); Lewis
S. Feuer, *The Conflict of Generations: The Character and Significance of
Student Movements* (New York: Basic Books 1960); Herbert Moller,
"Youth as a Force in the Modern World," *Comparative Studies in
Society and History* 4, no. 3 (Apr. 1968): 237–60; Aline Coutrot,
"Youth Movements in France in the 1930s," *Journal of Contemporary
History* 5, no. 1 (1970): 22–35; Arthur Marwick, "Youth in Britain,
1920–1960: Detachment and Commitment," ibid., 37–51; Brian Simon,
"The Student Movement in England and Wales during the 1930s,"
History of Education 13, no. 3 (Sept. 1987): 189–203; Seymour Martin
Lipset, *Rebellion in the University: A History of Student Activism in
America* (London: Routledge and Kegan Paul 1972); Philip Altbach,
Student Politics in America: A Historical Analysis (New York: McGraw
Hill 1974); Eileen Eagan, *Class, Culture and the Classroom: The
Student Peace Movement of the 1930s* (Philadelphia: Temple University
Press 1981); Ralph Brax, *The First Student Movement: Student Activism
in the United States during the 1930s* (London: National University
1981); R.L. Schnell, *National Activist Student Organizations in
American Higher Education, 1905–1944* (Ann Arbour: University of

238 Notes to pages 128–9

Michigan 1976); Eric W. Riser, "Red Menaces and Drinking Buddies: Student Activism at the University of Florida, 1936–1939," *Historian* 48, no. 4 (1986): 559–71. On Canada, there are scattered references to student politics in some of the institutional histories cited throughout this chapter.

2 Robert Falconer, "Do Our Graduates Make Worthy Citizens?" President's Address, University of Toronto, 30 Sept. 1931, UTA; "Life is Enriched by Universities," report of a speech by H.J. Cody, president of the University of Toronto, *Globe,* 3 June 1936, 9; R.C. Wallace, principal, Queen's University, Inaugural Address, *Queen's Journal,* 14 Oct. 1936; C.G. Stone and F. John Garnett, *Brandon College: A History, 1899–1967* (Brandon: Brandon University 1969), 127 (views of President R.J. Evans).

3 Michael Hayden, *Seeking a Balance: The University of Saskatchewan, 1907–1982* (Vancouver: University of British Columbia Press 1983), 139–46; James Pitsula, "Student Life at Regina Collge in the 1920s," in Paul Axelrod and John G. Reid, eds., *Youth, University, and Canadian Society: Essays in the Social History of Higher Education* (Montreal: McGill-Queen's University Press 1989), 122–39; Frederick W. Gibson, *To Serve and Yet Be Free: Queen's University,* vol. 2, 1917–1961, (Montreal: McGill-Queen's Press 1983), 66–82.

4 Reports, Findings and Minutes of a Conference of Representatives from Canadian Universities Held at McGill University, Montreal, 28–31 Dec. 1926, Canadian Union of Students Collection, MCMUA.

5 History of the National Federation of Canadian University Students, 1926–48, NFCUS Publicity Commmittee, McMaster University, M.J. Diakowsky, ed., ca 1948, University Historian's Collection, A-83–0036/031, Students: SAC General, History of NFCUS, UTA.

6 *Manitoban,* 22 Feb. 1935.

7 Memo prepared by H.A.R. Gagnon, Sup't. Commanding "C" Division, 24 Mar. 1939, Canadian Security Intelligence Service (CSIS) Files. The CSIS material cited in this article was obtained following application through the Access to Information Act. Much useful information on the surveillance of student organizations was retrieved, though it was heavily edited, with names of individuals usually blacked out.

8 Richard Allen, *The Social Passion: Religion and Social Reform in Canada, 1914–1928* (Toronto: University of Toronto Press 1973), 219–23; Margaret Beattie, *SCM: A Short History of the Student Christian Movement in Canada* (Toronto: Student Christian Movement 1975); Donald L. Kirkey, Jr., "The Decline of Radical Liberal Protestantism: The Case of the Student Christian Movement," paper presented to Canadian Historical Association, Windsor 1988, 4–5; Ernest A. Dale, *Twenty-one Years A-Building: A Short Account of the Student Christian*

Movement in Canada, 1920–41 (Toronto: Student Christian Movement, n.d.).

9 See Beattie, SCM, 38, 87–8; internal political debate reviewed in Jean J. Hunter to A.E. Morgan, 24 Mar. 1936, Student Christian Movement File, Principal's Papers, RG C52, MUA: "Should the Movement, as an organization, adopt definite stands and take united social action on live issues, or should it be primarily concerned with developing religious people, in the best sense, by a sound modern educational method? We discovered that as a group we were divided on this question so basic to our work." See also Kirkey, "The Decline of Radical Liberal Protestantism," 26–7.

10 Interviews with W.E. Mann, 17 Dec. 1985; Jean Woodsworth, 30 Dec. 1985; Jean Burnett, 19 Dec. 1985; and Kenneth Woodsworth, 7 Mar. 1986.

11 The Student Christian Movement of the University of Alberta, Annual Report, 1930–31, President's Papers, 1928–36, Student and Alumni Affairs, SCM: Correspondence, 3286–3, UAA; *Managra* (student publication of the University of Manitoba Agricultural College), 24, no. 1 (Nov. 1930); Harry Avison Papers, MG 30 D 102, vol. 13, file 71, NAC; Annual Report of the Student Christian Movement, 1933–34, President's Office Papers, Student Christian Movement File, DUA.

12 R.C. Wallace to J.H. Woods, 21 Nov. 1939, President's Papers, 1928–36, University of Alberta, Student and Alumni Affairs, SCM: Correspondence 3286, UAA. Frederick Gibson, *To Serve and Yet Be Free: Queen's University*, 2: 147, though Wallace did note his concern about SCM's increasingly political orientation. E.W. Beatty to Chas. H. Hale, 30 June 1934, Student Christian Movement, RG2 C52, MUA. See also positive comments of J.S. Thomson, president of the University of Saskatchewan, J.S. Thomson to Rev. Beverly L. Outen, 1 Sept. 1937, Presidential Papers, II B-175 (1), USA.

13 Quotation from correspondence with David Woodsworth, 21 Jan. 1986; also interview with John Webster Grant, 19 June 1985.

14 For information on the founding of the CSA, see Canadian Youth Congress Collection, box 8, file 5, MCMUA.

15 Briefs and conference resolutions from the CSA for 1939–40 are found in the CSIS files, in possession of the author. Reports of CSA activities also in student newspapers from 1938 to 1940. The events leading to the breakup of the CSA will be discussed below. Neil Morrison, a CSA proponent, explained the difference between NFCUS and the more "democratic" CSA in a talk at the University of Alberta, *Gateway*, 24 Nov. 1939.

16 State Scholarships for Canada: A Brief to the Royal Commission on Dominion Provincial Relations from the Canadian Student Assembly,

June 1938, Student Christian Movement Collection, 84–2-9, United
Church Archives, Toronto; Jack Chernick, "National Scholarships,"
Manitoba Arts Review 1, no. 2 (Fall 1938); information in CSA News
Letter, no. 2 (27 Feb. 1940): CSIS files; *Varsity*, 7 Mar. 1939; *Ubyssey*,
22 Sept. 1939; Report of Commission on the Extension of University
Education, Summary of Conference Resolutions, Third National
Conference of the Canadian Student Assembly, Dec. 1939, CSIS files.

17 Canadian Student Assembly, "A Brief on National Student Life," 6 Dec.
1939, CSIS files.

18 Kenneth Woodsworth, "The Canadian Youth Congress" (history and
background, 1943), box 1, file 1, Canadian Youth Congress Collection,
MCMUA,. It includes favourable comments cabled to the 1938 congress
conference from Prime Minister Mackenzie King. See *Toronto Star*, 26
May 1936; interview with Kenneth Woodsworth, national secretary of
CYC, and with Jean Woodsworth, 30 Dec. 1985; material also in the
Frank and Libby Park Papers, MG 31 K9, vol. 7, file 128a, NAC; and in
CYC magazine publication called *The Youth Forum*, National Library of
Canada; see also interview with Peter Hunter, 17 Dec. 1985, an
organizer for the Young Communist League, who was active in the CYC,
and Peter Hunter, *Which Side Are You On Boys: Canadian Life on the
Left* (Toronto: Lugus Productions 1988), 113–17. The latest and most
comprehensive historical accounts of the 1930s, by John Thompson with
Allen Seager, *Canada, 1922–1939: Decades of Discord* (Toronto:
McClelland and Stewart 1985), and Robert Bothwell, Ian Drummond,
and John English, *Canada: 1900–1945* (Toronto: University of Toronto
Press 1987), do not mention the Canadian Youth Congress and do not
discuss the youth movement.

19 This policy was followed internationally. See Richard Cornell, *Youth
and Communism: An Historical Analysis of International Communist
Youth Movements* (New York: Walker and Co. 1965), 59–71; *Canada's
Party of Socialism: History of the Communist Party of Canada, 1921–
1976* (Progress Books: Toronto 1982), 108–18. The latter, the official
history of the Canadian Communist Party, contended that "the Young
Communist League played a key role in establishing the Canadian Youth
Congress" (117), a claim that YCL's enemies did not dispute. See also
Norman Penner, *Canadian Communism: The Stalin Years and Beyond*
(Toronto: Metheun 1987), 146–8; and Hunter, *Which Side Are You On
Boys*, 103–9.

20 Lita-Rose Betcherman, *The Little Band: The Clashes between the
Communists and the Political and Legal Establishment in Canada,
1926–1932* (Ottawa: Deneau 1982). The University of Western Ontario
Gazette, 20 Feb. 1934, reports on members of the Student League being
ejected from a meeting where Communist A.E. Smith was speaking on

behalf of the Canadian Labour Defence League.

21 Thompson and Seager, *Canada, 1922–1939,* 223–9, 285.

22 On profesors attending scientific conference, F.J. Meade, Sup't Commanding "C" Division to the Commissioner, 6 June 1935; report of Forsey speech delivered on 14 Jan. 1932, file no. 175/6540; on David Lewis, J.W. Phillips to Cortlandt Starnes, 19 May 1931, CSIS files.

23 J.W. Phillips to Commissioner Cortlandt Starnes, 9 May 1931, CSIS files; Cortlandt Starnes to Arthur Currie, 13 May 1931. A charge in 1935 by Mr J.F. Pouliot, Liberal MP for Temiscouta, that McGill was filled with Communists, was denied by the university: *Ottawa Journal,* 3 Mar. 1935, clipping in CSIS files. Again in 1937 Montreal surgeon Henry Gray claimed there were communists at McGill, an accusation denied by Principal A.E. Morgan: *Montreal Gazette,* 9 Apr. 1937, clipping in CSIS files.

24 *Ubyssey,* 20 Nov. 1934; *Vancouver Sun,* 22 Nov. 1934.

25 *Varsity,* 5 Dec. 1935; *Mail and Empire,* 6 Dec. 1935; and *Gateway,* 10 Dec. 1935.

26 *Manitoban,* 5 Feb. 1937; *Manifesto of the Canadian Congress against War and Fascism* (Toronto 1934), Special Collections, York University Library.

27 For material on the Student League, see *Manitoban,* 13 Jan. 1933, 1 Feb. 1934; University of Western Ontario *Gazette,* 20 Feb. 1934; *Ubyssey,* 23 Nov. 1934; report of C.D. LaNauze, Sup't. Commmanding "O" Division, 21 Feb. 1935, CSIS files. The Student League's activities were covered in *Young Worker,* the publication of the Young Communist League. See R.S., "The Canadian Student Movement," 17 Apr., 13 May, and 30 June 1933, and other articles on 7 May, 16 July, 13 Aug. 1934, and 24 Aug. 1935. On the YCL, see Ivan Avakumovic, *The Communist Party of Canada* (Toronto: McClelland and Stewart 1975), 122–4; and interview with Peter Hunter, 17 Dec. 1985, a YCL organizer in southwestern Ontario. Communist youth acted in political plays through the Progressive Arts Club at the University of Toronto and elsewhere in the country: Dorothy Livesay, *Right Hand, Left Hand: A True Life of the Thirties* (Erin, Ont.: Press Porcepic 1977), 73–86; Gregory S. Kealey, "Stanley Brehault Ryerson: Revolutionary Intellectual," *Studies in Political Economy* 9 (Fall 1982): 105–6.

28 Minutes of third annual CCYM Convention, Edmonton, 26, 27 July 1938, CCF Records, CCYM, General 1935–38, MG 28 IV–1 vol. 344, NAC. This was confirmed by Ben Swankey in an article in *League Life,* Oct. 1938, a publication of the Young Communist League: "The healthiest section of the CCYM, as regards size, influence and activity, is undoubtedly in Alberta." The CCYM was weakest in French Canada, the Maritimes, Manitoba, and British Columbia. It was somewhat more

active in Ontario and Saskatchewan. See also Ernest Shulman, "The Co-operative Commonwealth Federation and Its Youth Movement in Ontario," MA thesis, University of Wisconsin, n.d., ca 1955, 39–40. Carney Morris, a University of Toronto student from 1932 to 1934 who joined the CCF, recalled listening to street-corner speeches by such CCF members as Morden Lazarus; interview, 20 Sept. 1985.

29 See the following sources: A.G. Bedford, *The University of Winnipeg: A History of the Founding Colleges* (Toronto: University of Toronto Press 1976), 197; *Alarm Clock* reports on socialist activity around the country, Feb., Mar. 1933, Student Activities, 1927–33, *Alarm Clock* magazine, RG2 C52, Principal's Papers, MUA; David Lewis, *The Good Fight: Political Memoirs, 1909–1958* (Toronto: Macmillan 1981), 28–9; John G. Reid, *Mount Allison University*, vol. 2 (Toronto: University of Toronto Press 1984), 150; Michiel Horn, *The League for Social Reconstruction: Intellectual Origins of the Democratic Left in Canada, 1930–1942* (Toronto: University of Toronto Press 1980); Arthur Currie to J.H.B. MacBrien, commissioner of the RCMP, 11 Feb. 1933; file no. 175/6540, CSIS files; *McGill Daily*, 7 Dec. 1933.

30 Interviews with Kenneth Woodsworth, 7 Mar. 1986, and W.E. Mann, 17 Dec. 1985. David Lewis, national secretary of the CCF, believed that the Canadian Youth Congress was dominated by Communists, and recommended that the CCYM consider withdrawing in 1938: Lewis to Eamon Park, 18 May 1938, CCF Records, CCYM, General, 1935–58, MG-28, IV.1, vol. 344, NAC. Officially, the Young Communist League policy involved criticism of but co-operation with reform groups like the CCYM: see *Young Worker*, 30 June 1933.

31 Kenneth Woodsworth to Don Sutherland, 10 Dec. 1936, and Sutherland to Woodsworth, 3 Dec. 1936, Canadian Youth Congress Collection, file 4, box 8, MCMUA.

32 *Manitoban*, 7 Jan. 1938.

33 For a vivid description of the conference, see Armour McKay, "Canadian Students Draw Together at Winnipeg," *Saturday Night*, 15 Jan. 1938. See also *Gateway*, 7 Jan. 1938; *Ubyssey*, 7 Jan. 1938. See also Student Christian Movement Records, 84–2-6, United Church Archives, and the *Montreal Star*, 5 Jan. 1938; interview with a Dalhousie delegate to the conference, Gene (Morison) Hicks, 12 Aug. 1983.

34 No precise figures are available, but my own rough estimate and one by a study for the Canadian Youth Commission are close. According to the latter, during the 1930s "perhaps not more than five per cent of the student body took part in discussions ... about the position their own nation should take in the coming world crisis": *Youth Speaks out on Citizenship* (Toronto: Ryerson Press 1948), 5.

35 Interview with Douglas Cherry, 11 July 1984; correspondence with Frank W. Park, 26 May 1986.
36 Dashan Singh was cited in *Ubyssey*, 8 Oct. 1937; similar message in a *Sheaf* editorial, 22 Oct. 1937.
37 Interview with Earl Beattie, 19 Dec. 1985; Gertrude Rutherford to graduate members and friends, 14 Apr. 1931, University of Alberta, President's Papers, 1928–36, Student and Alumni Affairs, SCM: Correspondence, 3286–3, UAA; UWO *Gazette*, 11 Oct. 1935, and 6 Mar. 1934. There are many other examples pointing to the political quiesence of most students, including the recollections of some forty ex-students interviewed by the author. Interviews with Marjorie (Montogmery) Bowker (an ex-University of Alberta student), 7 July 1984; Gene (Morison) Hicks (Dalhousie), 12 Aug. 1983; and interview with Olga Volkhoff, transcript, UBCA.
38 See chapter 2.
39 According to Canon Cody, president of the University of Toronto, "At present the hard times are impelling students to work harder than ever at their regular studies, so that there seems to be little inclination to go into sporadic journalism": Cody to Arthur Currie, 17 Feb. 1933, Student Activities: *Alarm Clock*, 1927–1933, RG2 C52, Principal's Papers, MUA. Carleton Stanley, president of Dalhousie, notes the same phenomenon: Paul Axelrod, "Moulding the Middle Class: Student Life at Dalhousie University in the 1930s," *Acadiensis* 15. no. 2 (Autumn 1985): 99.
40 Correspondence with J. Kenneth Bradford, 10 Jan. 1986; interview with Marjorie Montgomery Bowker, 7 July 1984; *Manitoban*, 19 Oct. 1933. See also *Sheaf*, 12 Oct. 1933.
41 *Sheaf*, 21 Mar. 1935; *Varsity*, 11 Oct. 1935. On the shift towards the Liberal party, see Thompson and Seager, *Canada, 1922–1939*, 331. Because the voting age was eighteen, large numbers of students could not vote in the election itself, and there were complaints from students attending university away from home about the lack of absentee voting rights.
42 *Gateway*, 27 Oct. 1929; *Pharos* (Dalhousie yearbook) 1931, 91–2; *Manitoban*, 16 Nov. 1932; *Evergreen and Gold* (University of Alberta yearbook) 1934–35, 115; *Ubyssey* 27 Nov. 1936; *Dalhousie Gazette*, 1, 15 Mar., 9 Nov. 1933; 27 Nov. 1936; *Queen's Journal*, 8 Nov 1938; 3 Feb. 1939.
43 *McGill Daily*, 1 Nov. 1930.
44 *Sheaf*, 6 Feb. 1930.
45 *Queen's Journal*, 9 Oct. 1931.
46 *Manitoban*, 5 Oct. 1934, defends students against a complaint by Professor W.H. Alexander, of the University of Alberta, that there was

not enough radical thinking on campus. Everywhere, the social life of the campus predominated. See various institutional histories, and Axelrod, "Moulding the Middle Class," 101–14.

47 Frank G. Swanson, report of the *Gateway* editor, 1936–37, Students' Council Minute Book, UAA.

48 *Globe*, 12, 19 Feb. 1929; *Varsity*, 3 Mar. 1931; Arthur Currie to Alec Edminson, 5 Jan. 1932, Principal's Papers, RG2 C52, Student Activities, MUA; Stanley B. Frost, *McGill University: For the Advancement of Learning*, vol. 2, *1895–1971* (Montreal: McGill-Queen's Press 1984), 195; Principal's Papers, Fascism and Communism (Feb. 1938), RG2 C44, MUA; *McGill Daily*, 22 Feb. 1938 and subsequent issues; *Ubyssey*, 13, 18, 20 Feb. 1931; *Sheaf*, 10, 17 Nov. 1938; Michael Hayden, *Seeking a Balance: University of Saskatchewan*, 182–3; *New Republic* incident in *McGill Daily*, 26 Jan. 1937. The *Oasis* of the Ontario Agricultural College in Guelph was suspended in 1932 because of its "critical attitude" towards the college's faculty: University of Western Ontario *Gazette*, 4 Feb. 1932.

49 *Sheaf*, 3 Dec. 1937; *Manitoban*, 18 Jan. 1937; *Gateway*, 10 Feb. 1932, 10 Feb. 1933; *Vancouver Daily Province*, 16 Nov. 1937. One way around these bans was the formation of social-problems or political-science clubs, where students could discuss political ideas, supposedly free of partisan affiliation. See AMS Records, Clubs: Social Problems Club, 1938, folder no. 15–32, UBCA.

50 On the limits to academic freedom for Canadian professors, see a revealing address by Sir Edward Beatty, "Freedom and the University," *Queen's Quarterly* 44, no. 4, (1937): 463–71. See also Michiel Horn, "Academic Freedom and the Canadian Professor," *CAUT Bulletin*, Dec. 1982; and Frank Abbott, "Academic Freedom and Social Criticism in the 1930s," *Interchange* 15, no. 1 (1983–84): 107–23.

51 *Gateway*, 18 Nov. 1938; it also noted that there is "absolutely no such thing as complete freedom of the press. And perhaps, after all, it is just as well."

52 There are many examples of this, particularly related to the incidents described above. Student newspapers carried stories of censorship elsewhere in the country, usually defending the right of free speech. An amusing example was the *McGill Daily*'s comment on the "atheism" controversy at the University of Toronto. It claimed that no one could charge that atheism was rampant at McGill because the university was a "theocracy" – the chancellor and vice-chancellor were "gods": *McGill Daily*, 1931, undated copy in Principal's Papers, Socialism: Professors and the CCF, RG2 C43, MUA.

53 In 1931 sixty-eight University of Toronto professors were widely criticized for publishing an open letter objecting to Toronto police

harassment of "allegedly" communist meetings. Victoria College students purchased an advertisement in the student newspaper defending the right of professors to free speech: *Globe*, 22 Jan. 1931. For a full discussion of the incident, see Michiel Horn, "Free Speech within the Law: The Letter of the Sixty-Eight Toronto Professors, 1931," *Ontario History* 72, no. 1, (March 1980): 35. In 1938 Carlyle King, a University of Saskatchewan professor, was defended by students after he was publicly attacked for making "anti-war" statements: Michael Hayden, *Seeking a Balance*, 183. In 1939 a group of University of Toronto students supported Professor Frank Underhill following similarly critical comments: R. Douglas Francis, *Frank Underhill: Intellectual Provocateur* (Toronto: University of Toronto Press 1986), 113. The University of Toronto and McGill appear to have had the largest number of such incidents among Canadian universities.

54 Murray to P.J. Philpott, president, Saskatoon Branch of Canadian Legion of the BESC, 1 Nov. 1935, Presidential Papers, ser. 1, B109, *Sheaf*, USA.

55 *McGill Daily*, 9 Nov. 1939, reports on such an event at the University of Alberta; *Dalhousie Gazette*, "Student Government History," article 54, 6 Nov. 1975; Charles Johnston and John Weaver, "Founding a Collegiate Atmosphere; Traditions at the Crossroads: 1930–1939," in *Student Days: An Illustrated History of Student Life at McMaster University from the 1890s to the 1980s* (Hamilton: McMaster University Alumni Association 1986).

56 Petition to the Board of Governors of the University, 2 March 1931, President's Papers, University of Alberta, 1928–36, General: Correspondence: Reports, 3285–1, UAA; also interview with ex-student, John W. Chalmers, 4 July 1984. Boarding costs were rolled back from thirty to twenty-seven dollars a month.

57 *Ubyssey*, 16 Feb. 1932; *Totem* 1932, 85; interview with Olga Volkhoff, transcript in UBC Archives, who describes the publicity campaign as "extraordinary"; see also David C. Jones and Timothy A. Dunn, "All of Us Common People and Education in the Depression," *Canadian Journal of Education* 5, no. 4, (1980): 41–56.

58 University of Western Ontario *Gazette*, 31 Mar., 6 Apr. 14 Apr. 1939.

59 Interview with Douglas Cherry (left-wing student at the University of Saskatchewan), 11 July 1984; and with W.E. Mann (University of Toronto), 17 Dec. 1985. On "school spirit," see *Manitoban*, reprinted in *McGill Daily*, 13 Feb. 1931.

60 The Student Peace Movement was formed in 1931, then appeared to lapse, and was revived in 1935. On the 1931 petition, see the Dalhousie *Gazette*, 24, 31 Oct. 1931; and *Manitoban*, 5, 12 Jan. 1932. On the Student Peace Movement, see Canadian Youth Congress Collection, box 9, file 3, MCMUA; interview with Kenneth Woodsworth, who recalled a

strong YCL presence in the organization; *Manitoban*, 18 Feb. 1936;
Charles M. Johnston, *McMaster University: The Early Years, 1930–
1957*, vol. 2 (Toronto: University of Toronto Press 1981), 75. For an
overview of peace-movement activities, which includes some reference to
student involvement, see Thomas P. Socknat, *Witness against War:
Pacifism in Canada, 1900–1945* (Toronto: University of Toronto Press
1987), esp. 153–7.

61 Cited in Eileen Eagan, *Class, Culture and the Classroom:*, 58–9. The
first "strike" occurred on 13 April 1934, when thousands of students
walked out of class for an hour. Possibly the largest was in 1936, when
up to five hundred thousand students joined peace demonstrations.
Historical estimates of the sizes vary. See Eagen, *Class, Culture and the
Classroom*, 135; James Weschler, *Revolt on Campus* (Washington:
University of Washington Press 1973), 171; Ralph Brax, *The First
Student Movement*, 40; Hal Draper, "The Student Movement of the
Thirties: A Political History," in Rita James Simon, ed., *As We Saw the
Thirties: Essays on Social and Political Movements of a Decade*
(Chicago: University of Illinois Press 1967), 169–71.

62 *Gateway*, 7 Dec. 1934. See also *Ubyssey*, 4 Dec. 1934; UWO *Gazette*,
23 Nov. 1934; *Sheaf*, 30 Nov. 1934.

63 *McGill Daily*, 15 Dec. 1936; *Dalhousie Gazette*, 10, 17 Oct. 1935.
Other peace activities included a conference sponsored by the Quebec
Student Peace Movment in November, 1935: Principal's Papers, Student
Activities: General, RG2 C52, MUA; and a "peace hour" on a number of
campuses in March 1936: *Manitoban*, 4 Mar. 1936. A "counter"
Remembrance Day demonstration was planned by the Student Christian
Movement at the University of Toronto in 1935: *Varsity*, 14 Oct. 1935.

64 Reid, *Mount Allison University* 2: 151–2; *Dalhousie Gazette*, 2 Oct.
1936; *Sheaf*, 25 Nov. 1938.

65 *Dalhousie Gazette*, 2 Nov. 1933; *L'Hebdo Laval*, 6 Mar. 1936.

66 *Vancouver Sun*, 16 Feb. 1934; *Gateway*, 9 Feb. 1934; on Arcand,
McGill Daily, 11 Feb. 1937. Arcand, who headed the National Social
Christian Party, seemed to temper his comments when he spoke at
McGill, giving "a polished and well delivered speech," according to
the *Daily*. For material on fascism in Canada, in which there is very
little discussion of the role played by university students in these
organizations, see Lita-Rose Betcherman, *The Swastika and the Maple
Leaf: Fascist Movements in Canada in the Thirties* (Toronto: Fitzhenry
and Whiteside 1975); Jonathan Wagner, *Brothers Beyond: National
Socialism in Canada* (Waterloo, Ont.: Wilfrid Laurier University Press
1981); Fred Rose, *Fascism over Canada: An Exposé* (Toronto: New Era
Publications 1938).

67 Montreal *Gazette*, 23, 24, 26, 27 Oct. 1936; *McGill Daily*, 23, 26 Oct.

1936; University of Western Ontario *Gazette*, 26 Oct. 1936. There were also reports of a demonstration several days earlier, consisting of some four hundred people, most of whom were thought to be Université de Montréal students, who marched through the streets and attacked the offices of a building housing a Communist bookstore: *McGill Daily*, 15 Oct. 1936.

68 Cited in Frank Scott, "The Nineteen Thirties in the United States and Canada," in Victor Hoar, ed., *The Great Depression: Essays and Memoirs from Canada and the United States* (Toronto: Copp Clark 1969), 184–5.

69 On discriminatory admission regulations, see chap. 2; see also Axelrod, "Moulding the Middle Class": 109–10. Vicious anti-Semitic slogans are found on a poster reprinted in a pamphlet called "Communauté juive," 18 Oct. 1932, Fonds D35 107, (Archives, Université de Montréal). For other examples of anti-Semitism in Quebec and elsewhere, see David Rome, *Clouds in the Thirties: On Anti-Semitism in Canada, 1929–1939*, vol. 7 (Montreal: Canadian Jewish Congress 1979), 36–55.

70 Betcherman, *The Swastika and the Maple Leaf: Fascist Movements in Canada in the Thirties*, 34–37; Andrée Lévesque, *Virage à Gauche Interdit: Les communistes, les socialistes et leurs ennemis au Québec, 1929–1939* (Montreal: Boreal Press 1984), 127–30; Lucienne Fortin, "Les Jeunes-Canada," in F. Dumont, J. Hamelin, J.P. Montminy, eds., *Idéologies au Canada français, 1930–1939*, (Quebec: Les Presses de L'Université Laval 1978), 215–33; Denis Chouinard, "Des contestataires pragmatiques: les Jeune-Canada, 1932–1938," *Revue d'histoire de l'Amérique française* 40, no. 1 (été 1986): 5–28; Mason Wade, *The French Canadians: 1760–1967*, vol. 2 (Toronto: Macmillan 1968), 901–3.

71 The Young Communist League published *l'Ouvrier Canadien* and had a small following among French Canadians. See Lévesque, *Virage à Gauche Interdit*, for a detailed discussion of Communist and socialist activity in Quebec during the 1930s. See also Norman Penner, *The Canadian Left: A Critical Analysis* (Toronto: Prentice-Hall 1977), 108–13.

72 F.R. Scott, "Freedom of Speech in Canada," offprint of paper from the *Papers and Proceedings of the Canadian Political Science Association* 5 (1933): 187.

73 Michael Behiels, "Le père Georges-Henri Lévesque et l'établissement des sciences sociales à Laval, 1938–1955," *Revue de l'Université d'Ottawa* 52, no. 3, (1982): 335–76, and translation of this article, "Father Georges-Henri Lévesque and the Introduction of Social Sciences at Laval, 1938–55,", in Paul Axelrod and John G. Reid, *Youth, University, and Canadian Society: Essays in the Social History of Higher Education*

(Montreal: McGill-Queen's University Press 1989), 320–42.

74 An examination of student newspapers and archival records at Laval, Université de Montréal, and a variety of English Canadian universities cited in this article shows great similarities in the extra-curricular and social activities of students throughout Canada.

75 Montreal *Gazette*, 24 Oct. 1936; *McGill Daily*, 3 Nov. 1936.

76 According to the Dominion censor's "Regulations," "any adverse or unfavourable statement, report or opinion likely to prejudice the defence of Canada or the efficient prosecution of the war ... or to interfere with the success of His Majesty's forces" was prohibited: cited in *Sheaf*, 29 Sept. 1939.

77 The program of Le Bloc Universitaire is published in *L'Hebdo Laval*, 10 Nov. 1939. See also *Le Quartier Latin*, "Nous voulons la paix," 28 Apr. 1939. According to a report in *Ubyssey* (12 Jan. 1940), 35 of the 185 students attending the CSA conference were French Canadians.

78 Canadian Student Assembly, Conference Report to Delegates, 9 Jan. 1940, CSIS files. By contrast, NFCUS, which held a conference at the same time as the CSA, "pledged student support to the Canadian government during the present period of national emergency": *Ubyssey*, 16. Jan. 1940.

79 CSA, Conference Report to Delegates, 9 Jan. 1940, CSIS files.

80 Cited in *Ubyssey*, 16 Jan. 1940. See also Reid, *Mount Allison*, 2: 153–4. Faculty members were involved in the conference as resource leaders.

81 CSA, Conference Report to Delegates, 9 Jan. 1940, CSIS files.

82 The following questions were included: Should compulsory service of manpower be introduced?; Indicate where you believe freedom of speech, press, pulpit, radio, assembly and association should be restricted as at present under the Defence of Canada Regulations; Do you believe that Government measures such as the Excess Profits Tax and the Price Control Board have prevented profiteering?; Do you believe that it is fair that youth with army rejection slips should be given preference for jobs in industry and for relief? *Queen's Journal*, 9 Feb. 1940, cited in Gibson, *Queen's University*, 2: 455.

83 *Montreal Gazette*, 7 Feb. 1940. The CSA attempted to put the events in a less dramatic light in its News Letter, no. 2 (27 Feb. 1940). The McGill episode was followed closely by the RCMP, C.W. Harrison to the commissioner, 21 Feb. 1940, CSIS files.

84 *Ubyssey*, 9 Feb. 1940. Dalhousie, Mount Allison, the University of British Columbia, the University of Saskatchewan, the University of Alberta, and Queen's all withdrew, though small groups of students attempted to carry on with "independent assemblies" on some of these campuses. See CSA News Letter, no. 2 (27 Feb. 1940), CSIS files.

85 Laval students opposed conscription, 2673 to 8, as did Université de

Montréal students, 935 to 35: *Le Quartier Latin*, 15 Mar. 1940.

86 The University of Manitoba voted on the questionnaire and solidly opposed conscription, 773 to 227: *Winnipeg Free Press*, 2 Mar. 1940, cited in CSIS files. The University of Toronto also held the survey: CSA News Letter, no. 2 (27 Feb. 1940). Among others, the University of British Columbia, Alberta, Queen's, and Mount Allison did not distribute it: various CSIS files.

87 V.A.M. Kemp, Sup't Commanding "O" Division to the Commissioner, RCMP, 26 Jan. 1940, CSIS files.

88 V.A.M. Kemp to the Commissioner, RCMP, 8 Mar. 1940, CSIS files.

89 H.A.R. Gagnon to the Commissioner, 15 Feb. 1940, CSIS files.

90 Kemp to the Commissioner, 26 Jan. 1940, CSIS files.

91 Kemp to the Commissioner, 8 Apr. 1940; E.F. Kusch to Sgt. Leopold, 12 Apr. 1940, CSIS files. The CSA issued defensive public statements that included supportive comments from several faculty resource leaders present at the 1939 conference, including Arthur Lower, who criticized C.A. Krug from Mount Allison for his "colonial sentiment" and accused Krug of taking refuge "in the weakest of all defences, name calling, [dragging] out a singularly weather-beaten bogey to frighten people with, to wit, communism": cited in *Manitoban*, 9 Feb. 1940. The Canadian Youth Congress was declared an "unlawful organization" during the war. See Reg Whitaker, "Official Repression of Communism during World War II," *Labour/Le Travail* 17 (Spring 1986): 143.

92 Reid, *Mount Allison*, 2: 153; W.A. Kerr to Norman Rogers, minister of National Defence, 5 Oct. 1939, President's Papers, 1936–42, 3388–1, Military: General Correspondence, UAA; University of Manitoba, *Brown and Gold* 1940, 60; Report of the President of the University of British Columbia for the year ending 31 Aug. 1940, 56–62, UBCA. University of Western Ontario *Gazette*, 13 Oct. 1939, cited increased COTC enlistments around the country, including a total of 1500 at the University of Toronto. See also Gibson, *Queen's*, 2, 181, where some 842 students had joined the COTC by Nov. 1939; for McGill, see Stanley B. Frost, *McGill University*, 2: 218–19.

93 Such students posed special problems for university authorities because males exempted from war service owing to their status as students were not officially entitled to refuse COTC training as conscientious objectors: Michael Hayden, *Seeking a Balance*, 184; Charles M. Johnston, *McMaster University*, 2: 90.

94 C.P. Tracy to Dr Kerr, 8 Nov. 1940, President's Papers, 1936–42, University of Alberta, 3388–1, Military: General Correspondence, UAA.

95 Discipline folder, UA 20, President's Papers, box 25, folder 11, ca Mar. 1941, UMA.

96 *McGill Daily*, 2 Nov. 1939. For accounts of patriotic campus activities,

see Stanley B. Frost, *McGill University*, 2: 216–29; Gibson, *Queen's University*, 2: chap. 8; Reid, *Mount Allison University*, 2: 152–9; *McMaster University*, 2: chap. 3.

97 While there has been a tendency to overstate the degree of student activism in Britain and the United States, it is likely that a larger proportion of students in those countries participated in the student movement than in Canada. The proximity of British universities to European hostilities, including the martydom of a Cambridge student in the Spanish civil war, gave a particular urgency to student politics there. In the United States student activism was especially evident in universities such as City College of New York, which drew its students from poor, immigrant, and working-class families less hostile to socialist or communist ideology than middle-class Anglo-Saxon Protestant Canadian or French Canadian Catholic families. Canadian universities enrolled both a narrower range of students with respect to class origins and a smaller proportion of college-aged youth in total. In addition, the Communist Party was at the centre instead of on the fringes of the American student movement. From 1932 to 1935, the Communist-led National Student League and the socialist League for Industrial Democracy were the most important national student organizations in the United States. In 1935 they united in the American Student Union, in which Communist influence was especially strong. For reasons that have not been adequately explained, the ASU, with a maximum of twenty thousand student members, was able to organize the massive student "strikes" for peace in the mid-thirties. Still, two contemporary studies, Maxine Davis, *The Lost Generation: A Portrait of American Youth Today* (New York: MacMillan 1936), and "Youth in College," *Fortune Magazine*, June 1936, both conclude that the degree of political awareness and activism on American campuses was wildly exaggerated by the media. In addition to the sources cited in nn 1 and 61, see Victor Kiernan, "Herbert Norman's Cambridge," in Roger W. Bowen, ed., *E.H. Norman: His Life and Scholarship* (Toronto: University of Toronto Press 1984), 27–45; H.S. Ferns, *Reading from Left to Right: One Man's Political History* (Toronto: University of Toronto Press 1983), chaps. 2–5; and Irving Howe, *A Margin of Hope: An Intellectual Biography* (New York: Harcourt Brace Jovanovich 1982), 63–73.

98 On the SCM, see Margaret Beattie, *SCM*, 23–5; NFCUS suspended activities in 1940 but was revived in 1944. It became the Canadian Union of Students in 1963 and played a leading role in the student movement of that decade, but dissolved in 1969. On the Communist Party, see *Canada's Party of Socialism*, 140–1, and Penner, *Canadian Communism*, chap. 6.

CHAPTER SEVEN

1 David O. Levine, *The American College and the Culture of Aspiration, 1915–1940* (Ithaca: Cornell University Press 1986).
2 *Queen's Journal*, 21 Feb. 1933.
3 "Many Graduates Afraid of Unemployment Bogey," *Globe*, 4 May 1933; Leonard Marsh, *Canadians In and Out of Work* (London: Oxford 1940), 395–6. See also *Globe*, 3 May 1933, which admitted in an editorial that employment prospects for graduates were "not bright"; Herb Hamilton, *Queen's* (Kingston: Alumni Association of Queen's University 1977), 23; John Macdonald, *The History of the University of Alberta, 1908–1958* (Edmonton: University of Alberta 1958), 41; John E. Robbins, Reminiscences 1929–40, John Robbins Papers, MG 31 D 91, vol 1., 7, NA; Prospective Employers of Graduates: Inquiries, Correspondence, Deans' Papers, 1914–1967, 41/12/11/424, UAA. See also Scott Wade and Hugh Lloyd, *Behind the Hill* (Fredericton: Student Representative Council, Associated Alumni, and Senate of the University of New Brunswick 1967), 182, which cited the *New Brunswickian*, Jan. 1933: graduates "will have qualified to assume positions where almost none are offered." University of Manitoba engineering graduates of 1932 found a "decreasing demand" for their services: Annual Report, University of Manitoba 1931–32, 5, UMA.
4 Abraham Rotson, "Refrain for a Bourgeois Child," *Alarm Clock* 1, no. 2 (Feb. 1933).
5 Robert Bothwell, Ian Drummond, and John English, *Canada: 1900–1945* (Toronto: University of Toronto Press 1987), 252; John Herd Thompson with Allen Seager, *Canada: Decades of Discord, 1922–1939* (Toronto: McClelland and Stewart 1985), 342–4.
6 University of Alberta, Report of the Board of Governors and the President, 1934–35, 20, and 1935–36, 17–18, UAA.
7 *Queen's Journal*, 29 Sept. 1936; University of Alberta *Gateway*, 15 Oct. 1937. See also DBS, *Higher Education in Canada, 1936–38* (Ottawa 1939), 27; "Plenty of Work in Future for UBC Chemistry Grads," *Ubyssey*, 24 Nov. 1936; "Mines Seen Using All Graduates," *Globe and Mail*, 26 Jan. 1937.
8 DBS, *Higher Education in Canada, 1936–38*, 31.
9 Department of Labour, *Women at Work in Canada: A Fact Book on the Female Labour Force, 1964* (Ottawa 1965), 34.
10 *Queen's Journal*, 4 Oct. 1932, 26 Jan. 1937.
11 Interview, Arthur Hackett, 10 Jan. 1987.
12 Correspondence with author, 6 Jan. 1986.
13 Correspondence with author, 4 Feb. 1986.

14 Interview, 7 July 1984.

15 Evelyn M. Eaton to Robert Stamp, private collection, 3 Apr. 1981.

16 Jean Courney to Robert Stamp, 11 Dec. 1980.

17 Interview, 15 Aug. 1983.

18 It should be kept in mind that holding a degree did not guarantee one a job in these professions, particularly in the case of women.

19 Department of Labour, *Women at Work in Canada*, 34. Other sources that reflect these patterns include some forty interviews conducted by the author with students primarily from Dalhousie, the University of Toronto, and the University of Alberta. See also *Hidden Voices*, Queen's University Oral History Project (Kingston: Queen's University 1978); letters to Robert Stamp from students of the 1939 graduating class, University of Western Ontario, private collection; Margaret Gillet and Kay Sibbald, *A Fair Shake: Autobiographical Essays by McGill Women* (Montreal: Eden Press 1984). Alumni magazines from most Canadian universities, which report on the activities of university graduates, also bear out these patterns, though because these sources almost always detail "success" stories only, they may not be entirely representative.

20 A survey of 478 women who graduated from the University of Toronto School of Social Work between 1914 and 1938 found that 121, or 25.3 per cent, of these graduates had since married and that only 6 of these remained in social work: James Struthers, "'Lord Give Us Men': Women and Social Work in English Canada, 1918–1953," Canadian Historical Association, *Historical Papers* 1983, 100.

21 See Ruth Roach Pierson, *'They're Still Women After All': The Second World War and Canadian Womanhood* (Toronto: McClelland and Stewart 1986), chap. 1.

22 Acadia University, *The Acadia Record, 1838–1953*, rev. and enlarged by Watson Kirckconnell (Wolfville, NS: Acadia University 1953). Popularly known as the Blue Book, this volume contains brief biographies of all Acadia graduates to 1953. The information for the years 1921, 1926, 1929, 1931, 1936, and 1940, which has been coded and entered on computer, provides the basis for statistical data used in the text. I would like to thank Myra Rutherdale for providing technical assistance.

23 Survey information adapted from correspondence solicited and received by Michael Hayden, USA. See also President's Report, University of Saskatchewan 1937–38, 92.

24 McMaster Graduating Class, 1936, private collection of Arthur Muter.

25 Marjorie Cohen, "Crisis and the Female Labour Reserve: The Canadian Depression Experience," paper presented to the Blue Collar Workers Conference, Windsor 1939; Department of Labour, *Women at Work in Canada*, 28–37.

26 *The Acadia Record*. See also Don Dowden, "Acadia University in the

1930s: Social Trends in Depression-Era Higher Education," graduate research paper, Acadia University 1988, 10.

27 On the upper class, see Leonard Marsh, *Canadians In and Out of Work* (London: Oxford 1940); John Porter, *The Vertical Mosaic*, chaps. 7–9 and app. I and II; Wallace Clement, *The Canadian Corporate Elite*, (Toronto: Mclelland and Stewart 1975), esp. chaps. 5–6; and Clement, *Class, Power and Property: Essays on Canadian Society* (Toronto: Metheun 1983), chap. 2; Jorge Niosi, *Canadian Capitalism: A Study of Power in the Canadian Business Establishment* (Toronto: James Lorimer and Company 1981), chap. 2; Peter Newman, *The Canadian Establishment* (Toronto: McClelland and Stewart 1975.)

28 These included those holding directorships in the 170 dominant Canadian corporations. Porter, *The Vertical Mosaic*, 274.

29 Ibid., 284.

30 Newman, *The Canadian Establishment*, 466–75.

31 This information was derived from biographical data on these individuals contained in various issues of *Who's Who in Canada* (Toronto: University of Toronto Press) , and *The Canadian Who's Who* (Toronto: Who's Who Canada Publications).

32 Of Newman's elite, 35 per cent attended one of these institutions. See also Porter, *The Vertical Mosaic*, 277.

33 Porter, *The Vertical Mosaic*, 277–8.

34 Newman, *The Canadian Establishement*, 509–21. See also Clement, *The Canadian Corporate Elite*, 242–5, on this point.

35 *The Vertical Mosaic*, 295. A study of University of British Columbia graduates found that 13 per cent of the graduates of 1939–43 achieved the position of major executive, compared to less than 10 per cent for the period 1916–39: Peter Z.W. Tsong, *The UBC Alumni, 1916–1969: Thoughts of 12.6% of the UBC Alumni* (Vancouver: Peter Tsong 1972), 119.

36 *The Vertical Mosaic*, 295.

37 A variety of sociological studies confirm these tendencies: Lorne Tepperman, *Social Mobility in Canada* (Toronto: McGraw-Hill Ryerson 1975), 187–91; Alfred Hunter, *Class Tells: On Social Inequality in Canada* (Toronto: Butterworth's 1986), chap. 6; Alexander Himelfarb and C. James Richardson, *Sociology for Canadians: Images of Society* (Toronto: McGraw-Hill Ryerson 1982), chaps. 10–12.

38 Sources: *The Canadian Who's Who*, various years; Evelyn Davidson, ed., *Who's Who of Canadian Women, 1984–85* (Toronto: Trans-Canada Press 1984); various university yearbooks and biographies.

39 Burton Bledstein, *The Culture of Professionalism: The Middle Class and the Development of Higher Education in America* (W.W. Norton and Co.: New York 1976), 43. See also: Randall Collins, *The Credential*

Society: An Historical Sociology of Education and Stratification (New York: Academic Press 1979), 135; Magali Sarfatte Larson, *The Rise of Professionalism: A Sociological Analysis* (Berkeley: University of California Press 1977), 44; Barbara and John Ehrenreich, "The Professional-Managerial Class," *Radical America* (March–April 1977): 22; C. Wright Mills, *White Collar: The American Middle Classes* (New York: Oxford University Press 1956), 246; and William J. Goode, *The Celebration of Heroes: Prestige as a Control System* (Berkeley: University of California Press 1978).

40 R.C. Wallace, "Higher Education on the Stand," *Queen's Quarterly* 46, no. 3 (Autumn 1939): 264. See also "Is the UBC Worth Rescuing?" *Vancouver Province*, 26 Sept. 1933; Sir Robert Falconer, "Academic Canada Comes of Age," *Saturday Night*, 1 Jan. 1938. Historian J.B. Brebner wrote, "Up to the present, it seems fair to say, Canadian universities have been regarded by the public, and to some degree by themselves, chiefly as service institutions of a rather narrowly utilitarian kind, with somewhat grudging tolerance for theoretical studies, normally in the faculty of arts": Brebner, *Scholarship for Canada: The Function of Graduate Studies* (Ottawa: Canadian Social Science Research Council 1945), 32.

41 On the "doctrine of utility," see Mario Creet, "H.M. Tory and the Secularization of Canadian Universities," *Queen's Quarterly* 88, no. 4 (Winter 1981): 718–36.

42 Sir Robert Borden's Address to the Graduating Class of Acadia University, 25 May 1932, Ernest Lapointe Papers, MG 27 III B10, vol. 6, file 1, NAC.

43 See, for example, Jerrold Siegel, *Bohemian Paris: Culture, Politics, and the Boundaries of Bourgeois Life, 1830–1930* (New York: Viking-Penguin 1986); Paul Avrich, *The Modern School Movement: Anarchism and Education in the United States* (Princeton: Princeton University Press 1980); Ephraim H. Mizruchi, *Regulating Society: Beguines, Bohemians and other Marginals* (Chicago: University of Chicago Press 1987).

44 A typically hysterical statement about the radicalism and irresponsiblity of youth was delivered in the Canadian House of Commons by F.H. Pickel, Conservative MP from Brome-Missisquoi. "There is no home life, absolutely none as a general rule. Children come and go as they please," and universities had become nothing more than "athletic recruiting grounds": cited in Toronto *Globe*, 3 Apr. 1935. See also a *Globe* editorial, headlined "Youth and the Red Peril," cited approvingly the views of Martin H. Carmondy, Supreme Grand Knight of the Grand Rapids Knights of Columbus, who charged that university youth were

being duped by "propaganda work being carried out by the agents of communism": 18 Feb. 1936.

45 *Queen's Journal*, 24 Jan. 1930. The Vancouver *Province* noted that besides teaching students practical skills, universities were a "bulwark against quacks and frauds and the periodic waves of fanantacism which sweep against the country; against everything from technocracy to Bolshevism": "Is UBC Worth Rescuing?" 26 Sept. 1933.

46 Ernest Lapointe, speech to University Catholic Clubs, 1935, Ernest Lapointe Papers, MG 27 III B10, vol. 61, file A5, NAC.

47 Convocation Address by Graham Murray, *Halifax Herald*, 11 May 1937.

48 *McGill Daily*, 18 Dec. 1933.

49 *Ubyssey*, 11 Oct. 1935. See also *McGill Daily*, 6, 9 Oct. 1930; 1, 16 Nov. 1936. University of Alberta *Gateway*, 21 Oct. 1932; 17 Feb. 1933; 20, 24 Nov. 1934; *Queen's Journal*, 7 Jan., 10 Nov. 1938; University of Western Ontario *Gazette*, 28 Feb. 1936.

50 Report of the President of the University of British Columbia 1939–40, 17.

51 Calculated from *The Acadia Record*.

52 From information provided by the Alumni Office through the University Archives, University of Saskatchewan, 25 July 1984.

53 On the perceived influence of American higher education on Canada, see Sir Robert Falconer, "American Influences on the Higher Education of Canada," *Proceedings and Transactions of the Royal Society of Canada*, 3rd ser., 24, section II (1930): 23–8. On general attitudes of Canadians, see Thompson and Seager, *Decades of Discord*, 192.

54 Stanley B. Frost, *McGill University: For the Advancement of Learning, vol. 2, 1895–1971* (Montreal: McGill-Queen's University Press 1984), chap. 15; Michael Hayden, *Seeking a Balance: The University of Saskatchewan, 1907–1982* (Vancouver: University of British Columbia Press 1983), chap. 7; Charles Johnston and John Weaver, *Student Days: An Illustrated History of Student Life at McMaster University from the 1890s to the 1980s* (Hamilton: McMaster University Alumni Association 1986), chap. 7.

55 See Clark Kerr and Marian L. Gade, "The Contemporary College President," in *The American Scholar* (Winter 1987): 29–45; H. Blair Neatby, "Visions and Revisions: The View from the Presidents' Offices of Ontario Universities since the Second World War," Canadian Historical Association, *Historical Papers* 1988, 1–15.

56 See Neil Guppy, Doug Balson, and Susan Vellutiini, "Women and Higher Education in Canadian Society," in Jane Gaskell and Arlene McLaren, eds., *Women and Education: A Canadian Perspective* (Calgary: Detselig

1987), 171–92; Alison Prentice et al., *Canadian Women: A History* (Toronto: Harcourt Brace Jovanovich 1988), 324–9; Paul Anisef, Norman Okihiro, and Carl James, *Losers and Winners: The Pursuit of Equality and Social Justice in Higher Education* (Toronto: Butterworth 1982); articles by Jane Gaskell, Randle W. Nelsen, and Gordon Shrimpton in Terry Wotherspoon, ed., *The Political Economy of Canadian Schooling* (Toronto: Metheun 1988).

57 Paul Axelrod, *Scholars and Dollars: Politics, Economics, and the Universities of Ontario, 1945–1980* (Toronto: University of Toronto Press 1982).

58 W.A. Neilson and Chad Gaffield, eds., *Universities in Crisis: A Mediaeval Institution in the Twenty-first Century* (Montreal: Institute for Research on Public Policy 1986).

59 Helen Lefkowitz Horowitz, *Campus Life: Undergraduate Cultures from the End of the Eighteenth Century to the Present* (New York: Alfred Knopf 1987), chap. 7; Charles Johnston and John Weaver, *Student Days*, chap. 8. Peter Stearns notes the enduring mood of insecurity in middle-class culture. See his *Be a Man! Males in Modern Society* (New York: Holmes and Meier Publishers Inc. 1979), 110.

60 Robert Bothwell, David Bercuson, and J.L. Granatstein, *The Great Brain Robbery: Canada's Universities on the Road to Ruin* (Toronto: McClelland and Stewart 1984); Allan Bloom, *The Closing of the American Mind* (New York: Simon and Schuster 1987).

APPENDIX A

1 For a discussion of this notion, see David Thomson, *The Aims of History: Values of the Historical Attitude* (London: Tames and Hudson 1969), chap. 3.

2 See the following discussions of this question: Leonard Marsh, *Canadians In and Out of Work* (London: Oxford 1940), 401; G.H. Cole "The Conception of the Middle Class," *British Journal of Sociology* 1, no. 4 (Dec. 1950): 275–90; Peter Stearns, "The Middle Class: Toward a Precise Definition," *Comparative Studies of Society and History* 21 (1979): 377–98; Lenore O'Boyle, "The Classless Society: Comment on Stearns," ibid., 397–413; C. Wright Mills, *White Collar: The American Middle Classes* (New York: Oxford University Press 1951); David Huehner, "The American Middle Class and Higher Education: A Critique of Current Sociological Theory and Historical Analysis," paper presented to Canadian History of Education Association Conference, London, Ont., Oct. 1988, 2–3; Dennis Forcese, *The Canadian Class Structure* (Toronto: McGraw-Hill Ryerson 1975), 24–5; Alexander Himelfarb and James Richardson, *People, Power and Process: Sociology for Canadians*

(Toronto: McGraw-Hill Ryerson 1979), 183.

3 Burton Bledstein discusses the etymology of the term in nineteenth- and early twentieth-century America in *The Culture of Professionalism: The Middle Class and the Development of Higher Education in America* (New York: W.W. Norton and Co. 1976), chap. 1. An otherwise fascinating study by John S. Gilkeson Jr., *Middle-Class Providence, 1820–1940* (Princeton: Princeton University Press 1986), is limited by the author's failure to define the middle class, and while Peter Stearns, in "The Middle Class," calls for a careful defintion of terms, he does not provide it. In Canada the term has been used frequently, without being specifically defined, by social historians of the late nineteenth and early twentieth centuries. See Alan Metcalfe, *Canada Learns to Play: The Emergence of Organized Sport, 1807–1914* (Toronto: McClelland and Stewart 1987), 20, 41, 64–5, 82–3, 98; Paul Rutherford, "Tomorrow's Metropolis: The Urban Reform Movement in Canada, 1880–1920," Canadian Historical Association, *Historical Papers* 1971, 203–24.

4 Michael Katz, Michael Doucet, and Mark Stern, *The Social Organization of Early Industrial Capitalism* (Cambridge: Harvard University Press 1982), chap. 1.

5 For a discussion of stratification literature, see Mary G. Powers, introduction to Mary G. Powers, ed., *Measures of Socioeconomic Status: Current Issues* (Boulder, Colo.: American Association for the Advancement of Science 1982), 1–28; Bernard R. Blishen, William K. Carroll, Catherine Moore, "The 1981 Socioeconomic Index for Occupations in Canada," *Canadian Review of Sociology and Anthropology* 24, no. 4 (1987): 466–8. An international "prestige" scale can be found in Donald Treiman, *Occupational Prestige in Comparative Perspective* (New York: Academic Press 1977). An exhaustive and stimulating discussion can be found in William J. Goode, *The Celebration of Heroes: Prestige as a Control System* (Berkeley: University of California Press 1978). For additional sources on occupational classification, see Michael B. Katz, "Occupational Classification in History," *Journal of Interdisciplinary History* 3, no. 1 (Summer 1972): 63–88; Bernard R. Blishen, "The Construction and Use of an Occupational Class Scale," *Canadian Journal of Economics and Political Science* 24 (November 1958): 519–31; Bernard R. Blishen, "A Socioeconomic Index for Occupations in Canada," *Canadian Review of Sociology and Anthropology* 4, no. 1 (Feb. 1967): 41–53; Bernard R. Blishen, William K. Caroll, "Socioeconomic Measures from Canadian Census Data," in Powers, ed., *Measures of Socioeconomic Status*, 43–54; Andrea Tyree and Billy G. Smith, "Occupational Hierarchy in the United States," 1789–1969," *Social Forces* 56, no. 3 (Mar. 1978): 881–9. On Marx's treatment of the middle class, see James F. Becker, *Marxian Political Economy: An Outline* (Cambridge: Cam-

bridge University Press 1977), 203–43. For an analysis of Canadian approaches, see Wallace Clement, "Canadian Class Cleavages: An Assessment and Contribution," in Clement, *Class, Power and Property: Essays on Canadian Society* (Toronto: Metheun 1983), 134–71; and Alfred Hunter, *Class Tells: On Social Inequality in Canada* (Toronto: Butterworth 1986), chap. 11.

6 E.P Thompson, *The Making of the English Working Class* (Harmondsworth, Middlesex: Penguin 1963). On Canada, see Bryan Palmer, *A Culture in Conflict: Skilled Workers and Industrial Capitalism in Hamilton, Ontario, 1860–1914* (Montreal: McGill-Queen's University Press 1979).

7 A critique of Marx can be found in John Porter, *The Vertical Mosaic* (Toronto: University of Toronto Press 1965), 18–28, and 3–7, 125–32, and 294, while a critique of Porter can be found in Clement, "Canadian Class Cleavages," 138–41. See also Becker, *Marxian Political Economy*, 203–43; George Ross, "Marxism and the New Middle Classes," *Theory and Society* 5, no. 2 (Mar. 1978): 163–90; Michael W. Apple, "Standing on the Shoulders of Bowles and Gintis: Class Formation and Capitalist Schools," *History of Education Quarterly* 28, no. 2 (Summer 1988): 230–41; Erik Olin Wright, *Class, Crisis, and the State* (London: Verso 1979); Nicolas Poulantizis, *Class in Contemporary Capitalism* (London: New Left Books 1975); Arthur Marwick, "The Upper Class in Britain, France and the USA since the First World War," in Marwick, ed., *Class in the Twentieth Century* (Brighton: Harvester Press 1986), esp. 4–5; R.W. Connell, *Ruling Class, Ruling Culture: Studies of Conflict, Power and Hegemony in Australian Life* (Cambridge: Cambridge University Press 1977); Katz et al., *The Social Organization of Early Industrial Capitalism*, 62.

8 A similar perspective is offered in a paper by David Huehner, in which he advocates the use of "closure theory" – an approach that combines neo-Marxist and Weberian approaches to history and sociology – to analyse the relationship between the middle class and higher education. See Huehner,"The American Middle Class and Higher Education."

9 See G.H. Cole, "The Conception of the Middle Class"; Stuart Blumin, "The Hypothesis of Middle-Class Formation in the Nineteenth Century: A Critique and Some Proposals," *American Historical Review* 90, no. 2 (April 1985): 299–338; Stuart Blumin, "Black Coats to White Collars: Economic Change, Nonmanual Work, and the Social Structure of America," in Stuart W. Bruchey, ed., *Small Business and American Life* (New York: Columbia University Press 1980), 100–21; Mary Ryan, *Cradle of the Middle Class: the Family in Oenida County, New York, 1790–1865* (Cambridge: Cambridge University Press 1981); John Gilkeson, *Middle Class Providence 1820–1940*; Clyde Griffen and Sally Griffen, *Natives*

and Newcomers: The Ordering of Opportunity in Mid-Nineteenth Century Poughkeepsie (Cambridge: Harvard University Press 1978); David O. Levine, *The American College and the Culture of Aspiration, 1915–1940* (Ithaca: Cornell University Press 1986); C. Wright Mills, *White Collar: The American Middle Classes* (New York: Oxford University Press 1956); Anthony Giddens, *The Class Structure of the Advanced Societies* (London: Hutchinson 1975); Barbara and John Ehrenreich, "The Professional-Managerial Class," *Radical America* (March-April 1977): 7–31; Magali Sarfatte Larson, *The Rise of Professionalism: A Sociological Analysis* (Berkeley: University of California Press 1977); Randall Collins, *The Credential Society: An Historical Sociology of Education and Stratification* (New York: Academic Press 1979); Hartmut Kaelble, *Social Mobility in the 19th and 20th Centuries: Europe and America in Comparative Perspective* (Washington: Berg Publishers 1985); Patrick Harrigan, "Social Mobility and Schooling in History: Recent Methods and Conclusions," *Historical Reflections* 10, (Spring 1983): 127–41; Daniel Horowitz, "Frugality or Comfort: Middle-class Styles of Life in the Early Twentieth Century," *American Quarterly* 37 (1985): 239–59. On Canada, see Robert Gidney and Wyn Millar, "From Voluntarism to State Schooling: The Creation of a Public System in Ontario," *Canadian Historical Review* 66, no. 4 (Dec. 1985): 443–73; Leonard Marsh, *Canadians In and Out of Work*, esp. 1–27, 383–94; Jean Barman, *Growing Up British in British Columbia* (Vancouver: University of British Columbia Press 1984); Porter, *The Vertical Mosaic*; Wallace Clement, *The Canadian Corporate Elite: An Analysis of Economic Power* (Toronto: McClelland and Stewart 1975); Wallace Clement, "Inequality of Access: Characteristics of the Canadian Corporate Elite," in Clement, *Class, Power and Property*; Jorge Niosi, *Canadian Capitalism: A Study of Power in the Canadian Business Establishment* (Toronto: James Lorimer 1981); Dennis Olsen, *The State Elite* (Toronto: McClelland and Stewart 1980). A useful and original account of the relationship between middle-class values and residential patterns in the first half of the twentieth century is John C. Weaver, "From Land Assembly to Social Maturity: The Suburban Life of Westdale (Hamilton), Ontario, 1911–1951," in Michael Piva, ed., *A History of Ontario: Selected Readings* (Toronto: Copp Clark Pitman 1988), 214–41.

10 There is a large literature on the distinguishing characteristics of working-class culture. See Edward Thompson and Bryan Palmer cited above; Paul Willis, *Learning To Labour: How Working Class Kids Get Working Class Jobs* (Farnborough, England: Saxon House, Teakfield Limited 1977); Stephen Humphries, *Hooligans or Rebels? An Oral History of Working-Class Childhood and Youth 1889–1939* (Oxford: Blackwell 1981); Richard Sennet and Jonathon Cobb, *The Hidden Injuries of*

Class (New York: Vintage 1973); Robert Roberts, *The Classic Slum: Salford Life in the First Quarter of the Century* (Penguin: Baltimore 1973); Richard Hoggart, *The Uses of Literacy* (Harmondsworth, Middlesex: Penguin 1958); Roy Rosenzweig, *Eight Hours For What We Will: Leisure in an Industrial City, 1870–1920* (Cambridge: Cambridge University Press 1983); Ian Mackay, "The Realm of Uncertainty: The Experience of Work in the Cumberland Coal Mines, 1873–1927," *Acadiensis* 16, no. 1 (Autumn 1986): 3–57. See also Peter N. Stearns, *Be a Man! Males in Modern Society* (New York: Holmes and Meier Publishers Inc. 1979), chaps. 4–5, which compare working-class and middle-class perceptions and expressions of masculinity in the nineteenth and early twentieth centuries. For a discussion of differences in "prestige allocation" among classes in modern times, see William J. Goode, *The Celebration of Heroes: Prestige as a Control System*, esp. chap. 6.

11 Clement, "Inequality of Access," also employs a three-class model: 35–41.

12 See Graham Lowe, "Women, Work and the Office: The Feminization of Clerical Occupations in Canada, 1901–1931," in Veronica Strong Boag and Anita Clair Fellman, eds., *Rethinking Canada: The Promise of Women's History* (Toronto: Copp Clark Pitman 1986), 118; Veronica Strong Boag, *The New Day Recalled: Lives of Girls and Women in English Canada, 1919–1939* (Toronto: Copp Clark Pitman 1988), chap. 2; Erik Olin Wright, *Class, Crisis and the State*, 80–1.

13 Bledstein's work, *The Culture of Professionalism* (see esp. chap. 3) is an example of this.

14 Comparing the culture of university-educated middle-class Canadians with those lacking post-secondary educational credentials would be an interesting direction for new research.

Index